Sustainable Development Goals Series

The **Sustainable Development Goals Series** is Springer Nature's inaugural cross-imprint book series that addresses and supports the United Nations' seventeen Sustainable Development Goals. The series fosters comprehensive research focused on these global targets and endeavours to address some of society's greatest grand challenges. The SDGs are inherently multidisciplinary, and they bring people working across different fields together and working towards a common goal. In this spirit, the Sustainable Development Goals series is the first at Springer Nature to publish books under both the Springer and Palgrave Macmillan imprints, bringing the strengths of our imprints together.

The Sustainable Development Goals Series is organized into eighteen subseries: one subseries based around each of the seventeen respective Sustainable Development Goals, and an eighteenth subseries, "Connecting the Goals," which serves as a home for volumes addressing multiple goals or studying the SDGs as a whole. Each subseries is guided by an expert Subseries Advisor with years or decades of experience studying and addressing core components of their respective Goal.

The SDG Series has a remit as broad as the SDGs themselves, and contributions are welcome from scientists, academics, policymakers, and researchers working in fields related to any of the seventeen goals. If you are interested in contributing a monograph or curated volume to the series, please contact the Publishers: Zachary Romano [Springer; zachary.romano@springer.com] and Rachael Ballard [Palgrave Macmillan; rachael.ballard@palgrave.com].

More information about this series at
https://link.springer.com/bookseries/15486

Tulus T.H. Tambunan

Fostering Resilience through Micro, Small and Medium Enterprises

Perspectives from Indonesia

Tulus T.H. Tambunan
Center for Industry, SME
and Business Competition Studies
Trisakti University
West Jakarta, Indonesia

ISSN 2523-3084 ISSN 2523-3092 (electronic)
Sustainable Development Goals Series
ISBN 978-981-16-9434-9 ISBN 978-981-16-9435-6 (eBook)
https://doi.org/10.1007/978-981-16-9435-6

Color wheel and icons: From https://www.un.org/sustainabledevelopment/, Copyright © 2020 United Nations. Used with the permission of the United Nations.
© The Editor(s) (if applicable) and The Author(s), under exclusive license to Springer Nature Singapore Pte Ltd. 2022
This work is subject to copyright. All rights are solely and exclusively licensed by the Publisher, whether the whole or part of the material is concerned, specifically the rights of translation, reprinting, reuse of illustrations, recitation, broadcasting, reproduction on microfilms or in any other physical way, and transmission or information storage and retrieval, electronic adaptation, computer software, or by similar or dissimilar methodology now known or hereafter developed.
The use of general descriptive names, registered names, trademarks, service marks, etc. in this publication does not imply, even in the absence of a specific statement, that such names are exempt from the relevant protective laws and regulations and therefore free for general use.
The publisher, the authors and the editors are safe to assume that the advice and information in this book are believed to be true and accurate at the date of publication. Neither the publisher nor the authors or the editors give a warranty, expressed or implied, with respect to the material contained herein or for any errors or omissions that may have been made. The publisher remains neutral with regard to jurisdictional claims in published maps and institutional affiliations.

Cover credit: Nikolay Pandev/getty images

The content of this publication has not been approved by the United Nations and does not reflect the views of the United Nations or its officials or Member States.

This Palgrave Macmillan imprint is published by the registered company Springer Nature Singapore Pte Ltd.
The registered company address is: 152 Beach Road, #21-01/04 Gateway East, Singapore 189721, Singapore

I dedicate to my wife, Maud Herati Tambunan-Sutrisno and my two sons, Priya and Adriel Tambunan

PREFACE

It has been recognized worldwide that Micro, Small and Medium Enterprises (MSMEs) play a vital role in the economic development of developing countries, including those in Indonesia, as the enterprises have proved to be the primary source of job/employment creation and output growth. MSMEs are important not only from the economic perspective but also socially and politically because of their potential contributions to poverty reduction, improvement of income distribution, and rural development. For this reason, governments in many developing countries including Indonesia are supporting capacity building in their MSMEs largely through direct interventions with a variety of programs, of which subsidized credit schemes are the most important one. In Indonesia, for instance, government has intervened to support MSMEs' development in a number of ways such as subsidized credit including the very popular scheme, i.e. the Community Business Credit or known in Indonesia as KUR (*Kredit Usaha Rakyat*) introduced in 2007, human resource development trainings in production techniques, management, entrepreneurship, provision of total quality control, and technical assistance. Internet facility, advisory extension workers, subsidized inputs, marketing and promotion facilitation, establishments of business development services and common service facilities inside industry clusters, establishment of special small-scale industrial estates, partnership program, establishment of the export support base of Indonesia (DPE), and implementation of an incubator system for promoting the development of new entrepreneurs.

viii PREFACE

Various government departments such as the Ministry of Cooperative and Small Medium Enterprise, the Ministry of Industry, and the Ministry of Trade have taken the lead in MSME development policies.

Many international institutes such as the World Bank, the Asian Development Bank (ADB), and the United Nation Industry and Development Organisation (UNIDO) as well as many industrialized/rich countries through bilateral cooperations have played a crucial role in empowering MSMEs through a variety of forms such as co-funding, technical assistance, and trainings in Indonesia and many other developing countries.

With its title *Fostering Resilience through Micro, Small and Medium Enterprises: Perspectives from Indonesia*. This book is about development of MSMEs in Indonesia based on recent secondary data and primary data from field surveys (for some issues discussed in this book). The book is divided into seven chapters, including the introduction in Chapter 1. Chapter 2 discusses the recent development of MSMEs in Indonesia and, as a regional comparative, those in other economies in the Asia-Pacific (AP) region. This chapter deals with a number of important issues including their contributions to the employment generation and the formation of gross domestic product (GDP), export development, development constraints they face, productivity, and investment.

Chapter 3 examines empirically the development of MSMEs' export in Indonesia and also in some other countries in the AP region. This chapter also reviews the literature on important factors that influence the ability or decision of MSMEs to export, especially direct exports. In addition, this chapter also analyzes empirically the role of partnerships between MSMEs, for example, large companies, banks and government institutions, and the role of cooperatives in supporting the export of MSMEs.

Chapter 4 deals with the issue of women entrepreneurs in MSMEs. As in other parts of the world, women's entrepreneurship in Indonesia also has a great potential not only in empowering women but also society at large in the country. Yet, as in many other developing countries, in Indonesia this potential remains largely untapped. This chapter tries to identify and discuss the main factors that influence the role of women as entrepreneurs in Indonesia.

Chapter 5 is based on a study on the impacts of the 1998/1999 Asian financial crisis, 2008/2009 global financial crisis, and the 2020 Covid-19 pandemic crisis on the enterprises in Indonesia. It examines theoretically the transmission channels through which those crises affected MSMEs.

It also identifies the business risks of the affected MSMEs and explores the crisis mitigating measures (CMMs) widely adopted by the affected MSMEs.

Chapter 6 examines the development of Financial Technology (FinTech), in particular Peer-to-Peer (P2P) lending and explores the importance of P2P lending as an alternative source of funding for Micro and Small Enterprises (MSEs) in Indonesia. This Indonesian case is very important for two main reasons. First, most small businesses in Indonesia do not have access to bank financing. Second, P2P lenders have grown rapidly in recent years, which are expected to become an alternative funding for small businesses in the country. It is also confirmed by a 2020 report on development of FinTech companies in ASEAN which emphasized that P2P lending platform providers are especially needed in Indonesia (and the Philippines and Vietnam) because there are so many MSEs that cannot obtain loans from mainstream commercial banks (including government-assisted loans), which forces them to struggle with day-to-day business.

Finally, as the overall conclusion of this book, Chapter 7 gives some theoretical contributions and policy implications with respect to the nature of development of MSMEs in developing/low-income countries and the impact of economic crises on MSMEs.

West Jakarta, Indonesia   Tulus T.H. Tambunan

PRAISE FOR *FOSTERING RESILIENCE THROUGH MICRO, SMALL AND MEDIUM ENTERPRISES*

"Amid current global trends and economic upheavals, the importance and/or contribution of MSMEs cannot be emphasized enough, given that they make an impact economically, socially, and politically. The most salient feature of the book is that information provided is designed to justify this very powerful stance, bringing a unique blend of knowledge which offers new concepts, and content that is grounded profoundly in the intellectual rigor of the author."

—Dr. Dev Raj Paneru, *IQAC-Director of Global College International, and Principal of Global College of Management (TU affiliated), Kathmandu-31 Nepal*

"MSMEs are gaining immense global importance. They are the backbone of various economies as they generate huge employment and act as a driving force behind achieving certain sustainable development goals. In this context, the book focuses on exploring new developments, global challenges, and the resilience of MSMEs in Indonesia. The book is aptly designed to embrace crucial contributions and challenges of MSMEs in the country, which will be very much useful to policymakers, academicians, researchers, and entrepreneurs. The book is commendable in all respects, and it is a treasure of knowledge."

—Professor Himachalam Dasaraju, *Sri Venkateswara University, Tirupati, India*

"The book on the topic entitled 'Fostering Resiliences through Micro, Small and Medium Enterprises- Perspectives from Indonesia' gives a detailed picture of how MSMEs are defined in Indonesia and other countries. It covers various aspects of MSME in Indonesia in particular and other countries in general. It is a best combination of theory and practice as it is based on the analysis of primary as well as secondary data."

—Professor Krishn A. Goyal, *Jai Narain Vyas University, Jodhpur, India*

CONTENTS

1	Introduction	1
2	Development of MSMEs and Their Main Constraints	13
3	Internationalization	37
4	Women Entrepreneurs	75
5	MSMEs in Times of Economic Crisis	101
6	Development of Financial Technology with Reference to Peer-to-Peer (P2P) Lending	147
7	Theoretical Contributions: General Conclusions	179

References	193
Index	213

LIST OF FIGURES

Fig. 2.1	Number of MSMEs in the AP region by economy* (*Note* the number of MSMEs is rounded up in thousand. The numbers in brackets are percentages of total enterprises. *Source* APEC [2020])	15
Fig. 2.2	Share of employment in MSMEs in the AP region by economy (*Source* APEC [2020])	20
Fig. 2.3	Employment growth in MSMEs in the AP region by economy (%) (*Note* Compound annual growth rates [CAGR] were used. *Source* APEC [2020])	20
Fig. 2.4	Share of GDP by business size in Indonesia, 2016–2018 (constant 2000 prices; %) (*Source* Menegkop and UKM and BPS)	21
Fig. 2.5	Labor productivity by business size in Indonesia, 2018 (IDR billion) (*Source* Menegkop and UKM/BPS)	26
Fig. 2.6	Productivity of firm by business size in Indonesia, 2018 (IDR billion) (*Source* Menegkop and UKM/BPS)	26
Fig. 2.7	Total investment value in MSMEs as a percentage of the total investment value of all business size groups, 2018 (*Source* Menegkop and UKM/BPS)	27
Fig. 2.8	Types of MSIs constraints, 2017 (*Source* BPS [2018])	29
Fig. 3.1	Export development of Indonesian MSMEs, 2007–2019 (percent of total exports) (*Source* Menegkop & UKM [online])	38
Fig. 3.2	MSME export values in the AP region by economy (*Source* APEC, 2020)	40

xvi   LIST OF FIGURES

Fig. 3.3	Percentage of MSIs involved in Export by group of industry, 2019 (*Note* KBLI Code: 10: food, 11: beverages, 12: tobacco processing, 13: textiles, 14: apparel, 15: leather, leather goods and footwear, 16: wood, wood products and cork (excluding furniture), woven articles from rattan, bamboo and the like, 17: paper and paper articles, 18: printing and reproduction of recorded media, 20: chemicals and articles of chemical substances, 21: pharmaceuticals, chemical medicinal products and traditional medicine, 22: rubber, articles of rubber and plastics, 23: non-metal minerals, 24: base metals, 25: non-machined metal goods and their equipment, 26: computers, electronic and optical goods, 27: electrical equipment, 28: YTDL machinery and equipment (excluding others), 29: motor vehicles, trailers and semi-trailers, 30: other means of transportation, 31: furniture; 32: other processing; 33: repair and installation of machinery and equipment. *Source* BPS [2020])	50
Fig. 3.4	MSME indirect export model in Indonesia	52
Fig. 3.5	Parties involved in partnerships with MSIs, 2019 (*Source* BPS, 2020)	56
Fig. 3.6	Percentage of types of partnership conducted by MSIs, 2019 (*Source* BPS, 2020)	56
Fig. 3.7	Scatter plot of number of MSIs doing export and MSIs doing marketing partnership (*Source* BPS, 2020)	57
Fig. 3.8	Development of Cooperatives in Indonesia, 2000–2019 (*Source* The Indonesian Ministry of Cooperative and SME [www.depkop.go.id])	60
Fig. 3.9	Scatter plot of number of MSIs doing export and MSIs that are members of a cooperative	65
Fig. 3.10	Scatter plot of percentage of MSIs doing export and MSIs that are members of a cooperative	65
Fig. 3.11	Percentage of MSIs as members of cooperatives by type of service received	66
Fig. 4.1	Percentage of MSEs in all sectors owned by female by province, Indonesia, 2016 (%) (*Source* BPS)	81
Fig. 4.2	Total MSEs in the manufacturing industry by gender of the owner, 2003–2019 (%) (*Source* BPS, 2020)	83
Fig. 4.3	Respondents from both categories by main constraints (*Source* Field survey: February–April 2016)	97

Fig. 5.1	Indonesian GDP growth rates during the Asian Financial Crisis and the Recovery Periods, 1997–2007 (%) (*Sources* BPS [*Berita Resmi Statistik: Pertumbuhan Ekonomi Indonesia; Laporan Bulanan Data Sosial-Ekonomi; Statistik Indonesia*], various issues)	110
Fig. 5.2	Output growth rates of the three key sectors in Indonesia during the Asian Financial Crisis and the Recovery Periods, 1997–2007 (%) (*Sources* BPS [*Berita Resmi Statistik: Pertumbuhan Ekonomi Indonesia; Laporan Bulanan Data Sosial-Ekonomi; Statistik Indonesia*], various issues)	110
Fig. 5.3	Development of Indonesian Income per Capita, 1970–2002 (US dollar) (*Sources* BPS [*Statistik Indonesia*] various issues; ADB [*Key Indicators Asia and the Pacific*], various issues)	111
Fig. 5.4	Poverty rate in Indonesia, 1976–2000 (%) (*Source* BPS [*Statistik Indonesia*], various issues)	111
Fig. 5.5	Examining empirically the effects of the 1997/1998 crisis on MSMEs in Indonesia with the first approach	113
Fig. 5.6	Examining empirically the effects of the 1997/1998 crisis on MSMEs in Indonesia with the second approach	113
Fig. 5.7	Total number of MSMEs in Indonesia (units) (*Source* Menegkop and UKM [www.depkop.go.id])	116
Fig. 5.8	Percentage changes of real GDP and total number of MSMEs in Indonesia (*Source* Indonesian State Ministry of Cooperative and SME [www.depkop.go.id])	117
Fig. 5.9	Theoretical framework of the effects of the 2008/2009 crisis on MSMEs in Indonesia	119
Fig. 5.10	Annual growth of Indonesian real GDP, 2000–2021 (%) (*Source* BPS [https://www.bps.go.id/])	122
Fig. 5.11	Number of visiting foreign tourists in Indonesia during the Period January 2020–January 2021 (thousand visitors) (*Source* BPS [https://www.bps.go.id/])	123
Fig. 5.12	Trend of open unemployment rate by gender in Indonesia between August 2018 and August 2020 (percent) (*Source* BPS [https://www.bps.go.id/])	124
Fig. 5.13	Trend of underemployment rate by gender in Indonesia, August 2018–August 2020 (percent) (*Source* BPS [https://www.bps.go.id/])	124
Fig. 5.14	Poverty rate in Indonesia, 2011–2020 (%)* (*Note* *September. *Source* BPS [http://www.bps.go.id])	127

xviii   LIST OF FIGURES

Fig. 5.15	Development of the Gini Ratio, September 2014–September 2020 (*Source* BPS [http://www.bps.go.id])	129
Fig. 5.16	Impact of COVID-19 pandemic on MSMEs in Indonesia	130
Fig. 5.17	The impact of COVID-19 on MSMEs through its effects on tourism	131
Fig. 5.18	Number of respondents by category of cost increases (*Source* Field survey 2020)	134
Fig. 5.19	Number of respondents by category of sales decline (*Source* Field survey 2020)	135
Fig. 5.20	Number of respondents by form of CMM (*Source* Field survey 2020)	139
Fig. 6.1	Total accumulated KUR distribution, 2007–2020 (Rp billion) (*Source* Bank Indonesia [BI] [http://www.bi.go.id/id/umkm/kredit/data/Default.aspx])	164
Fig. 6.2	The MSME funding ecosystem in Indonesia	165
Fig. 6.3	MSMEs' outstanding commercial loans of MSMEs in Indonesia, 2013–2018 (percent of total commercial loans) (*Source* Bank Indonesia [https://www.bi.go.id/id/pencarian/Default.aspx?k=kredit%20UMKM])	166
Fig. 6.4	Total number of MSME bank credit accounts 2013–2018 (*Source* Bank Indonesia [https://www.bi.go.id/id/pencarian/Default.aspx?k=kredit%20UMKM])	166
Fig. 6.5	Ecosystem of MSEs funding with the emergence of P2P lending provider in Indonesia	173
Fig. 7.1	"Classical" hypothesis on the link between the importance of MSMEs and economic development	182
Fig. 7.2	"Modern" hypothesis on the link between the importance of MSMEs and economic development	183
Fig. 7.3	Company growth theory based on life cycle theory (*Source* Degenhardt et al. [2002], Mao [2009], William [2017])	187
Fig. 7.4	"Pull" and "Push" determinant factors of the growth of MSEs in developing countries	189
Fig. 7.5	Hypothesis on the link between the importance of MSEs and poverty	189

LIST OF TABLES

Table 1.1	Summary of MSME classification criteria in APEC economies	6
Table 1.2	Main characteristics of MIEs, SEs, and MEs in Indonesia	8
Table 2.1	Number of MSMEs and their workers by sub-category in Indonesia, 2016–2018	14
Table 2.2	Growth in the number of MSMEs and MSME density in the AP region by economy (%)	16
Table 2.3	Distribution of manpower in MIEs and SEs by business field in Indonesia, 2016	19
Table 2.4	Number and percentage of poor population by region September 2019–September 2020	33
Table 2.5	Percentage and number of poor people by island in Indonesia, September 2020	33
Table 2.6	Distribution of MSEs and MLEs by Island, 2016 (%)	34
Table 3.1	Share of MSME exporters in the AP region by economy	39
Table 3.2	Main findings from selected important research papers on determinants of MSMEs' ability to do direct export	44
Table 3.3	Number of MSIs' involved in export by percentage export and group of industry, 2019	51
Table 3.4	Number and percentage of MSEs involved in export by group of industry and partnership, 2019	55
Table 3.5	Development of active cooperatives (all types) in Indonesia, 2019	61
Table 3.6	Number and percentage of MSEs involved in export by group of industry and cooperative, 2019	64

xix

xx   LIST OF TABLES

Table 4.1	Indonesian women as employers and own-account workers 2001–2020 (% of total employment by gender)	80
Table 4.2	Gender Development Index (GDI) and Gender Inequality Index (GII) in selected Asian developing countries, 2020	84
Table 4.3	The Global Gender Gap Index 2007 ranking and 2006 comparisons in selected Asian developing countries	85
Table 4.4	The Global Gender Gap Index rankings in ASEAN by member country, 2020	86
Table 4.5	Necessity-motivated entrepreneurship by gender in selected Southeast Asian Countries, 2015	88
Table 5.1	The hypotheses of the DS effects on MSMEs of the income declines in the final	115
Table 5.2	Studies on the impact of the 1997/1998 crisis on MSMEs in Indonesia	117
Table 5.3	Most affected exports by the 2008/2009 crisis in some other Southeast Asian Countries	118
Table 5.4	Impact of COVID-19 on the working-age population by sex and region of place live, August 2020 (million people)	125
Table 5.5	Percentage of change in commuter workers entering big cities August 2019–August 2020	126
Table 5.6	Number and percentage of poor population by region September 2019–September 2020	127
Table 5.7	Percentage and number of poor population by Island in Indonesia, September 2020	128
Table 5.8	Evidence on the impact of COVID-19 on MSMEs, March–April 2020	133
Table 5.9	Different types of business risks and different appropriate forms of CMMs by type of crisis, 1997/1998, 2008/2009, and 2020	136
Table 5.10	Evidence on CMMs adopted by affected MSMEs during the three crises	138
Table 6.1	Company profile of P2P lending providers in Indonesia, December 2019 and April 2020	160
Table 6.2	Profile of the surveyed ten small business' owners	169
Table 6.3	Number of MSEs granted loans by the interviewed P2P lending providers	171
Table 6.4	Constraints faced by P2P lending companies when collaborating with banks	172

CHAPTER 1

Introduction

1.1 The Importance of Micro, Small and Medium Enterprises

It has been recognized worldwide that micro, small and medium enterprises (MSMEs) play a vital role in economic development, as the enterprises have proved to be the primary source of job/employment creation and output growth, not only in developing countries but also in developed countries. In his various publications, based on reviews of many empirical studies, Tambunan (2006, 2009a, 2009b, 2015) shows that, for example, 12 million or about 63.2 percent of total labor force in the United States (US) worked in 350,000 firms employing less than 500 employees, which considered as MSMEs. These enterprises made up more than 99 percent of all business entities and employed more than 80 percent of total workforce in the country. They, often called the foundation enterprises, are the core of the US industrial base. MSMEs are also important in many European countries. In the Netherlands, for example, these enterprises accounted for 95 percent or more of total business establishments. In other industrialized/OECD countries like Japan, Australia, Germany, French and Canada, MSMEs, and micro and small enterprises (MSEs), are also acted as an important engine of economic growth and technological progress.

© The Author(s), under exclusive license to Springer Nature Singapore Pte Ltd. 2022
T. T.H. Tambunan, *Fostering Resilience through Micro, Small and Medium Enterprises*, Sustainable Development Goals Series, https://doi.org/10.1007/978-981-16-9435-6_1

1

In developing countries, MSMEs have also a crucial role to play because of their potential contributions to poverty reduction, improvement of income distribution, employment creation, industrial development, rural development, and export growth. For this reason, governments in many developing countries are supporting capacity building in their MSMEs largely through a variety of programs, of which subsidized credit schemes are the most important one. International institutes such as the World Bank, the Asian Development Bank (ADB), and the United Nation Industry and Development Organisation (UNIDO) and many donor countries through bilateral cooperations have also played a crucial role in empowering MSMEs in many developing countries.

It is widely suggested in the literature that the importance of MSMEs in developing countries is because of their characteristics, which include the following ones:

1. their number is large, especially MSEs, and they are scattered widely throughout the rural areas and therefore they may have a special "local" significance for the rural economy;
2. as being populated largely by firms that have considerable employment growth potential, their development or growth can be included as an important element of policy to create employment and generate income. This awareness may also explain the growing emphasis on the role of these enterprises in the rural areas. The agricultural sector has shown not to be able to absorb the increasing rural population. As a result, rural migration increased dramatically, causing high unemployment rates and its related socio-economic problems in the urban areas. Therefore, rural non-farm activities, especially rural industries being a potentially quite dynamic part of the rural economy have often been looked at their potential to create rural employment, and in this respect, MSMEs could play an important role;
3. not only that the majority of MSMEs, especially MSEs, in developing countries are found in the rural areas, they are also mainly agriculturally based activities. Therefore, government efforts to support MSMEs could also be considered as efforts, indirectly, to support the agricultural sector;
4. MSMEs use technologies that are in a general sense more "appropriate" (as compared to modern technologies used by large enterprises [LEs]) to factor proportions and local conditions in developing

countries, namely quite many raw materials being locally available and scarcity of capital, including human capital;

5. many MSMEs, especially small and medium enterprises (SMEs) expanded significantly. Therefore, they are regarded as enterprises having the "seedbed LEs" function;

6. although in general rural people are poor, available evidence showed that poor villagers were able to save a small amount of capital and invest it; they were willing to take risks by doing that. So, in this respect, MSMEs provide a good starting point for the mobilization of rural saving/investment; while, at the same time, these enterprises could function as an important sector providing an avenue for the testing and development of entrepreneurial ability of villagers. In fact, owners of many MSMEs financed their operations overwhelmingly by their own savings, supplemented by gifts or loans from relatives or from local informal moneylenders, traders, suppliers of raw materials and other inputs, and payments in advance from their consumers. These enterprises could therefore play another important role, namely a means to allocate rural savings that otherwise would be used for unproductive purposes. In other words, if productive activities are not available locally (in the rural areas), rural/farm households having money surplus might keep or save their money without any interest revenue inside their home because in many rural areas there are no banks. That is why, in many cases they used their wealth to buy lands, cars or houses and other unnecessary luxury consumption goods that often considered by the villagers as a matter of prestige;

7. although many goods produced by MSMEs are also for the middle- and high-income groups of population, it is generally evident that the primary market for MSMEs' products is overwhelmingly simple consumer goods, such as clothing, furniture and other articles from wood, footwear, household items made from bamboo, rattan, and wood, and metal products. These goods catered to the needs of local low-income consumers. MSMEs are also important for securing the basic need goods for poor/non-wealthy people/households. However, there are also many MSMEs engaged in the production of simple tools, equipments, and machines for the demands of small farmers and small producers in the industrial, trade, construction, and transport sectors;

8. as part of their dynamism, MSMEs, especially SMEs, often achieved rising productivity over time through both investment and technological change; although different countries may have different experiences with this, depending on various factors. The factors may include the level of economic development in general and development of related sectors in particular; accessibility to main important determinant factors of productivity, particularly capital, technology and skilled manpower; and government policies that support the development of production linkages between MSMEs and LEs as well as with foreign direct investment (FDI);

9. as often stated in the literature, one advantage of MSMEs was their flexibility relative to their larger competitors. These enterprises are construed as being especially important in industries or economies facing rapidly changing market conditions, such as the sharp macroeconomic downturns that have bedeviled many countries in Southeast Asia, including Indonesia, over the past one decade.

Therefore, given their vital role as discussed above, especially for poverty eradication, mostly among women, the United Nations (UN) has assigned a great role to MSMEs for taking a lead in achieving most of the economic-related sustainable development goals (SDGs), including promoting inclusive and sustainable economic growth, increasing productive employment opportunities and decent work especially for the poor and vulnerable, particularly women and youth, advancing sustainable industrialization and innovation, and creating a positive push for a higher quality of life, better education and good health for all (OCED, 2017, cited from Dasaraju et al., 2020).

This role of MSMEs has become more important considering the fact that the recovery efforts of the COVID-19 pandemic in many developing countries so far have been uneven and insufficient to reverse the economic and social consequences, especially to the livelihood of the most vulnerable. Even before the COVID-19 pandemic, the SDGs were already off-track, and SDGs financing was falling short in developing countries. The world has only less than a decade to achieve the 2030 Agenda for Sustainable Development. This effort demands, among others, productive and highly competitive MSMEs that also resilience to face future challenges.

1.2 Definition and Concept of MSMEs

What constitutes an MSME varies widely between countries. There is no common agreement on what distinguishes a microenterprise (MIE) from a small enterprise (SE); a SE from a medium enterprise (ME); and a ME from a LE. MSMEs may range from a part time business with no hired workers or a non-employing unincorporated business, often called self-employed units, such as traditional business units making and selling handicrafts in rural Java in Indonesia, to a semiconductor manufacturer employing hundreds of people in Japan. They may range from fast growing firms to private family firms that have not changed much for decades or stagnated. They range from enterprises, which are independent businesses, to those, which are inextricably part of a large company, such as those which are part of an international subcontracting network. The only true common characteristic of MSMEs is that they are "not-large"; that is whether a firm is really an MSME or not is relative.

Moreover, definitions and concepts used for statistical purposes can vary from those used for policy or program purposes (for example, to determine eligibility for special assistance). Many countries have definitions for policy purposes, and to complicate matters further, these definitions often differ from the definition used for statistical purposes, as also differ by industry and policy program. As an example, there is considerable diversity in the definitions on MSMEs even for statistical purposes among countries/economies in the Asia–Pacific region or officially known as the APEC economies. However, many economies in the region also use a monetary measure such as initial investment or asset, including or excluding land and building, annual sales or turnover to define MSMEs. About half of APEC member economies have a classification standard that is a factor in the sector or industry in which the business operates. In some APEC economies, companies must meet all the criteria to be classified as MSME, while in other economies, companies must meet only one or two criteria. Some APEC members, like Mexico and Papua New Guinea, use a formula or assessment matrix based on specific criteria standards to classify MSMEs (Table 1.1).

Even with the number of workers, there is considerable diversity between the economies in the region. In most economies, an MSME is defined as a business entity having less than 100 employees (and even fewer in specific sectors such as services or retail), but in some larger economies like the United States and Canada the ceiling is raised to 300

Table 1.1 Summary of MSME classification criteria in APEC economies

Economy	Total workers	Sales/Revenues	Assets/Capital	Sector/Industry
Australia	X	X		
Brunei Darussalam	X			
Canada	X			
Chile	X	X		
China	X	X	X	X
Hong Kong, China	X			X
Indonesia		X	X	
Japan	X		X	X
Korea		X	X	X
Malaysia	X	X		X
Mexico	X	X		X
New Zealand	X			
Papua New Guinea	X	X	X	X
Peru		X		
Philippines			X	
Russia	X	X		
Singapore	X	X		
China Taipei	X	X	X	X
Thailand	X		X	X
United States	X	X		X
Viet Nam	X	X	X	

Source APEC (2020)

or even 500 employees. In Indonesia, MIEs employ less than five (5) full time equivalent employees; SEs are enterprises with 5 to 19 workers; and MEs are those with 20 to 50 employees more.

Most enterprises from this MSME category are actually very small and about 70 to 80 percent of them employ less than five (5) people. There are only a very small percentage of firms, typically ranging from about 1 to 4 percent, which have more than 100 employees. Unfortunately, there is no consistent definition of an MIE among the economies in the region. Only some economies have definitions or categories of MIEs, and most of these use 5 employees as a cut off. In practice, however, most MIEs were likely to be non-employing workers (i.e. self-employment). They did not actually employ anyone, but they created jobs and some incomes, even if only part time jobs, for the entrepreneurs. These MIEs made up the great majority of enterprises, and usually comprised around 60 to 80 percent of all business establishments. Their contribution to employment was usually disproportionately small, and they typically contributed only about 10 to 40 percent of available jobs. However, as stated in the report, the role of MIEs in creating jobs will be greater in the future in some economies, where they will provide a higher proportion of jobs, or where they create job opportunities that would not otherwise be available.

In Indonesia, there are several definitions of MSMEs, depending on which agency provides the definition. However, Indonesia also has a national law on MSMEs. The initial law was issued in 1995 by the State Ministry of Cooperative and SME, namely the Law on Small Enterprises Number 9 of 1995. It defines a small enterprise (SE) as a business unit with total initial assets of up to 200 million rupiah (IDR), not including land and buildings, or with annual sales of a maximum of IDR1 billion, and a medium enterprise (ME) as a business unit with annual sales of more than IDR 1 billion but less than IDR 50 billion. Although the law does not explicitly define a microenterprise (MIEs), data from the State Ministry on SEs also include MIEs. In 2008, the State Ministry issued the new Law on MSMEs Number 20. According to this new law, MSMEs are those with annual sales/turnovers up to IDR 50 billion and fixed investments (excluding land and building) of less than IDR 10 billion.

1.3   CHARACTERISTICS

But in reality, the sub-categories of MSMEsin Indonesia as in many other developing countries do not only differ in the total number of employees, annual income, or the value of capital/assets invested as criteria for defining them. It lso easy to differentiate them with each other with reference to their different characteristics. These character-istics include formality or way of doing business, market orientation, owner/producer socio-economic profile, nature of work, organization and management system, degree of mechanization (nature of production processes), sources of main raw materials and capital, location, external relations, owner's motivation and entrepreneurial level, and the level of involvement of womenas entrepreneurs (Table 1.2).

In Indonesia, and possibly in many other countries as well, more women entrepreneurs are found in MSMEs than in LEs, and within the MSMEs group, MIEs have more women as business owners than SEs

8   T. T.H. TAMBUNAN

Table 1.2   Main characteristics of MIEs, SEs, and MEs in Indonesia

Aspects	\MIEs	SEs	MEs
Formality	Operate in informal sector, and unregistered	Some operate in formal sector, registered and pay taxes	All operate in formal sector, registered and pay taxes
Location	Majority in rural areas	Many in urban areas	Mostly in urban areas
Organization and management	• Run by the owner • No internal labor division • No formal management and accounting system	• In some, run by the owner • Labor division in some • Formal management and accounting system in some	• Many hire professional managers, • Many have labor division, formal organizational structure and formal accounting system
Nature of employment	Majority use unpaid family members	Some hired wage laborers	All hire wage laborers and have formal recruitment system
Nature of production process	• Degree of mechanization very low/mostly manual • Low level of technology	Some use advanced machines	Many have high degree of mechanization and have access to modern technology
Market orientation	Majority sell to local market and for low-income consumers	• Many sell to national market and export • Many serve also middle to high-income group	• All sell to national market and many also export • All serve middle and high-income consumers
Owner's profiles	Low or uneducated and from poor households	Some have good education, and from non-poor households	Majority have good education and are from wealthy families

(continued)

Table 1.2 (continued)

Aspects	\MIEs	SEs	MEs
Sources of inputs	Majority use local raw materials and use own money	Some use imported raw materials, and have access to bank	Majority use imported raw materials and have access to formal credit sources
External networks	Majority have no access to government programs and no business linkages with LEs	Many have good relations with government and have business linkages (e.g. subcontracting) with LEs	Majority have good access to government programs and have business linkages with LEs
Motivation of the owners	To survive	Some are looking for profit	All are looking for profit
Level of entrepreneurship of the owners	Low	Medium	High
Female owner	Majority	Many	Few

Source Tambunan (2016)

and MEs for two main reasons: (1) In order to carry out MIE activities, advanced technologies and high formal skills are not really necessary because, in general, MIEs are relatively simple business activities that generate not much income, depending on the type of business, such as food production, food stalls, shops that sell basic goods, retail and handicrafts; and (2) because of this simple and very small activity, no special room is required (such as a factory building) and, especially for married women, they can easily divide their time between serving customers and carrying out their primary duty of taking care of their household.

In addition, there are differences in the background or motivation of business owners between MIEs, SEs and Mes. The difference in owner's personal motivation should actually be seen as the most important characteristic to differentiate MSMEs from LE, as well as between the sub-categories within the MSME group itself. According to Tambunan (2015), most micro-entrepreneurs in Indonesia have more economic motivation than profit, that is, they conduct these activities not for profit but as a means of survival, namely to earn money (for the unemployed) or to increase their total income (for example farmers whose their primary income from farming is not sufficient) to meet their daily needs. However, there are also micro entrepreneurs whose motivation is to continue their family business. Compared to small and even medium-sized entrepreneurs, few micro-entrepreneurs have the motivation to seek profit. In addition, another reason for becoming a micro-scale entrepreneur is that there are no opportunities for careers in other fields (Tambunan, 2015).

The motivations of small-sized entrepreneurs are more diverse than their micro counterparts. Although economic motivation is also the main reason, some others have a more realistic motivation by looking at future business prospects with their limited capital. Most of the small-sized entrepreneurs in Indonesia have a reason to do business because of the existence of business opportunities and a secure large market share. There are also a number of small-sized entrepreneurs doing business with the main reason being heredity/inheritance, being equipped with skills and creating new jobs for local residents. Although there are still a number of entrepreneurs who argued that they do not have opportunities in other fields for various reasons, such as low formal education, or poor physical conditions. This shows that small-sized entrepreneurs have a better reason than micro-sized entrepreneurs.

Meanwhile, the motivations of medium-sized entrepreneurs in Indonesia are largely the same as those of most small-sized entrepreneurs, namely seeing future business prospects, opportunities, and a great market opportunity. There are also some entrepreneurs from this group who do business because of heredity/inheritance, have expertise, or others. In general, it can be said that the motivation of small-sized and medium-sized entrepreneurs is more business oriented than micro-sized entrepreneurs.

Another characteristic is the age structure of the entrepreneur/business owner. Based on national data, the age structure of MSME owners according to age groups in Indonesia shows that more than a third of the number of MSME owners were over 45 years old, and only a few were under 25 years old. On average, MSME owners were over 40 years old. This age structure of entrepreneurs/business owners shows that MIE and SE owners tend to be younger than ME owners. One of the reasons could be that MEs are business units which are not only bigger but also more complex and they require more capital compared to MIEs and SEs, and such businesses can only be conducted by persons who are more established and have enough money, long experience, and broad insight, and all of these are age related. Another suggestion is that many ME owners started many years earlier from much smaller-sized businesses, so that as their businesses grow and become MEs, the owners will also get older.

The difference between MSMEs and LE can also be seen from the status of their workers. In LEs and MEs there are no unpaid workers; all workers are legally recruited and paid monthly. In contrast to this, in MIEs and SEs there are many unpaid workers. Thus, the composition of unpaid labor tends to be inversely proportional to the scale of the business, meaning that the larger the size of the business, the smaller the composition of unpaid workers. This also shows that in most MIEs and SEs, the owners are directly involved in all activities in running their businesses, and that many of them employ family members as workers, often referred to as "helpers".

From the gender perspective of workers, there are also differences between LEs and MSMEs. In LEs, the role of female workers is relatively smaller than that in MSMEs, although there are variations by sector or subsector. Within the MSME group, MIEs and SEs tend to have more female workers than MEs. The structure of the workforce according to sex is closely related to the differences in types of business between the two sub-business groups. In the manufacturing industry, for example, the nature of production activities in MIEs and SEs is generally simpler than that in most MEs, such as in the textile and clothing industry, food processing, footwear, and handicrafts which do not require too much physical burden and special skills that make it easier for women to do it.

The most striking difference between LE and MSMEs is the gender of the entrepreneurs or business owners. In Indonesia, although currently the level of emancipation and development of women is much better than, say 50 years ago, until now formal jobs are still dominated by men. In MSMEs, especially MIEs, most of which are in the informal sector, the role of women entrepreneurs is much bigger than that in LEs. In this latter group of enterprises, the level of participation of women as entrepreneurs is relatively low. This gender structure suggests a positive correlation between the level of participation of women as entrepreneurs and the size of the business, which means that the larger the size of the business, the fewer women entrepreneurs.

Lastly, the difference between LEs and MSMEs can also be seen in the average level of formal education of entrepreneurs/owners. The number of business owners in MIEs and SEs with only primary school education is more than that in MEs and LEs. Whereas for the category of entrepreneur/owner of who graduated from college the percentage is higher in LEs than in MSMEs. This entrepreneurial/owner structure according to their formal education level suggests a positive relationship between the average level of education of the owner and the size of the business: the larger the size of the business, which is usually positively related to the level of business complexity that requires higher skills and managers with broader business insight, the more entrepreneurs/owners with higher formal education.

REFERENCES

APEC. (2020, April). *Overview of the SME sector in the APEC region: Key issues on market access and internationalization.* APEC Policy Support Unit, Asia-Pacific Economic Cooperation Secretariat.

Dasaraju, H., Somalaraju, K., & Kota, S. M. (2020). MSMEs in developing economies and their role in achieving sustainable development goals in the context of Covid19: A theoretical exposition. *International Journal of Small and Medium Enterprises and Business Sustainability, 5*(2), 93–120.

Tambunan, T. T. H. (2006). *Development of small & medium enterprises in Indonesia from the Asia-Pacific perspective.* LPFE-Usakti.

Tambunan, T. T. H. (2009a). *SME in Asian developing countries.* Palgrave Macmillan.

Tambunan, T. T. H. (2009b). *Development of small and medium enterprises in ASEAN countries.* Readworthy Publications.

Tambunan, T. T. H. (2015, May). *Utilisation of existing ASEAN-FTAs by local micro-, small- and medium-sized enterprises* (ARTNeT Policy Brief, No. 45). ESCAP (UN).

Tambunan, T. T. H. (2016, September). *The importance of credit guarantee scheme as a financing alternative for MSMEs in ASEAN in the era of ASEAN economic community.* The Study of Credit Guarantee Schemes in ASEAN Member States. Unpublished report, US-ACTI Grants Program. USAID.

CHAPTER 2

Development of MSMEs and Their Main Constraints

2.1 Number of Enterprise and Labor

The data from the State Ministry of Cooperatives and SMEs (Menegkop and UKM) as well as the Central Statistics Agency (BPS) showed that there were approximately 39.765 million MSMEs which represents 99.8 percent of the total business establishments in Indonesia in 1997. The number was observed to be growing every year except in 1998 when the Asian financial crisis of the 1997–1998 period hit Indonesia which caused the Indonesian rupiah (IDR) exchange rate to depreciate against the United States dollar (USD) by more than 200 percent. This forced several domestic companies out of business while some others reduced their production volume due to various reasons such as the high cost of foreign debt (loan repayment plus interest) in rupiah, high domestic inflation, high-interest rates on the domestic money market which, along with many domestic banks experiencing financial difficulties due to bad debts and losses in USD trading, made it difficult for domestic businesses to obtain credit at the time, and high import prices for raw materials and other production inputs in rupiah.

The crisis also caused the national economy to experience the biggest recession in Indonesian history since the 1945 independence and even the

© The Author(s), under exclusive license to Springer Nature
Singapore Pte Ltd. 2022
T. T.H. Tambunan, *Fostering Resilience through Micro,*
Small and Medium Enterprises, Sustainable Development Goals Series,
https://doi.org/10.1007/978-981-16-9435-6_2

13

Dutch colonial period as indicated by a negative GDP rate of 13 percent. The number of MSMEs at the time reduced to approximately 36.8 million units which is a 7.42 percent reduction. Moreover, Menegkop and UKM estimated that nearly 3 million MSEs stopped doing business during the crisis while the MEs and LEs that closed down were estimated to be 4.2 and 12.7 percent, respectively, of the total enterprises (Tambunan, 2019). However, when the national economy began to recover in 1999, the number of MSMEs started growing again to 37.9 million units which is an increase of 2.98 percent and the growth continued afterward.

Table 2.1 shows the number of MSMEs was nearly 61.7 million companies which is approximately 99 percent of the total business units in Indonesia in 2016 and the number increased to more than 64 million in 2018. The findings showed that the MIEs were dominant as indicated by almost 98 percent while the SE portion was only about 1 percent and MEs were even less, not up to 0.1 percent. This means the discussion of Indonesian MSMEs is usually concerning MIEs.

A comparison with other economies in the Asia and Pacific (AP) region, based on the most recent data available at that time in the period 2015–2018 from the APEC Secretariat, showed that more than 98 percent of companies are considered MSMEs with more than half of the economies, including Indonesia, holding a share of more than 99 percent as indicated in Fig. 2.1. This share has remained constant over the past decade for all economies. This means nearly 150 million businesses in the region are considered MSMEs based on how each economy defined

Table 2.1 Number of MSMEs and their workers by sub-category in Indonesia, 2016–2018

Description	Unit of measure	2016		2018	
		Total	Share (%)	Total	Share (%)
MSMEs	Unit	61,651,177	99.99	64,194,057	99.99
LEs		5370	0.01	5550	0.01
Total companies		61,656,547	100.00	64,199,607	100.00
MSMEs	People	112,828,610	97.04	116,978,631	97.00
LEs		3,444,746	2.96	3,619,507	3.00
Total workers		116,273,356	100.00	120,598,138	100.00

Source Menegkop and UKM (http://www.depkop.go.id/)

2 DEVELOPMENT OF MSMES AND THEIR MAIN CONSTRAINTS   15

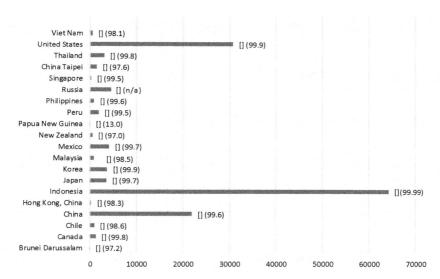

Fig. 2.1 Number of MSMEs in the AP region by economy (*Note* the number of MSMEs is rounded up in thousand. The numbers in brackets are percentages of total enterprises. *Source* APEC [2020])

its MSMEs and the availability of most recent data and this represents approximately 99.8 percent of all businesses in the region. It is important to note that what is considered MSME in one economy may not be considered as MSME in other economies due to the difference in their definitions of the concept.

The actual number of MSMEs in different economies of the region is calculated not only based on different classification standards but also through the use of data collected using different methodologies. For example, the data for Australia includes individual and company ownership without workers as MSMEs while those from Canada do not. Likewise, Indonesia includes the informal sector while other countries with a large share of the informal sector such as Peru and the Philippines do not. Therefore, the examination of the figures presented in this chapter requires observing the changes in each economy over time and analyzing the trends being shown across regions instead of comparing the economies.

The number of MSMEs tends to grow by 1.0–2.5 percent per year in most economies including Indonesia as indicated in Table 2.2. Several economies have experienced strong growth rates in the number of MSMEs over the past 5–10 years as observed in Malaysia, Peru, Russia, Vietnam, and China while the growth rate was observed to be faster in other economies. It was only Japan that experienced a decline and this reflects the overall reduction in the number of firms as a whole due to ongoing demographic changes.

The contribution of the MSMEs to the net growth of the number of companies is, however, very large as observed in Australia and Malaysia despite the significant decrease in the number of LEs. MSMEs accounted

Table 2.2 Growth in the number of MSMEs and MSME density in the AP region by economy (%)

Economy	MSME growth		MSME density	
	%	Period	Density	Period
Australia	1.4	2008–2009 to 2017–2018	92.4	2017–2018
Brunei Darussalam	1.1	2010–2017	13.8	2017
Canada	1.9	2011–2018	34.6	2018
Chile	2.7	2009–2017	51.2	2017
China	115.0	2013–2018	15.8	2017
Hong Kong, China	2.0	2009–2018	45.4	2018
Indonesia	2.5	2010–2018	239.8	2018
Japan	−2.3	2009–2016	28.2	2016
Korea	2.5	2009–2017	72.5	2017
Malaysia	7.1	2010–2015	30.0	2015
Mexico	1.0	2015–2018	33.0	2018
New Zealand	1.1	2009–2018	106.2	2018
Papua New Guinea	N/A	N/A	6.0	2016
Peru	6.7	2009–2017	60.4	2017
Philippines	2.5	2010–2017	8.8	2017
Russia	6.0	2010–2014	31.5	2014
Singapore	2.0	2014–2018	46.6	2018
China Taipei	2.0	2009–2018	62.2	2018
Thailand	0.7	2009–2018	44.3	2018
United States	1.6	2009–2016	95.4	2016
Viet Nam	8.8	2012–2017	5.4	2017

Source APEC (2020)

for more than 98 enterprises of the net growth in the number of enterprises for most of the economies in the region during the reference period, with most observed to owned shares of more than 99 percent. This is consistent with the findings indicated earlier that MSMEs constitute the majority of firms in the AP region and this share has remained stable over the past decade. It also helps to illustrate the importance of MSMEs as a source of job creation and economic growth in an economy.

The report on MSMEs in the AP region published by the APEC Secretariat (APEC, 2020) showed that another way to observe the prevalence of MSMEs in an economy is through the analysis of the density or intensity which is defined as the number of MSMEs per 1000 people. This is often seen as an indicator of the overall business environment in an economy reflecting the ease with which new businesses enter the market. However, with the previous discussion about the MSME data collection methodology and the boundaries of cross-economic comparison, the data for only one period does not always provide a complete picture of the number of MSMEs in an economy. Therefore, it is more useful to study changes in the density of MSMEs in an economy from one period to another (APEC, 2020). Table 2.2 showed Indonesia as the economy with the highest density of MSMEs in the region.

The dominance of MSEs in the MSMEs group is not only in Indonesia but also in other economies in the AP region. It is also important to note that microenterprises (MIEs) make up the largest share of total MSEs followed by small enterprises (SEs) while medium enterprises (MEs) are the smallest. Moreover, the economies that collect separate data on individual or employer entrepreneurs and enterprises without paid workers showed the companies from these two categories are the highest in MSMEs. For instance, individual entrepreneurs constitute more than 50 percent of all MSMEs in Japan and Russia while employers without employees made up almost 81 percent of the total in the United States. In Vietnam almost 80 percent of total MSMEs are MIEs, and in China approximately 85 percent (APEC, 2020). In the AP region, Indonesia has the largest share with almost 100 percent and this automatically means its workers are dominated by those working with MIEs (Menegkop and UKM, http://www.depkop.go.id/).

The latest data from the Minister of Cooperatives and Small and Medium Enterprises presented in Table 2.1 showed that the number of paid workers in Indonesian MIEs was more than 107 million out of an estimated total of 117 million workers in MSMEs in 2018. Moreover, most of the MIEs workers were generally observed to have only had primary school or at most high school education. According to gender, women are mostly employed, especially in low-tech industrial groups which does not require too many physical burdens such as food processing and beverage, apparel, and different kinds of handicrafts companies.

The results of business/company registration in the 2016 economic census (SE2016) also showed that the workforce outside agriculture, forestry, and fisheries sectors in Indonesia was 70.32 million and this was dominated by those in MSEs with 53.6 million which is 76.28 percent of the total workforce while medium and large enterprises (MLEs) only absorbed 23.72 percent. Although an MSE has a small workforce compared to an MLE but the significantly higher number of MSEs in the country allows the absorption of a large workforce. Meanwhile, MLEs also require a large number of workers but they are significantly lesser in Indonesia compared to MSEs and are usually concentrated in big cities, thereby, making their absorption of labor lesser. Furthermore, the existence of almost 99 percent of companies in the country as MSEs indicates they can be a forum for community empowerment and a driver of the economy. However, the number and percentage of workers in microenterprises (MIEs) and small enterprises (SEs) by sector in 2016 are presented in Table 2.3.

The share of the total workforce in MSMEs varies widely between economies in the region. For example, Russia has only approximately 25.2 percent as indicated in Fig. 2.2 as against the higher percentage recorded in Indonesia. Moreover, the number of workers in MSMEs comprises more than 60 percent of total workers in most economies with some recorded to have more than 80 percent. It was also discovered that there are more than 950 million people employed by MSMEs across the region depending on how each economy defines MSMEs and most recent data and this value accounts for nearly two-thirds of the total employment in the region. This proportion has also remained constant for the past 5 to 10 years across the economies in the AP region with only Malaysia and Thailand observed to have experienced a substantial change over the reference period as indicated by an increase of 13.3 and 7.3 percentage points, respectively.

The employment opportunities in MSMEs were observed to have grown by 1.0–2.5 percent per year in more than half of the total

2 DEVELOPMENT OF MSMES AND THEIR MAIN CONSTRAINTS 19

Table 2.3 Distribution of manpower in MIEs and SEs by business field in Indonesia, 2016

Sector	Size		
	MIEs	SEs	Total
Mining, Energy, Water and Waste Management	620,851 (1.51)	141,056 (1.12)	761,907 (1.42)
Processing industry	6,424,952 (15.66)	2,926,753 (23.21)	9,351,705 (17.43)
Construction	1,202,851 (2.93)	838,962 (6.65)	2,041,813 (3.81)
Wholesale and Retail Trade, Car and Motorcycle Repair and Maintenance	16,403,030 (39.98)	3,606,960 (28.61)	20,009,990 (37.30)
Transportation and Warehousing	1,612,370 (3.93)	128,158 (1.02)	1,740,528 (3.24)
Provision of Accommodation and Provision of Food and Drink	6,808,195 (16.59)	996,472 (7.90)	7,804,667 (14.55)
Information and Communication	876,527 (2.14)	62,187 (0.49)	938,714 (1.75)
Finance and Insurance Activities	295,474 (0.72)	254,593 (2.02)	550,067 (1.03)
Real Estate	561,628 (1.37)	30,251 (0.24)	591,879 (1.10)
Company Services	754,687 (1.84)	180,620 (1.43)	935,307 (1.74)
Education	2,871,679 (7.00)	2,916,023 (23.13)	5,787,702 (10.79)
Human Health Activities and Social Activities	593,074 (1.45)	311,996 (2.47)	905,070 (1.69)
Other Services	2,006,980 (4.89)	215,195 (1.71)	2,222,175 (4.14)
Total	41,032,298 (100.00)	12,609,226 (100.00)	53,641,524 (100.00)

Source BPS (2017)

economies in the AP region based on the available data for the period between 2008 and 2018 as indicated in Fig. 2.3. Several economies have also experienced strong growth in the employment created by MSMEs, including the Philippines, Thailand, and Vietnam over the past years while Indonesia recorded a relatively low rate which was only 2.5 percent and this is lower than the percentage increase in the number of workers in LEs.

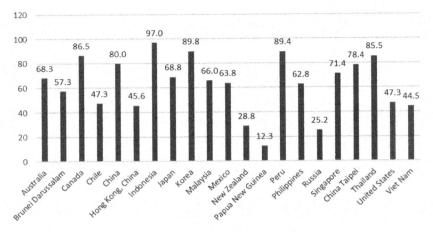

Fig. 2.2 Share of employment in MSMEs in the AP region by economy (*Source* APEC [2020])

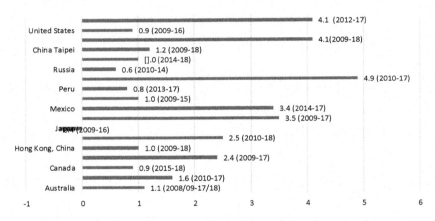

Fig. 2.3 Employment growth in MSMEs in the AP region by economy (%) (*Note* Compound annual growth rates [CAGR] were used. *Source* APEC [2020])

2.2 Contribution to GDP

The contribution of MSMEs to GDP is always smaller than their role as job creators in all economies in the AP region. This is observed from their absorption of more than 90 percent of the total workforce as well as their contribution of lesser than 90 percent to the GDP with the economies having different ratios. Figure 2.4 shows that MSMEs collectively contributed more than 50 percent to Indonesia's GDP and even though this is greater than the value for LEs, their actual contribution is much smaller considering the fact that they have a significantly higher number compared to the LEs. Moreover, there are also differences within the MSME group such that the total contribution of MIEs and SEs is lesser than those for MEs which is also smaller than the ones provided by the LE.

Several studies have been conducted on factors determining the low and high production or GDP share growth of MSMEs. For example, Joomunbaccus and Padachi (2019) investigated the factors affecting the growth of MSMEs in Mauritius using a descriptive-based survey approach and found entrepreneurial skills, access to finance, and effective marketing to be the most significant factors. Bari et al. (2005) also used a sample of 54 MSMEs in Pakistan and identified lack of financing and poor business support as the biggest challenges facing these firms in the country. Moreover, Moktan (2007) studied 168 MSEs in Bhutan and found that

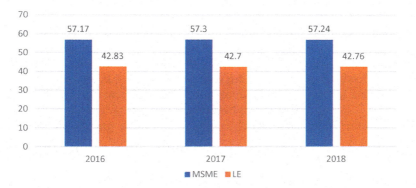

Fig. 2.4 Share of GDP by business size in Indonesia, 2016–2018 (constant 2000 prices; %) (*Source* Menegkop and UKM and BPS)

access to finance, proper business regulations, and the right infrastructure were the main determinants of MSEs success while the evidence from Chilipunde (2010) showed that the current problems faced by MSMEs in Malawi are due to the lack of a trained workforce, financial incapacity, poor managerial skills, and information technology (IT). The owner-managers were also found to have inadequate training, poor entrepreneurial skills, and unethical project behavior.

Suroso et al. (2017) examined the relationship between human capital (the dimensions used include the level of formal education, business management training, previous work experience, experience in parent's business, and owner experience) and entrepreneurial competence (the dimensions used include regulatory competence, strategic competence, relationship competence, and opportunities to seek business competencies) and its influence on the performance of MSME businesses in Central Java province in Indonesia. The study was conducted through a quantitative approach with the use of a questionnaire as the survey instrument and the results showed that human resource competence and entrepreneurial competence had a simultaneous significant effect on the success of MSME businesses but a partial test showed that entrepreneurial competence did not affect business performance. These results indicate the ability of entrepreneurial characteristics, especially human capital and entrepreneurial competencies, to influence the performance of MSMEs. Therefore, it was recommended that entrepreneurs or owners of MSMEs increase their knowledge through both formal and informal education and training and also acquire managerial experience.

Macphersona and Holt (2007) systematically reviewed existing empirical studies which focus on the influence of knowledge possessed by entrepreneurs or owners of MSMEs on business performance and the results showed that quality human resources, strong social capital, good organizational systems, and extensive knowledge networks together have a positive impact on their business growth. Rihayana et al. (2018) also examined the factors influencing the output growth of MSMEs with special attention on entrepreneurial factors and relationships with consumers in strengthening marketing capabilities toward achieving marketing success in the *endek* weaving and embroidery handicraft industry in Denpasar City in Bali. The research was conducted using a structural equation model (Smart-PLS) in 2016 and the results showed that entrepreneurial orientation affected marketing performance but did not affect the marketing ability. The company's ability to develop and maintain customer relationships was also observed to have affected its marketing capabilities and this further influenced the marketing performance. The study concluded that the company-designed products, efforts to produce products tailored to customer tastes, and the creation of new breakthroughs in the production process were unable to significantly improve marketing performance. Meanwhile, the performance was improved through the implementation of strategies focused on creating customer satisfaction and relationships by integrating several functional areas of the company to achieve a competitive advantage. This, therefore, means there is a need to improve the choice in the use of promotional media.

Sidek et al. (2019) were also motivated by the resource-based view (RBV) theory which indicates the high significance of resources and capabilities at the firm level in maintaining competitive advantage and performance to examine the factors influencing business performance. They also determined the effect of serial mediation by mapping the entrepreneurial orientation as the ability and access to external finance and the resource with the ability to produce competitive advantage required to ultimately improve the performance of MSMEs. The data obtained from 284 randomly selected MSMEs were analyzed using a structural equation model (AMOS-SEM) and the relationship between entrepreneurial orientation and MSME performance was observed to be partly mediated by the access to external finance and competitive advantage. The study concluded that entrepreneurial orientation and access to external financial resources are two important factors determining the ability of MSMEs to increase production due to the fact that they enhance competitive advantage.

Malaeb (2017) researched the barriers to the growth of MSMEs in Lebanon in Master's dissertation and found political, economic, and security situation as well as excessive administrative burdens and a less conducive business and regulatory environment to be the factors hampering the development of the industry in the country. Moreover, the results drew a line from the close ties between the lack of a specific government policy for MSMEs and the growth of these firms in the country. It was also concluded that the obstacles faced by MSMEs in Lebanon are different from those in most other developing countries because are not related to the nature of these business but rather controlled by external factors such as the political and security situation of the country.

There is also quite a lot of studies on the development of MSME businesses with the focus on those owned or managed by women. This is considered important due to the fact that most MSMEs, especially MSEs, in developing countries including Indonesia are run by women. Sallah and Caesar (2020) investigated the impact of intangible assets available to women entrepreneurs/business owners on their business performance and found three intangible resources including social capital, humans, and reputation to have the most significant contribution to the growth of businesses.

Rahman (2010) also assessed the key factors affecting the performance of women MSME entrepreneurs in Bangladesh using cross-sectional data from 375 MSME entrepreneurs. Moreover, descriptive statistics were used to describe the relationship between the dependent and independent variables. The dependent variable was the business performance of the female respondents which was measured by the average income earned, net expenditure, average investment, and the average number of the labor force while the independent variables include the factors affecting the performance such as the personal attributes of the respondents, entrepreneurial characteristics, business capacity, and the strengths and weaknesses of women entrepreneurship including the environmental factors such as the institutional supports and services. Some other variables were also considered to have a moderate role and these include entrepreneurship training and education for women entrepreneurs while government, policy, use of advanced technology, and the role of trade organizations were considered as important intervening variables. The findings showed that women entrepreneurs in MSMEs were mostly young but literate housewives with low business experience, inadequate expertise to run their businesses, low education or knowledge, and most of them suffer from a lack of capital. Moreover, most environmental factors, political situations as well as the law and taxation were found to have a negative impact on the performance of these women entrepreneurs. All of these factors ultimately contributed to their poor business performance.

Islam et al. (2019) also studied the businesses managed by women in Bangladesh using surveys and in-depth interviews with 201 women entrepreneurs in MSEs involved in various business sectors. A structured questionnaire was designed to collect relevant information from the respondents and the results showed that some socio-economic factors significantly influenced the development of MSME businesses managed by women. These factors include the availability of MSME authority services, difficulties in obtaining initial capital, community relations, family problems and gender discrimination, availability of training centers, availability of service tools, and availability of raw materials.

Bhuyan and Pathak (2019) also investigated the inequality faced by women entrepreneurs in different countries and the factors associated with the variations. The specific objectives of the study were to (i) identify the factors creating entrepreneurial gender disparities, (ii) identify the barriers faced by women entrepreneurs, and (iii) compare women's entrepreneurial activities in different countries. This research was based on secondary data retrieved from several reports such as the Global Entrepreneurship Monitor (GEM), the Women's Entrepreneurship Index, and the 2007–2015 report from the Organization for Economic Cooperation and Development (OECD). The results showed that the unavailability of women's networks, technical training, access to finance, fear of failure, and the absence of supportive policies were some of the key factors hindering the growth of women's entrepreneurship or the development of MSMEs managed by women.

It has been previously stated that the higher GDP share of MSMEs, when compared to LEs, is not due to a higher level of productivity (partially by individual factors of production such as labor productivity or based on all factors of productivity) compared to LEs but rather due to the fact that almost all the firms in the country are MSMEs. Moreover, it is possible to calculate the level of productivity of MSMEs using two methods with the first being the productivity level of the inputs or factors used in their production, either partial or total, while the second is the level of business unit productivity or output per firm. Meanwhile, the data constraint associated with the first approach indicates only the level of labor productivity which includes the value or volume of output or value-added generated by labor divided by the number of labors can be calculated. This means a worker averagely produces a certain number of outputs and the quantity produced per day or hour reflects the productivity of such worker. Figure 2.5 shows that the value-added ratio (based on constant market prices) to the number of labors in the LE group is greater than the same ratio in the MSME group as generally expected. Moreover, there are other differences in the productivity of labor within the MSME group with the MIEs which use a lot of unpaid workers found to have the lowest while the highest was recorded in MEs.

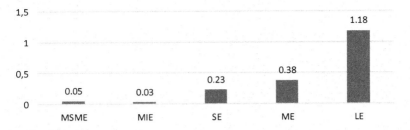

Fig. 2.5 Labor productivity by business size in Indonesia, 2018 (IDR billion) (*Source* Menegkop and UKM/BPS)

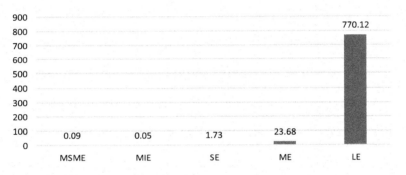

Fig. 2.6 Productivity of firm by business size in Indonesia, 2018 (IDR billion) (*Source* Menegkop and UKM/BPS)

The second approach is the ratio of output or value-added to the number of firms such as the ratio of value-added generated by MSMEs to the number of MSMEs. Figure 2.6 shows that there is a much greater difference in terms of productivity of firms between MSMEs and LEs when compared to the productivity of labor. This is observed from the fact that the number of firms from the LE group is much lesser. It is also important to note that the level of productivity of the firms also varies between sub-groups as reported in labor productivity.

The low productivity of MSMEs is not only evident in Indonesia but also considered to be one of the general features of this business group in developing countries when compared with those in developed countries. This is due to the fact that these MSMEs, especially the rural

MSEs, are limited by the unavailability of the main sources of productivity growth such as capital, particularly human resources and investment capital required to purchase advanced technologies, new machines, and other production facilities or to finance factory expansion, difficulties in marketing and procuring raw materials, lack of information, and poor management and organization within the company.

The lower productivity of MSMEs compared to LEs is also attributed to several factors such as the investment capital to purchase new machines, expand production capacity, conduct research and development (R&D) to produce new or innovated products, or improve the production process. Moreover, the cost or funding/loan structure of MSMEs generally shows these firms pay more attention to working capital than investment capital. Meanwhile, the volume of production (or productivity) is closely related to the volume of investment.

The 2018 data presented in Fig. 2.7 shows the percentage of total investment by business size and according to different sub-categories of MSMEs and LEs as a percentage of the total investment of all business sizes (including investments made by LEs). The total investment value in MSMEs was found to be greater than the gross fixed capital formation in LEs. However, there were investment differences between the sub-groups of MSME with the smallest investment recorded in MIEs due to the fact that they are characterized by a manual or low level of mechanization during the production process depending on the type of goods or services. This, therefore, makes the MIEs have a lesser level of productivity compared to SEs, MEs, and LEs.

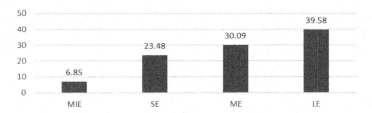

Fig. 2.7 Total investment value in MSMEs as a percentage of the total investment value of all business size groups, 2018 (*Source* Menegkop and UKM/BPS)

2.3 Main Constraints

Evidence from several other countries, especially developing ones, shows that the development or growth of MSMEs in Indonesia is hindered by many obstacles which differ in intensity based on regions, rural and urban areas, sectors, and even between companies in the same sector. However, there are some problems considered to be common to all MSMEs in any country, especially developing countries and these include limited working capital and investment; difficulties in marketing, distribution and procurement of raw materials and other inputs; limited access to information about market opportunities and others; limited skilled personnel or low quality of human resources; low technological capabilities; high transportation and energy costs; limited communication; high costs due to complicated administrative and bureaucratic procedures, especially in business licensing; and uncertainty due to unclear or uncertain economic regulations and policies.[1]

The data from the 2010 National Survey on MSIs showed that approximately 78 percent of all MSIs which represents 2,732,724 units experienced difficulties in running their businesses and the most prevalent ones were associated with funding, marketing, and raw materials with 806,758 units, 495,123 units, and 483,468 units respectively. Moreover, the MSIs in the food industry had the greatest difficulties with 745,824 units (34.96%) which include those related to the capital with 255,793 units, raw materials with 206,309 units, and marketing with 146,185 units. The same trend was also observed in the data from the 2017 National Survey on MSIs as indicated by Fig. 2.8.

With respect to funding, there were several special credit schemes for MSIs at the period with some still existing but most of the respondents, especially those in rural areas, said they have never received credit from banks or other financial institutions. This means they depended entirely on their own money or savings, financial assistance from relatives, and

---

[1] Unfortunately, there are no studies or national surveys on LEs with empirical evidence on the problems facing these enterprises that could be used as a comparison. Although several reports, studies, or reviews in newspapers regarding the business climate and competition in Indonesia could also provide a clue about the obstacles faced by LEs such as high loan interest rates or banks that are not smooth in channeling their funds to the business sector, increasing prices of certain raw materials and energy, labor issues, market distortions, bureaucracy, tax system that is not pro-business, poor infrastructure condition, and large numbers of legal and illegal levies.

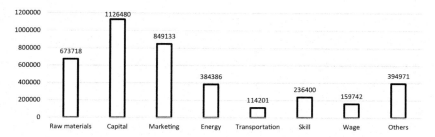

Fig. 2.8 Types of MSIs constraints, 2017 (*Source* BPS [2018])

loans from informal money lenders to finance their business activities. Some of the reasons provided for not dealing with banks include not having information on the existence of such special credit schemes, some tried to apply but were rejected because their business was deemed unfit for funding, some resigned due to complicated administrative procedures or inability to fulfill requirements including the provision of guarantees or collateral such as house or land certificates. There are also others that did not wish to borrow from formal financial institutions because they felt uncomfortable or afraid of defaulting (BPS, 2018).

With respect to marketing, the MSIs generally did not have the resources to seek, develop or expand their markets. Instead, they relied heavily on their trading partners such as mobile traders, collectors, or trading houses to market their products, also on consumers visiting their production sites, and through production linkages or subcontracting arrangements with larger enterprises which contribute a small percentage to the marketing efforts.

2.4 Nature of Development of Indonesian MSMEs

The development of MSMEs as well as the changes in their employment and output shares, output composition, market orientation, and location over time are usually thought to be related to many factors including the level of economic development, changes in real income per capita, population growth, and technological advancement. This was the basis for the formulation of a key question that "Is there a general or a systematic pattern of transformation of MSMEs over the time in the course of economic development?" or, more specifically, "Will MSMEs, especially MSEs, die out or on the contrary go along with the increase in real income per capita?"

There is a need for a complete understanding of the nature of MSMEs' development to answer this question. This is due to the fact that economic development creates a natural place to develop and grow different sizes of enterprises including MIEs, SEs, MEs, and LEs. Meanwhile, the size of a business establishment depends on certain factors with the two most important being market and technology. Concerning the first factor, only small or micro-scale economic activities such as MIEs and SEs are viable in a small or very small market. Moreover, this market size is determined by the level of real income per capita and the size of population which combined to determine the actual number of buyers.

MSMEs in the manufacturing industry produce a variety of products that can be grouped into two categories due to their nature or characteristics and these include consumer goods and industrial goods. The first category involves MSMEs manufacturing final products to be sold in the market and surviving the competition with LEs producing similar products by differentiating their products, thereby, creating a market niche for themselves. For instance, MSMEs, particularly MIEs and SEs, in many developing countries are specialized in different simple items made by hand such as handicrafts which are not within the competitive area of similar items produced with sophistication through machines by LEs. This means they have a better chance to survive, grow, and develop. Meanwhile, there is a tendency for the firms to be outpriced in the market when they try to compete with LEs for exactly the same products which are prescribed by the economic scale of output as a large industry that depends on modern technologies.

The second category involves MSMEs manufacturing products for other manufacturers or serving as ancillaries to LEs. It is observed in recent years that the relationship between MSMEs and LEs has become increasingly important because of the trend toward diverticalization which involves LEs increasingly placing focus on their core competencies and buying other products and services in order to remain competitive. These production linkages which are mainly in the form of subcontracting arrangements often expose the MSMEs to the muscle power of large firms, thereby, leading to unpleasantness and problems for them. One obvious problem is the difficulties they experience in meeting the tight schedules and product specifications when acting as supplies for LEs. This technical, managerial, and organizational problem is observable not only in developing countries but also in developed ones.

In relation to technology, Panandikaer, 1996 (cited by Tambunan, 2009) explained that a large economic size dictated by technology has the ability to force MSMEs out of competition due to their inability to produce efficiently because of lack of economies of scale. For instance, the state of the art of technology in electronics industries can indicate a large size and this makes LEs viable. It is, however, important to note that neither the market nor the technology is fixed for a lifetime, there is usually constant change. This is indicated by the rapid innovations in technology witnessed globally in the last 5–10 years in some fields such as bioprocessing of materials, information, telecommunication, TV, satellite, fax, cellular, phones and pagers, as well as computer and automation. Several LEs experienced serious problems in adapting to these changing technologies and business environment in terms of the planned production, investment, and labor division including the recruitment of new workers with the skills needed by new technology, thereby, leading to the inability of many of them to compete in the market. In such circumstances, the MSMEs have a better chance to survive.

To sum up, these discussions imply that a complex interaction between the demand-side factors such as the market and the supply-side factors such as technology affects the development of MSMEs. Therefore, analysis of the development of these firms needs to be approached from the supply- and demand-sides of the industries or sectors they operate as indicated by the theoretical framework supported by some evidence. This analytical approach allows better examination of the main supply-side and demand-side determinant factors, the interactions between the factors, and the effects of the individual as well as interacted factors on the MSMEs' development.

In addition to the market and technology factors, MSEs in Indonesia are booming because of poverty. Theoretically, the relationship between changes in the share of MSEs in total employment or GDP, and changes in real per capita income can be positive as well as negative. It is positive when an increase in the average income per capita creates more market opportunities which further encourage the emergence of new businesses and production growth in all lines of business including MSEs, and negative when an increase in income which reflects better employment opportunities in other sectors leads to a negative growth rate in labor supply to MSEs. This means MSE activities act merely as a "last resort" for the poor with most of the people involved in micro and small activities observed to be from poor households that are unable to find better jobs because they are a poorly educated workforce. Therefore, they "must" do these activities as a primary, secondary, or temporary/seasonal source of income in order to survive. MSEs are indeed the most important rural non-agricultural activities for the rural poor in developing countries.

A World Bank study in 1980 (cited by Tambunan, 2009) pointed out that the relative expansion of rural non-farm employment is susceptible to favorable or unfavorable interpretation. This led to the formulation of a question that "is the growth of rural MSEs reflecting an 'involutionary' pattern of rural development as increasingly impoverished rural or farm households try to maintain their minimum incomes through increased participation of household members in non-farm activities, or, is it a result of economic development or diversification of economic activities in the rural area?" This simply means that "is the increased involvement of rural people in MSMEs, especially in MIEs, a symptom of distress or a sign of progress or development?"

This question is very important due to the fact that the most intractable component of rural poverty in developing countries is the indigence of the landless and near-landless laborers and the marginal farmers with no or very little access to agricultural land, thereby, leading them to non-farm activities and this is often classified under self-employment to avoid unemployment and starvation.

This leads to the argument that the increased involvement of rural poor farm households in non-farm activities, especially in more densely populated agricultural areas where the number of poor households is likely to be relatively higher, is a sign of distress adaptation to growing poverty and landlessness, since these activities are undertaken only as a "last resort".

As can be seen in Table 2.4 the total poor people in rural areas are more than those in urban areas and this is consistent with the fact that most of the MSEs in Indonesia are located in rural areas and most of them focus on handicrafts from bamboo, wood, and rattan, simple household items such as kitchen utensils, processing of agricultural commodities into food and beverage ingredients, motorcycle repair shop, and agricultural tools.

Table 2.5 also indicates the percentage and number of poor people by island and the highest, 20.65 percent, was recorded in the Maluku and Papua region while the lowest, 6.16 percent, was in Kalimantan. It is also

Table 2.4 Number and percentage of poor population by region September 2019–September 2020

Region/year	Total poor population (million people)	Percentage of poor population
Urban		
September 2019	9.86	6.56
September 2020	12.04	7.88
Rural		
September 2019	14.93	12.60
September 2020	15.51	13.20
National		
September 2019	24.79	9.22
September 2020	27.55	10.19

Source BPS (http://www.bps.go.id)

Table 2.5 Percentage and number of poor people by island in Indonesia, September 2020

	Percentage of poor people			Number of poor people (000 men)		
	Urban	*Rural*	*Total*	*Urban*	*Rural*	*Total*
Sumatera	8.80	11.34	10.22	2306.81	3759.37	6066.18
Java	8.03	13.03	9.71	8105.76	6646.27	14,752.03
Bali and Nusa Tenggara	8.99	18.18	13.92	633.96	1482.53	2116.49
Kalimantan	4.72	7.51	6.16	375.55	640.56	1016.11
Sulawesi	5.95	13.45	10.41	477.07	1584.44	2061.51
Maluku and Papua	5.49	28.51	20.65	139.34	1398.02	1537.36
Indonesia	7.88	13.20	10.19	12,038.50	15,511.19	27,549.69

Source BPS (http://www.bps.go.id)

important to note that the majority of poor people in the country are on the island of Java due to the fact that more than 50 percent of the country's total population live on this island. This is consistent with the data from the 2016 National Economic Census which showed that the majority of MSMEs in Indonesia are in Java which is the most densely populated island and the center of national economic activities with the focus on the manufacturing industry, trade, finance, construction, agriculture, and services in the country. This means most of the companies in the non-agricultural sector reaching 16.2 million units are on this island

Table 2.6 Distribution of MSEs and MLEs by Island, 2016 (%)

Island	MSEs	MLEs
Java	60.7	65.2
Sumatera	18.6	16.6
Sulawesi	8.1	5.6
Kalimantan	5.1	6.0
Bali and Nusa Tenggara	5.7	4.9
Papua and Maluku	1.8	1.7
Total	100.0	100.0

Source http://www.depkop.go.id/berita-informasi/data-informasi/data-umkm/; http://www.lisubisnis.com/2016/12/perkembangan-jumlah-umkm-di-indonesia.html

and dominated by MSEs with 15.9 million units which are approximately 61 percent of all non-agricultural MSEs as indicated in Table 2.6. Moreover, most of the MLEs in non-agricultural sectors which are up to 291.7 thousand units or 65.2 percent of the total in the country were also found in Java while Papua and Maluku Islands considered to be the least developed regions have a very low number of non-agricultural businesses as indicated by only 451.9 thousand MSEs and 7.5 thousand MLEs which are estimated at 1.8 and 1.7 percent of the total non-agricultural business in the country. It was also observed from field observations that most MSEs are in rural areas while most MLE are in urban or semi-urban areas although the exact figure is not known due to the unavailability of data.

REFERENCES

APEC. (2020, April). *Overview of the SME sector in the APEC region: Key issues on market access and internationalization.* APEC Policy Support Unit. Asia-Pacific Economic Cooperation Secretariat.

Bari, F., Ali, C., & Haque, E. (2005). *SME development in Pakistan: Analyzing the constraint on growth* (Pakistan Resident Mission Working Paper Series, No. 3). Asian Development Bank.

Bhuyan, M., & Pathak, P. (2019). Entrepreneurship development and bridging gender gaps. *International Journal of Advance and Innovative Research, 6*(1), 56–65.

BPS. (2017, November). *Analisa Ketenagakerjaan Usaha Mikro Kecil* [Micro and small business employment analysis], *Sensus Ekonomi 2016, Analisa Hasil Listing.* Badan Pusat Statistik Nasional.

BPS. (2018, June). *Profil Industri Mikro dan Kecil 2017* [2017 micro and small industry profile]. Badan Pusat Statistik.

Chilipunde, R. (2010). *Constraints and challenges faced by small, medium and micro enterprise contractors in Malawi* [Thesis Master, Port Elizabeth: Nelson Mandela Metropolitan University].

Islam, N., Fariha, R., Shreya, N. Z., Sabaa, F. T., Faiaz, M. D., & Yusuf, I. (2019, December 10). *Socioeconomic factors of women entrepreneurship development in Bangladesh*. Paper presentation, International Conference.

Joomunbaccus, S., & Padachi, K. (2019). The impediments to small and medium sized enterprises' development in Mauritius. *Journal of Small Business and Entrepreneurship Development, 7*(2), 86–98.

Macphersona, A., & Holt, R. (2007). Knowledge, learning and small firm growth: A systematic review of the evidence. *Research Policy, 36*, 172–192.

Malaeb, O. R. (2017). *An investigation into the obstacles facing small and medium enterprises in Lebanon: Toward a national SME policy* [Master dissertation, University of Liverpool].

Moktan, S. (2007). Development of small and medium enterprises in Bhutan: Analysing constraints to growth. *South Asian Survey, 14*(2), 251–282.

Rahman, M. A. (2010). *An assessment of the factors affecting performance of women entrepreneurs in SMEs of Bangladesh* [M. Phil thesis, Department of Management University of Dhaka].

Rihayana, I. G., Salain, P. P. P., & Adhik, N. R. (2018). Determining factors for marketing success in *endek* and embroidered textile industry through the integration of entrepreneurship orientation and customer relationship marketing in marketing capabilities. *Review of Marketing and Entrepreneurship, 2*(1), 31–48.

Sallah, C. A., & Caesar, L. D. (2020, January). Intangible resources and the growth of women businesses. Empirical evidence from an emerging market economy. *Journal of Entrepreneurship in Emerging Economies*. https://www.emerald.com/insight/content/doi/10.1108/JEEE-05-2019-0070/full/html.

Sidek, S., Mohamad, M. R., & Nasir, W. M. N. W. (2019). Entrepreneurial orientation and SME performance: The serial mediating effects of access to finance and competitive advantage. *International Journal of Academic Research in Business and Social Sciences, 9*(9), 81–100.

Suroso, A., Anggraeni, A. I., & Andriyansah (2017). Optimizing SMEs' business performance through human capital management. *European Research Studies Journal, XX*(4B), 588–599.

Tambunan, T. T. H. (2009). *SME in Asian developing countries*. Palgrave Macmillan Publisher.

Tambunan, T. T. H. (2019). The impact of the economic crisis on micro, small, and medium enterprises and their crisis mitigation measures in Southeast Asia with reference to Indonesia. *Asia Pacific Policy Study, 6*(1), 1–21.

CHAPTER 3

Internationalization

Global markets are an important source of growth for MSMEs but there is only a small number of exports in developing countries with very few being conducted directly without intermediaries such as trading companies or large-scale export companies due to some constraints. It is important to note that exporting is one way of internationalization for MSMEs while the two other ways include engaging directly or indirectly in regional or global production processes or supply chains and investing or opening branches abroad. Meanwhile, the MSMEs in developing countries are very weak especially in investing abroad and this is the reason most of the studies on internationalization generally focus on their ability to export.

3.1 Export Development

Micro, small, and medium enterprises (MSMEs) play a very important role in economic development in Indonesia as in many other developing countries. They are the main drivers of national economic activities as indicated by their over 50 percent contribution to the country's gross domestic product. They are also very numerous, reaching 99 percent of the number of companies of all sizes, and accounting for 92 percent of job creation in the country with the micro and small enterprises (MSEs)

© The Author(s), under exclusive license to Springer Nature
Singapore Pte Ltd. 2022
T. T.H. Tambunan, *Fostering Resilience through Micro,
Small and Medium Enterprises*, Sustainable Development Goals Series,
https://doi.org/10.1007/978-981-16-9435-6_3

37

discovered to be the main source of employment opportunities for low-skilled workers as well as married women from poor households in rural areas that own small businesses such as food stalls, selling of simple items needed by the villagers daily, as well as handicrafts from bamboo, rattan, and wood. The main purpose of these activities is to increase family income (Tambunan, 2018).

MSMEs are also expected to contribute to export growth in addition to their contributions to employment generation and gross domestic product (GDP). However, available data and literature showed that MSMEs, especially MSEs, in Indonesia have lesser ability to participate in export compared to their larger counterparts. This is indicated by the national data provided by the Minister of Cooperatives & UKM which showed that the share of MSME exports in the country's total exports is always very small with 17.7 percent recorded in 2007 observed to have dropped to 15.7 percent in 2019 as indicated in Fig. 3.1.

The export share of Indonesia's MSMEs is also observed to be much lower than the values recorded for their counterparts in several other countries. In Southeast Asia (SEA), for instance, Malaysia MSMEs accounted for nearly 19.0 percent, Viet Nam 20.0 percent, the Philippines 25.0 percent, and Thailand approximately 30.0 percent (ADB, 2015; APEC, 2020; ASEAN, 2015a, 2015b; OSMEP, 2015; SME Corp Malaysia, 2015; Tambunan, 2015a, 2015b; UN-ESCAP, 2010; Wignaraja, 2012; Yoshino & Wignaraja, 2015). This regional data from SEA also confirmed that most exports in the region were contributed by the LEs.

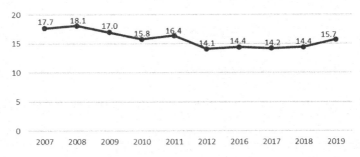

Fig. 3.1 Export development of Indonesian MSMEs, 2007–2019 (percent of total exports) (*Source* Menegkop & UKM [online])

Table 3.1 Share of MSME exporters in the AP region by economy

Economy	Share of total exporters (%)	Share of total MSMEs (%)	Year
Australia	87.2	2.0	2017–18
Canada	96.6	2.7	2018
Chile	55.3	0.5	2017
Mexico	83.1	3.6	2017
New Zealand	67.9	1.4	2018
Peru	70.5	0.3	2017
Thailand	71.0	0.9	2018
United States	97.5	0.9	2017

Source APEC (2020)

In the wider region of Asia Pacific, a report from the APEC Secretariat in 2020 showed that the contribution of MSMEs as part of total exporters varied from 55.3 percent in Chile to 97.5 percent in the United States as indicated in Table 3.1. The share remained stable over the reference period of 5–10 years with only Thailand showing a large increase from 59.6 percent in 2010 to 71.0 percent in 2018. Moreover, it was discovered that the involvement of MSMEs in the export of goods was very low in all economies with an average of less than 2 percent. It is important to note that this data is focused only on goods without services.

The data on the value of exports of goods by business size from half of the total economies in the region showed that the share of MSMEs in the total value of goods exported varied greatly from just over 2 percent in Chile to nearly 40 percent in Canada as shown presented in Fig. 3.2. The trend was observed to have fluctuated during 5–10 years usually in the range of three percentage points but there have not been any major changes between the economies in the region. One important fact discovered from this APEC report is that even though Indonesia is the largest economy in the region from the perspective of the area, number and variation of natural resources, nominal GDP values, and population, it is not the largest economy in terms of MSME exports. This is due to the fact that the country's MSMEs are traditionally oriented toward the domestic market as previously discussed.

Figure 3.2 also indicates that the LEs generally have a much larger export volume than MSMEs in all countries. It was also observed that LE tends to export while MSMEs, especially MIEs, tend to be oriented toward the domestic market due to several constraints which vary based

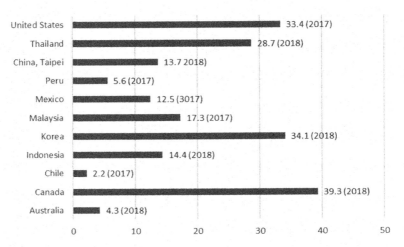

Fig. 3.2 MSME export values in the AP region by economy (*Source* APEC, 2020)

on economies. This means it is more useful not to measure the extent of internationalization of MSMEs but rather the share of their total sales exported directly in order to determine whether they export more than they sell to the domestic market more accurately. The data required of this are, however, often very difficult to collect by statistical agencies and this means they are not widely available.

The 2020 APEC report also showed that, based on data available for certain periods in individual economies, the annual growth in the number of large-sized exporters exceeded that of smaller-sized exporters except for New Zealand and Thailand. In Thailand, for instance, the number of exporters from the MSME category was responsible for the overall net growth of the number of exporters of goods because the number of exporters from the LE group has declined during the reference period. Although the number of exporters from the MSME group tended to grow more slowly per year compared to large-sized exporters, MSME exporters contributed a substantial share of the net growth of the number of goods exporters, with almost all economies having data owning shares above 70 percent.

For certain years the rate of growth in the value of goods exported by MSMEs was quite strong, with most economies in the region experienced annual growth rates of more than 4 percent. However, the growth in the value of exports of goods by LEs surpassed MSMEs in more than half of the economies. The share of net growth in the value of goods exports associated with MSMEs varied considerably across economies during certain periods, ranged from only 0.7 percent in Australia, 12.1 percent in Indonesia, to 41.0 percent in Canada. In general, MSMEs accounted for a greater share of net growth in the value of exports in these economies where annual growth in the value of exports of MSMEs exceeded that of LEs.

The World Bank Enterprise Survey also showed that the share of MSMEs in Indonesia that perceived customs and trade regulations as the main barrier to export was nearly 28 percent. As a comparison, in China 1.4 percent, Malaysia nearly 40 percent, and Thailand almost 29 percent. It was observed that more than 20 percent of MSMEs in most economies in the AP region identified these regulations as one of their main export barriers. Moreover, a much larger share of MSMEs in more than half of the number of economies in the region included in the World Bank dataset also have the same belief compared to the LEs. The exception, in this case, was also Papua New Guinea where nearly half of the LEs surveyed identified the factors as a constraint compared to about a quarter of the number of MSMEs.

3.2   LITERATURE REVIEW

The market orientation of MSME is generally different from those of their larger counterparts. This is due to the fact that most of them, especially the MSEs, produce simple and cheap consumer goods which are often considered inferior goods for local poor-or low-income buyers. There is, however, evidence that some of these tiny enterprises especially those selling furniture, foods and beverages, textile and garment, footwear, and handicrafts export, either directly or indirectly, through subcontract or marketing arrangements with larger exporting companies.

It was also discovered from several countries that the export share of MSMEs is not only relatively small but the exporting activities of most of them, especially MSE exporters, are usually indirect through intermediate agencies such as trading companies or export-oriented LEs. According to Wattanapruttipaisan (2005), the direct contribution of MSMEs to total export earnings in ASEAN was significantly lesser than 50 percent but the figures vary by country. This was also supported by the 2020 APEC report that MSMEs averagely contributed less than 30 percent of direct exports and this means they were underrepresented in the international economy relative to their role in the domestic economy. However, the consideration of the indirect exports of these firms is expected to increase their contribution to total exports above the stated proportion. It was further explained that many MSMEs in some member countries, especially those in the manufacturing industry, made up a significant part of the value chain in the production process but were not included in direct exports.

The World Bank Enterprises Survey in the AP region showed that the share of MSMEs engaged in direct exportation with the products exported constituting at least 10 percent of total annual sales ranged from as little as 5.6 percent in Thailand to as high as 23.5 percent in Malaysia while Indonesian MSMEs had 13.2 percent. It was discovered that it was only in Papua New Guinea that the share exported directly by MSMEs was higher than the figures for LEs. Moreover, in terms of the share of total sales exported directly by the company, the value was reported to have ranged from an average of 2.8 percent for MSMEs in Thailand to 9.8 percent for MSMEs in Malaysia while only Papua New Guinea had LEs exported a higher share of their total sales than MSMEs. This strongly confirms that direct export is much more difficult than indirect export for the majority of export-oriented MSMEs, especially the MSEs.

The literature on MSMEs' export has been growing in the past few decades with a general conclusion that their potential for full exportation activities is limited by some constraints. Some of these studies include Julien and Ramangalahy (2003), Leonidou (2004), Jones and Coviello (2005), Belso-Martinez (2006), Laghzaoui (2007), Leonidou et al. (2007), Arteaga-Ortiz and Fernandez-Ortiz (2010), Mpunga (2016), Alam (2017), Breckova (2018), Ribau et al. (2018), Dabić et al. (2019), and Chandra et al. (2020). Most of them conclude that the weakness of MSMEs, especially MSEs, in export compared to LEs is closely related to their size. For instance, Julien and Ramangalahy (2003) showed that the limited ability to acquire information and knowledge on foreign markets and to manage foreign activities is largely responsible for MSMEs' relatively low level of exporting commitment and poor performance. Belso-Martinez (2006) found that these limitations made industrial districts or clusters to be increasingly recognized as an organizational model enabling MSMEs to become exporters and to compete internationally. Moreover, findings from Laghzaoui (2007), Ribau et al.

(2018), and Dabić et al. (2019) showed that the small size and limited resources of these firms have the ability to constrict their involvement in international business activities and make them susceptible to the risk of failure in international market operations. Chandra et al. (2020) also reviewed the literature on internationalization barriers of MSMEs from developing countries in order to (1) explicitly point out specific factors influencing the growth and internationalization of MSMEs from developing countries and (2) identify the research gaps to provide lucid and succinct directions for future research in this area. They found many questions unanswered regarding the factors determining the growth and internationalization of these firms.

Suwandi (2012) outline three main motivations for MSMEs in Indonesia to export based on experience and these include (i) 100 percent business motivation which involves expanding markets and increasing turnover, (ii) business and social motivation which involves promoting the local community's businesses, and/or (iii) "trial and error" by trying oversea market while still selling in the domestic market.

Revindo et al. (2019) also investigated the main factors influencing Indonesian MSMEs' decisions and ability to engage in direct export activities by surveying 271 exporting and 226 non-exporting MSMEs in seven provinces in Java, Madura, and Bali. The findings showed that MSMEs have lesser ability to explore the growing export opportunities created through increasingly free world trade compared to large enterprises (LEs). They also discovered that the relatively poor export performance of these firms persists despite various policy measures launched by the Indonesian government such as the general assistance including access to credit, technical, and managerial training as well as specific export-related assistance including trade promotions, business matching, and training in export procedures.

Most of the export-oriented MSMEs in the country were found in clusters previously serving only local or national markets and later sold their products, directly or indirectly, abroad. Some clusters are more developed than others in export activities mainly because they have well-developed long-term subcontracting arrangements with domestic exporting big companies or trade contracts with domestic trading companies or agents or distributors in importing countries (Perry & Tambunan, 2009; Tambunan, 2010c, 2013, 2015a, 2015b).

Table 3.2 presents the main findings of other studies on the determinant factors or main constraints of MSMEs' exports with some discovered

Table 3.2 Main findings from selected important research papers on determinants of MSMEs' ability to do direct export

Research paper	Main findings
Madushanka and Sachitra (2021)	72.6% of the variation in export engagement can be explained by financial capability, management capabilities and government policies. However, marketing information was not a significant determinant of export engagement of MSMEs. Among the factors, management capability recorded the highest beta value (beta = 0.487) followed by financial capabilities
Kharel and Dahal (2020)	Major challenges include an inadequately trained/skilled workforce; onerous collateral requirements and high interest rates when accessing credit; an inadequately funded concessional export credit scheme, with an insufficient term length; procedural difficulty in accessing a cash export subsidy program; high tariffs on raw materials and intermediate goods coupled with an ineffective duty drawback system; the lack of an efficient arrangement for consolidating less-than-container-load cargoes; poor dissemination of information about existing incentives and facilities; inadequate provision of trade and market intelligence; restrictions on online payment solutions; a weak capacity of the public administration to coordinate and implement trade and industrial policies, lack of policy supports in the form of fiscal incentives and policy uncertainty
Revindo et al. (2019)	Positive factors: having network relationships with formal and informal institutions, firm age, size (number of employees), the owners have been overseas or have experience working for a multinational company or an exporting large-sized firm, produce merchandise that comprises a large share of Indonesia's national exports (foreign buyer), receive assistances from central government agencies or non-governmental sources (including promotion, business management, finance, and production) Negative factors: perceive difficulties in overcoming any tariff and non-tariff barriers, informational and human resource barriers, distribution, logistic, promotional, business environment, procedural and competitor barriers in host countries

(continued)

3 INTERNATIONALIZATION   45

Table 3.2 (continued)

Research paper	Main findings
Yean and Tambunan (2018)	Compliance with international quality standards, networks, training, and market information are very important factors
Haddoud et al. (2018)	Possession of resources and capabilities such as innovative and marketing factors are not necessarily drivers of MSMEs' export propensity. But, these should be complemented by decision makers that are export oriented who have the relevant attributes in terms of export knowledge and experience
Alam's (2017)	Important factors: foreign ownership, international certification, foreign technology, establishment in export processing zones
Mpunga (2016)	Important factors: adequate and stable financial capital, knowledge on foreign language, production technology, information and communication technology (ICT), information search competencies, standard products, restrictive entrance procedures into the country, export market characteristics (e.g. complicated business laws/regulations, customers' indifference with foreign goods, price uncertainty in the export markets, product competition in the export market, and complicated travel accreditation)
Revindo and Gan (2016)	Very important positive factors: the presence of foreign buyers, the confidence in the products, the aspiration to find alternative markets, networking and information dispersion
Harchegani et al. (2015)	Environmental factors (e.g. stability in political, economic and legal environment, database to access taste of export markets, and attractiveness of export markets), managers' commitment to export (e.g. a separate export unit, regular visit of export markets, and using export market research), managers' export marketing strategy (e.g. product adaptation strategy, pricing adaptation strategy, product innovation strategy, foreign advertisement, new products), export incentives (e.g. export motives, export problems, and competition), objective characteristics of the firm (e.g. size, export experience, expert human resource and sufficient financial)
Nyatwongi (2015)	Important factors: policy and legal framework, market information, tax, technology, finances and management skill
Fakih and Ghazalian (2014)	Positive effects: private foreign ownership, information and communication technology, and firm size. Negative effects: government ownership & domestic market size

(continued)

Table 3.2 (continued)

Research paper	Main findings
Hoekman and Shepherd (2013)	Positive factors: trade facilitation, firm size, firm ownership
Mupemhi et al. (2013)	Positive factors: availability of funds, management attitudes, knowledge of the market risk perception, international networks, intensity of competition Factors with no effects: age and size of the firms, technical ability of managers
Amornkitvikai et al. (2012)	Positive effects: government assistance, foreign ownership, municipal location, R&D, skilled labor. Mixed effects: firm size and age, labor productivity
Cardoza et al.'s (2012)	Negative effects: limited access to finance, domestic inefficiencies in logistics and distribution, high international transport costs and payment collection costs, and adverse regulatory frameworks. Three other factors, namely, government assistance, state participation, and public procurement, are not statistically significant
Petrit et al. (2012)	Positive factors: firm size, ownership, sector of activity, the availability of external finance, affiliation with business organizations, education of the workforce and, to a lesser extent, technology-related factors
Wignaraja (2012)	Important positive factors: firm size, foreign ownership, worker with high skills, obtaining international-agreed certificates (such as ISO), having access to foreign technology, having access to bank's credit
Ottaviano and Martincus (2011)	Positive factors: technology, training (human resource development), investment in product improvement
De Dios (2009)	Besides positive effects of supply-side determinant factors such as skill, technology and access to finance, ICT-based trade facilitation measures are also a positive factor
Li and Wilson's (2009)	Positive factors: trade facilitation, access to finance, skilled workers, technology, and market information
Hessels and Terjesen's (2007)	Adopting legitimate business or industry practices, and access to key resources (e.g. technology, capital, market information, raw materials, international marketing knowledge) are very important for MSMEs to be able to export
Valodia and Velia (2004)	Negative factors in domestic economy: cost of imported inputs/raw materials, poor business linkages, exchange rate movements, niche markets where demand was not price sensitive, lack of production capacity, disability to produce high or international standard quality goods. licensing/patent rights, firm size, lack of knowledge of international markets. Negative factors in foreign markets: high tariffs, import licensing and other non-tariff barriers, anti-dumping actions, unreliable firms as overseas suppliers, illegal custom control procedure

(continued)

Table 3.2 (continued)

Research paper	Main findings
Sandee and Ibrahim (2002)	Obstacles on the supply side: high transaction costs, high wage of workers, lack of access to formal credit. Obstacles on the demand side: increasing competitions from other exporting countries
Hine and Kelly (1997)	Positive internal factors inside firms: attitudes, values, perceptions of risk, continuous learning, managerial and marketing skills, availability of resources (including financial resources), adjustment of organizational structure, and the availability and effective use of information

to have provided comprehensive literature reviews while others used field surveys with the focus on different parts of the world.

3.3 THE ROLE A PARTNERSHIP AND COOPERATIVE: A RESEARCH

Aim

The literature review showed that lesser attention has been placed on the importance of partnership between MSMEs and other parties such as LEs, banks, departments and agencies of the government, and cooperatives to support exportation. Therefore, a study was conducted to assess the importance of partnership and cooperatives in supporting MSMEs to export with a focus on the MSEs in the manufacturing industry.

The study was based on two reasons with the first associated with the very rare or absence of empirical research on the role of partnership and cooperatives in the development of MSMEs' exports while the second is the plea made by the Indonesian government for MSMEs, especially MSEs, to collaborate with large enterprises (LEs) through subcontracting arrangements. The government has long realized that having production or marketing linkages with LEs can significantly assist the MSEs to increase their production as well as marketing and export capabilities. All state-owned companies are required to support MSMEs in their sectors through partnership arrangements while foreign direct investment-based companies are also required to have production linkages with local MSMEs in some sectors to operate in the country. Moreover, the

48   T. T.H. TAMBUNAN

government encourages MSMEs to form cooperatives and this is indicated by the Community Business Credit which is known as People's Business Credit (KUR) designed by the government to provide special loans for micro and small enterprises (MSEs) through cooperatives. This means the owner of an MSE that needs a credit scheme is required to form a cooperative with other MSEs or be a member of existing cooperative societies.

Theoretical Framework

The literature review showed several direct and indirect factors affecting the export performance or capability of MSMEs simultaneously. The direct factors are related to the internal aspects of the companies such as the human resource or skills of managers or owners regarding export and international marketing, workers' production and technological capabilities, capital, networking, company's culture, experience, export market demand, trade policies in both home and host countries, and several others. Meanwhile, the indirect factors include infrastructures and logistics, social and political stability, weather (for agricultural commodities), exchange rate, inflation, and others.

The factors affecting MSMEs' ability to export were also grouped into two categories and these include the demand and supply factors which are related to the demand-side and supply-side of the market, respectively. The demand factors were further divided into policy factors such as import tax and trade regulations and non-policy factors such as buyer's taste, buyer's income, exchange rate, and market competition in the importing countries. Similarly, supply factors were also categorized as policy and non-policy factors as previously mentioned in the literature review.

Partnership and cooperative aspects are included in the non-policy supply-side factors and it is expected that the MSMEs engaging subcontracting arrangements or other forms of partnership with LEs or other agencies and with adequate knowledge of exportation activities have better ability to export compared to those without these capabilities, *ceteris paribus*. Similarly, the formation of a cooperative also has the ability to assist MSEs in cooperating with each other especially regarding the marketing of their products and services in the overseas market and procuring raw materials.

Method and Source of Data

The research is descriptive. It used secondary data from the results of the 2019 Survey of MSEs in the manufacturing sector (called as micro and small industries or MSIs) with a workforce of less than 20 conducted by the Indonesian Central Statistics Agency (BPS). The data includes the number of companies, workforce, worker remuneration, expenses, income, capital, business difficulties, business services and guidance, as well as marketing distribution. The survey also provides information on the number of MSEs which have partnerships with LEs. The data is presented according to The Indonesian Standard Classification Code for Business Fields (KBLI) is two-digit and by province. Based on KBLI, the manufacturing sector consists of 23 groups of industry including food industry, textile and garment industry, leather industry, and so on. In this survey, microenterprises (MIEs) are defined as enterprises with 1–4 workers, and small enterprises (SEs) 5–19 workers.

Results

Export Performance

The 2019 data showed that the marketing of MSIs' products was dominated by local marketing in districts/cities where the companies are sited as indicated by 89.15 percent even though there are variations in the values by industry group. Meanwhile, the marketing outside these areas either within the province or other provinces was found not to be developed as indicated by 7.57 and 2.79 percent respectively. It was, however, observed that the exports made by MSIs to foreign markets were relatively small as represented by only 0.50 percent of their total products.

The results also showed that only 29,071 units of the MSIs exported their products and this was only approximately 0.66 percent of the total 4,380,176 MSIs even though the ratio varies by industry group. Figure 3.3 also indicates that the MSIs with the highest percentage of export were in the non-machined metal goods and equipment industry group (KBLI 25) with almost 5.9 percent of the total 3743 MSIs in the industry apart from the other processing industry group (KBLI 33). Meanwhile, the non-metal mineral industry group (KBLI 23) was placed second with almost 2.55 percent of the total 14,324 MSIs. This variation was believed to be caused by several factors ranging from production capacity, types of goods which determine the level of complexity in

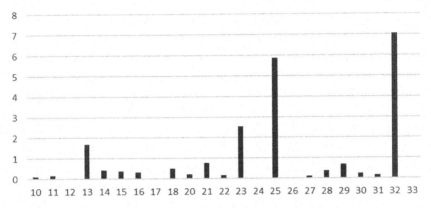

Fig. 3.3 Percentage of MSIs involved in Export by group of industry, 2019 (*Note* KBLI Code: 10: food, 11: beverages, 12: tobacco processing, 13: textiles, 14: apparel, 15: leather, leather goods and footwear, 16: wood, wood products and cork (excluding furniture), woven articles from rattan, bamboo and the like, 17: paper and paper articles, 18: printing and reproduction of recorded media, 20: chemicals and articles of chemical substances, 21: pharmaceuticals, chemical medicinal products and traditional medicine, 22: rubber, articles of rubber and plastics, 23: non-metal minerals, 24: base metals, 25: non-machined metal goods and their equipment, 26: computers, electronic and optical goods, 27: electrical equipment, 28: YTDL machinery and equipment (excluding others), 29: motor vehicles, trailers and semi-trailers, 30: other means of transportation, 31: furniture; 32: other processing; 33: repair and installation of machinery and equipment. *Source* BPS [2020])

producing and marketing them abroad, types and availability of required raw materials, level of competition and opportunities in the export market, differences between industry groups based on the level of development in the export-oriented MSIs clusters, and the proximity of the company to the ports. Furthermore, it was observed that there were industry groups where no MSI was involved in export activities for various reasons. This is possible because their exports were not recorded due to their inactivity in the areas of export for the whole year, occasional and small quantities of goods exported based on the order of an export-oriented trader, local industry-specific regulations which are not business-friendly, and the preference of the owners to sell only to local or domestic markets because of the continuous high demand.

It is, however, important to note that not all of them sold all their products to international markets as indicated by the variation in the proportion of exported goods in Table 3.3. The number of MSIs that exported more than 80 percent was only approximately 44 percent of the total MSIs involved in exports and despite the unavailable of further information, several reasons were suggested to have caused the trend of not selling all products to international markets. These include short of funds to finance export costs because selling abroad is certainly more expensive than selling locally and the international market not being the main destination. For instance, the main target for most small furniture producers

Table 3.3 Number of MSIs' involved in export by percentage export and group of industry, 2019

Industry[a]	Percentage			
	1–24	25–49	50–79	≥80
10	1395	12	92	149
11	–	–	–	153
12	–	–	–	–
13	817	863	332	3023
14	1024	696	181	759
15	96	7	114	–
16	401	44	381	1201
17	–	–	–	–
18	154	4	–	–
20	11	–	8	57
21	15	4	–	–
22	25	–	–	–
23	220	2	20	123
24	17	–	–	–
25	110	14	20	78
26	–	–	–	–
27	–	82	–	36
28	5	–	–	–
29	12	6	–	–
30	–	–	–	17
31	37	36	98	52
32	479	53	8385	7153
33	–	–	–	–

Note [a]See Fig. 3.3 for KBLI codes
Source BPS (2020)

in rural Java has always been the local or domestic markets considering the very large population of 269 million people in the country which makes the domestic market very attractive to these sellers. The fact that some of them sold overseas is possibly associated with an opportunity to export the products at the time due to the orders made by small or medium-sized traders or collectors from surrounding cities that visited certain MSI clusters in rural areas or through trading houses that ordered a certain amount but the demands were not met thereby requiring products from individual sellers from outside. This means the export was not a routine not large order from a company or organization. Moreover, foreign market opportunity can also stem from a foreign tourist owning or managing a small hotel home in his or her home country and making a business contract with a manufacturer to supply a certain number of chairs, tables, beds, or cabinets after visiting the furniture industry cluster in Indonesia. This is mostly observed among furniture producers in the city of Jepara located in Central Java Province which is considered the most popular center for the furniture industry in the country.

Another important characteristic of Indonesian MSMEs involved in export activities is that most of them do not export by themselves or not directly but indirectly through several intermediaries such as collectors, partnerships with exporting, international, regional trading companies, and cooperatives as indicated in Fig. 3.4. The indirect exports, for instance, through a trading company can be conducted in different forms such as subcontracting where the MSMEs only make a certain part such as 75 percent of the good while the trading company completes it into a finished good or in a situation where the MSMEs produce 100 percent of the good ordered while the trading company only packages and brands the product. In most cases, the trading company determines almost everything involved in the production process ranging from the shape and

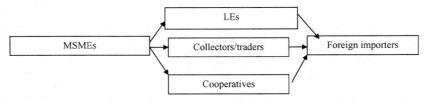

Fig. 3.4 MSME indirect export model in Indonesia

volume of goods, color, quality standard, and type of raw materials to be used.

The survey conducted by Urata (2000) on MSMEs in several industry groups in seven big cities of Java showed that not all respondents exported directly with some observed to be exporting through different types of intermediaries. The beginners in export without prior experience were discovered to be very dependent on trading companies or export-oriented large-sized companies.

The exportation in Indonesia is usually experienced through furniture manufacturers selling mainly to Europe and sponge rubber footwear or sandals manufacturers selling to several Arab countries and the Netherlands. It was discovered that the Indonesian MSMEs in the furniture and apparel industries were very active in export before the Asian financial crisis of 1997–1998 and these firms were reported by Berry and Levy (1999) to be mainly engaged in subcontracting linkages with LEs. They further stated that the export growth of MSMEs in these industries was clearly a reflection of the increasing importance of subcontracting with LEs or other commercial intermediaries. Moreover, Berry et al. (2001) concluded that linking production with trading companies through a subcontracting system is a good way to assist the exportation activities of MSMEs in the short term because the system frees them from bothering on the management of all administration related to exports, allows the firms to learn a lot on export, and also to produce goods that meet international standards in order to ensure they have high competitiveness in the global market.

The reasons the MSMEs do not export directly were observed to vary ranging from the insufficient quantity of goods produced due to limited production capacity which makes the exportation costs, especially transportation, very expensive, lack of experience to export directly to unavailability of foreign buyers to patronize these local producers. This makes it much cheaper and profitable for these firms to export by partnering with international trading companies with enough experience and market networks abroad.

It is also important to note that MSMEs that export directly without intermediaries do not always sell their products directly in foreign markets. Most of them sell the goods to foreign tourists and this is also classified in the International Monetary Fund's (IMF) version of the balance of payments as a category of exports. Those engaged in this kind of operation are often referred to as market-oriented MSMEs for foreign buyers. For example, Cole (1998a, 1998b) and Sandee et al. (2000) found that most of the export-oriented MSMEs in clusters across some industries including furniture and apparel in Jakarta, apparel in Bali province, and wood furniture in Jepara in Central Java province operate on commodity-driven buyers such as visiting foreign tourists. This means these firms found it relatively easy to penetrate global markets through trade networks. This study also showed the important role of foreign tourists in connecting the producers in these clusters with foreign markets, modernizing production methods, and improving the quality of goods produced in these clusters.

The Importance of Partnership

One of the government's efforts to support the development of MSMEs, especially MSEs, in Indonesia is by issuing some regulations and providing incentives to promote partnership between MSIs, larger enterprises, and other agencies. The partnership is designed to be mutually beneficial to both parties involved. However, the 2019 data showed the number of MSIs engaged in the partnership was relatively small at approximately 8.28 percent of the total 4.38 million MSIs and the ratio was observed to vary by industry groups as indicated in Table 3.4.

The most popular partnership was associated with product marketing which was recorded to be 37.59 percent followed by the procurement of raw materials with 37.56 percent and the partnership related to capital goods with 16.72 percent. Moreover, private larger companies were found to be the biggest party partnering with MSs as indicated by 36.8 percent while the involvement of government through state-owned companies at the central (BUMN) and local/regional (BUMD) levels as well as local government agencies/departments such as the regional office of cooperative and SMEs was observed to be very small as represented by only 3.3 and 5.65 percent respectively. This means the government needs to participate more in order to have a direct contribution toward finding the appropriate solution to the problems and difficulties being faced by these manufacturing enterprises. The other institutions and agencies discovered not to be partnering with MSIs include the banking and non-government organizations such as business associations, vocational training agencies, and chamber of commerce and industry as indicated in Fig. 3.5.

Table 3.4 Number and percentage of MSEs involved in export by group of industry and partnership, 2019

Industry[a]	Number of MSEs	Exporter		Partnership	
		Number	%	Number	%
10	1,587,019	1648	0.10	121,200	7.64
11	98,901	153	0.16	6583	6.66
13	296,154	5035	1.7	34,284	11.58
14	613,668	2660	0.43	64,298	10.48
15	57,332	217	0.38	9633	16.8
16	658,426	2027	0.031	33,865	5.14
18	31,598	158	0.5	4301	13.61
20	34,590	76	0.22	1283	3.71
21	14,597	19	0.78	1154	47.18
22	14,324	25	0.17	4733	32.43
23	240,141	365	2.55	11,309	78.95
24	3743	17	0.01	81	0.03
25	120,732	220	5.88	9685	8.02
27	1331	118	0.1	327	24.57
28	2631	5	0.38	291	11.06
29	2466	18	0.68	111	4.54
30	7202	17	0.24	587	8.15
31	144,775	223	0.15	10,816	7.47
32	227,408	16,070	7.07	24,603	10.82

Note [a]See Fig. 3.3 for KBLI codes
Source BPS (2020)

The majority of MSIs observed to have established partnerships indicated by 93.93 percent stated that the process has been very profitable especially in marketing while only 6.07 percent declared a loss. There are, however, certain factors to be improved to ensure more profitability and these include the guarantee of timely payment, assurance of production yield absorption, profit sharing proportions, and quality assurance of raw materials and other inputs as indicated in Fig. 3.6.

Unfortunately, the 2019 data from the MSI survey does not provide further information on the number of firms engaged in partnerships and involved in exports, especially in relation to marketing. However, it showed that the most serious obstacle experienced by most MSIs was marketing and this means the marketing partnership was very helpful for export-oriented MSIs. This is indicated by the scatter plot in Fig. 3.7

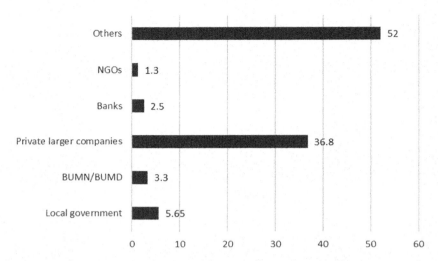

Fig. 3.5 Parties involved in partnerships with MSIs, 2019 (*Source* BPS, 2020)

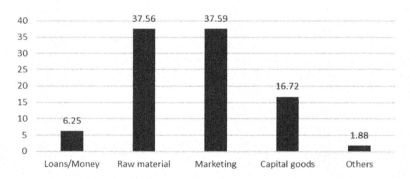

Fig. 3.6 Percentage of types of partnership conducted by MSIs, 2019 (*Source* BPS, 2020)

which showed a statistically significant and positive correlation coefficient between the number of MSIs engaged in export (y) and those engaged in marketing partnerships (x).

A case of the successful partnership between MSEs and LEs which created export opportunities is an agricultural cooperative of small banana

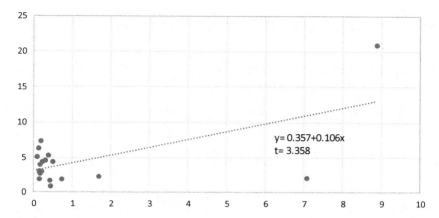

Fig. 3.7 Scatter plot of number of MSIs doing export and MSIs doing marketing partnership (*Source* BPS, 2020)

farmers known as the *Koperasi Tani Hijau Makmur* in Tanggamus District, the Province of Lampung in South Sumatera, Indonesia. The cooperative with 820 banana farmers partnered with a large company called PT Great Giant Pineapple (GGP) to cultivate more than 400 hectares of banana tree land and this led to the exportation of 64 tons of bananas or 14,266 boxes per month in 2020 to China, Malaysia, Singapore, and the Middle East. It is important to note that the farmers originally do not have the ability to build a corporate farm with the capacity to produce in large quantities, meet international quality standards, and ensure continuous cultivation to meet foreign market demands (Ubaidillah, 2021).

The Importance of Cooperative
There are three types of companies in Indonesia which include state-owned enterprises (BUMN), private-owned enterprises (BUMS), and cooperatives. A cooperative is an organization formed for the welfare of its members and considered by Article 1 of Law no. 25/1992 of Indonesia as a business entity with members including individuals or cooperative legal entities founded on the principles of cooperation and maintenance of economic movements based on the principle of kinship. The most

popular type of cooperative in the country is the saving and loan cooperative (KSP) which is also known as a credit cooperative or a cooperative legal entity-based microfinance which is one of the institutions capable of financing business activities of MSMEs due to its ability to adjust to the rhythm and character inherent in these enterprises.

According to the Decree of the Minister of Cooperatives and Small and Medium Enterprises No. 96 of 2004 concerning Guidelines for Supervision of Savings and Loans and Savings and Loans Cooperative Units, KSPs are cooperative institutions designed to conduct business activities through the collection and distribution of funds from and to prospective members, other cooperatives, and/or their members that need to be managed professionally in accordance with the cooperative principles as well as prudence and health principles in order to increase trust and provide maximum benefit to members and the surrounding community. Meanwhile, Regulation of the Minister of State No. 20 of 2008 defines deposits as the funds entrusted by members, prospective members, other cooperatives and/or their members to cooperatives in the form of savings and term cooperative savings. A loan is explained as money or an equivalent bill provided based on an agreement between the cooperative and another party that requires the borrower to repay the debt after a certain period accompanied by the payment of a certain amount of compensation.

The first cooperative in Indonesia engaged in the credit sector due to its ability to adapt to the conditions of the people entangled by loan sharks (Siregar, 2019). However, cooperatives also have other types of businesses over time due to different community problems and this led to the establishment of at least types as indicated by Siregar and Jamhari (2013) to include industrial crafts, tourism, savings and loans, markets, business, employees, services, women, fisheries, livestock, agriculture, transportation, Islamic boarding schools, KUD, KOPTI, KPRI, ABRI, BMT, retirees, students, youth, street vendors, and fishermen. These were further grouped into four types which include consumption, production, saving and loan (or KSP), and multi-business cooperatives (Susanti, 2010). The consumption cooperatives were established to provide the daily needs of members and the community such that the members generally enjoy certain incentives exclusive only to them when shopping. Production cooperatives assist the production process activities of the members while savings and loan cooperatives provide loans and serve as the institutions to save money. Multi-business cooperatives run more than one business through the combination of production with consumption or savings and loans with consumption. According to Zulhartati (2010), people also need an institution to assist producers to market their products to consumers in addition to the efforts provided to fulfill consumption, facilitation of production activities, provision of facilities for saving and borrowing. This, therefore, led to the establishment of the marketing cooperative to ensure the products of the members reach a wider market.

Cooperatives in Indonesia have experienced several challenges and recorded different achievements since they were first initiated in 1895. Some of these challenges include the dynamics of economic development, changes in policies, laws, and regulations, globalization and trade liberalization, and business competitions between cooperatives and non-cooperative-based firms. Meanwhile, the most important achievement made was their contribution to self-sufficiency in rice in the mid-1980s.

The national data of registered cooperatives from the Indonesian Ministry of Cooperatives and Small and Medium Enterprises for the 2000–2016 period showed that the number of cooperatives in Indonesia continued to increase every year except in 2016 when there was a slight decrease as indicated in Fig. 3.8. It is also important to note that not all registered cooperatives are active based on the definition of the Ministry that an active cooperative is required to hold an annual member meeting (RAT) for at least three consecutive years. Meanwhile, the focus on the figure due to the absence of data led to the assumption that the number of active cooperatives each year is much less than the total number of registered cooperatives. This is observed for the 2017–2019 period where the available data focuses only on the number of active cooperatives which is discovered to be much less than the average number of registered cooperatives per year. Some factors were suspected by Amini and Ramezani (2008), Sushila Devi et al. (2009, 2010), Mahazril'Aini Ya et al. (2012), and Maulana (2015) to be associated with the inactiveness of several cooperatives and they include low management managerial skills, lack of strategic planning, low member participation, lack of solidarity among members, limited resources especially finance, lack of market network, and heavy market competitions especially for producer cooperatives.

Sari and Susanti (2010) showed the two most important factors influencing the development of cooperatives are (a) capital and (b) member participation. Capital, in this case, is associated with the principal savings, mandatory savings and grants as well as loan capital from cooperative

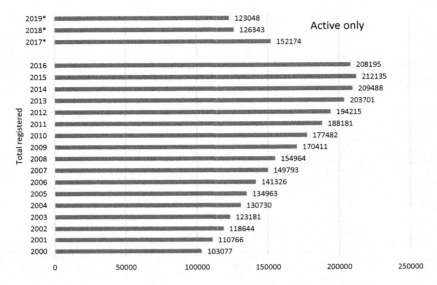

Fig. 3.8 Development of Cooperatives in Indonesia, 2000–2019 (*Source* The Indonesian Ministry of Cooperative and SME [www.depkop.go.id])

members and from outside the cooperative which is legal and does not contradict the articles of association and/or provisions of laws and regulations. It has been discovered that the ownership of a greater capital by a cooperative increases its chances of developing faster and vice versa. Meanwhile, participation, in this case, is related to the activeness of the members in the capital provision, decision-making, supervision, and utilization of services from the cooperative. This means a greater level of member participation also has the ability to improve the opportunity of cooperatives to develop. However, Yasri (1996) showed that the most important factors affecting savings and loans cooperatives include (a) interest rates, (b) loan period, and (c) length of the loan application process.

Table 3.5 shows the number of active cooperatives, the number of members, as well as the difference in the asset value and business volume by provinces in Indonesia. This difference is associated with several factors directly or indirectly influencing business dynamics in a location as generally observed in business activities and these include the level of economic

3 INTERNATIONALIZATION 61

Table 3.5 Development of active cooperatives (all types) in Indonesia, 2019

Province	Number of unit	Number of members	Assets (IDR million)	Business volume (IDR million)
Aceh	4115	122,459	741,191.95	858,341.07
North Sumatera	4199	929,962	7,958,317.86	5,658,111.70
Sumatera Barat	1919	313,950	4,278,835.52	4,147,748.59
Riau	2946	354,314	3,211,437.50	2,961,365.85
Jambi	2540	102,262	766,346.23	896,054.82
South Sumatera	3888	283,238	2,474,049.64	1,934,588.12
Bengkulu	1883	79,182	700,504.68	468,544.91
Lampung	2075	909,361	3,265,911.84	2,804,702.47
Kep. Bangka Belitung	651	68,069	500,300.59	504,961.62
Kepulauan Riau	884	63,523	662,658.92	593,464.97
DKI Jakarta	3447	1,264,944	13,350,612.75	16,564,902.94
West Java	13,247	2,040,509	16,072,554.05	17,670,557.18
Central Java	13,164	5,742,018	25,967,911.02	24,287,935.21
D.I. Yogyakarta	1751	857,104	4,061,898.99	4,491,040.78
East Java	21,757	3,620,213	26,275,314.66	28,116,735.18
Banten	3881	875,844	4,427,885.30	4,338,462.17
Bali	4244	1,108,238	14,294,454.95	13,444,457.16
West Nusa Tenggara	2396	317,182	1,548,605.07	1,276,627.33
East Nusa Tenggara	2697	703,337	3,022,143.15	2,590,375.49
West Kalimantan	2935	1,203,533	5,968,757.18	8,529,436.10
Central Kalimantan	2510	235,002	2,296,638.38	2,577,494.19
South Kalimantan	1721	198,855	1,562,382.65	1,015,792.74
East Kalimantan	2906	211,495	2,792,577.07	2,019,612.39
North Kalimantan	476	26,981	350,418.26	176,301.91

(continued)

Table 3.5 (continued)

Province	Number of unit	Number of members	Assets (IDR million)	Business volume (IDR million)
North Sulawesi	3620	65,765	335,192.12	337,208.98
Central Sulawesi	1429	132,214	805,554.66	1,022,220.56
South Sulawesi	4966	374,806	2,923,259.25	3,326,599.39
Southeast Sulawesi	3051	65,999	436,738.30	917,726.06
Gorontalo	884	46,193	243,249.39	198,286.68
West Sulawesi	837	18,788	109,905.85	273,968.89
Maluku	2373	33,786	168,238.68	186,116.15
North Maluku	917	24,434	137,721.98	182,908.98
Papua	2131	59,836	347,064.57	297,558.55
West Papua	608	10,342	54,504.03	48,321.01
Total	123,048	22,463,738	152,113,137.04	154,718,530.14

Source Indonesian Ministry of Cooperative and SME (www.depkop.go.id)

development, level of community welfare, poverty, market opportunities, institutions, infrastructure, population, regulation, and community average education.

Most studies on the role of cooperatives in developing MSMEs do not provide evidence on the relationship between cooperatives and the export activities of these MSMEs. For example, Mabula et al. (2020) only focused on the role of cooperatives in fostering entrepreneurial skills, awareness, and appropriate knowledge while several others such as Oluyombo (2013), Nembhard (2014), OECD (2015), Bakare and Akinbode (2016), and Adekunle et al. (2021) focused on the role of cooperatives in financing MSMEs. It is important to note that the major area of intervention implemented by cooperatives for several MSMEs in developing countries is finance due to the difficulties associated with the use of conventional banks to source funds for businesses. Another option for cooperative societies is to mobilize individual funds to establish and promote enterprises due to their ability to fundamentally protect the interest of their members.

Adedayo et al. (2020) studied the importance of cooperatives in Nigeria in supporting local economic activities through the provision of several services to members operating small businesses and the results showed the cooperatives perform an essential duty in aiding connection to sources of capital, procurement, stockpiling and circulation of inputs, and marketing of commodities. However, there was no further information on whether the commodities were exported. A report issued by APEC in 2014 was observed to be the only study that provides some evidence on the relationship between cooperative and MSMEs' export due to its focus on the verification of the implementation of the cooperative business model (CBM) in the developed and developing economies in Asia–Pacific (APEC) region. It also analyzed the successful experiences with the possible contribution to the identification of the most important socio-economic drivers needed to propose an effective model in the CBM to enhance the competitiveness of MSMEs. The report was based on research, international symposium, and workshop with one of the research questions focused on determining whether MSMEs are considered by cooperative societies as strategic partners to compete in local or global markets. Moreover, 9 out of the 21 APEC economies including Canada, Chile, Indonesia, Japan, Korea, Malaysia, Peru, Thailand, and Vietnam were selected to understand the role of the cooperative movement in the region, and the findings showed that several cooperatives in Canada are very active in traditional export sectors such as manufacturing and industry and those in Chile were also reported to be assisting MSMEs to be competitive in exporting business lines such as agricultural as well as food and flower growing industries. This means most of them are familiar with the export culture and were discovered to be adding momentum to the agricultural sector in order to expand their exporting capabilities and foster relationships with MSMEs. This is necessary considering the fact that exporting companies are one of the serious challenges facing cooperatives in Chile.

The Indonesian government has been trying to encourage MSMEs, especially MSEs, to form or become members of cooperatives but 2020 MSIs data showed that not all MSIs are members of cooperatives but the ratio varies by industry group. The largest percentage was recorded in Table 3.6 to be found only in the pharmaceuticals, chemical medicinal products, and traditional medicine industries (KBLI21) as well as the food industry (KBLI10) while the other industry groups had an average of less than 2 percent.

This survey data did not provide further information on the number of the members of a cooperative engaged in export activities but the scatter plots in Figs. 3.9 and 3.10 suggest the existence of an insignificant statis-

Table 3.6 Number and percentage of MSEs involved in export by group of industry and cooperative, 2019

Industry[a]	Number of MSEs	Exporter		Member of cooperative	
		Number	%	Number	%
10	1,587,019	1648	0.10	47,903	3.02
11	98,901	153	0.16	1113	1.13
13	296,154	5035	1.7	8827	2.98
14	613,668	2660	0.43	9511	1.55
15	57,332	217	0.38	569	0.99
16	658,426	2027	0.031	8282	1.26
18	31,598	158	0.5	256	0.81
20	34,590	76	0.22	239	0.69
21	14,597	19	0.78	511	3.50
22	14,324	25	0.17	28	0.20
23	240,141	365	2.55	5354	2.23
24	3743	17	0.01	9	0.24
25	120,732	220	5.88	2143	1.78
27	1331	118	0.1	13	0.98
28	2631	5	0.38	43	1.63
29	2466	18	0.68	1	0.04
30	7202	17	0.24	54	0.75
31	144,775	223	0.15	3172	2.19
32	227,408	16,070	7.07	4859	2.14

Note [a]See Fig. 3.3 for KBLI codes
Source BPS (2020)

tical positive relationship between the percentage of MSIs engaged in export (y) and those that are members of a cooperative. The findings showed that several other factors have stronger influences on the ability of MSEs to export but cooperatives also assist them in the process to some extent.

Cooperatives generally provide different types of services depending on the type and these range from marketing, procurement of raw materials and/or capital goods, technical assistance to funding. The 2019 survey showed most MSIs which are members of cooperatives used the opportunity of these services in sourcing for funds or credit as indicated in Fig. 3.11 where a little above 50 percent received credit from their cooperatives. This is not surprising due to the fact that the most common

3 INTERNATIONALIZATION   65

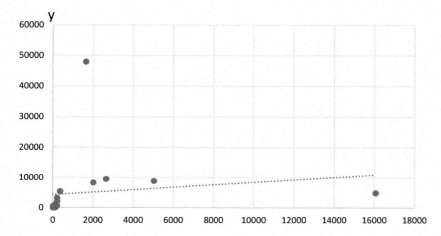

Fig. 3.9 Scatter plot of number of MSIs doing export and MSIs that are members of a cooperative

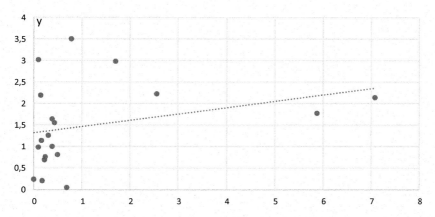

Fig. 3.10 Scatter plot of percentage of MSIs doing export and MSIs that are members of a cooperative

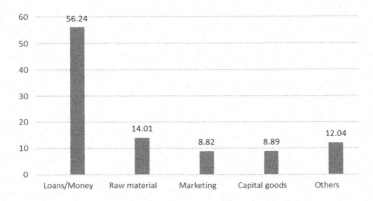

Fig. 3.11 Percentage of MSIs as members of cooperatives by type of service received

type of cooperative in Indonesia is KSP which has a significantly higher number than the others including the production, consumption, and multi-business types as previously explained. As the name implies, KSP provides loans and a place for its members to save their money and this means it is a business organization focused on the accumulation of savings from its members in order to loan it back to those in need of capital for business among them.

Although the results of the 2019 MSI Survey cannot fully prove the role of cooperatives in the export growth of MSIs because there is no further information regarding what percentage of those who are cooperative members export, there are many cases that can be found in Indonesia that show cooperatives are very helpful for their members to sell their products abroad. Some can be mentioned here. The Moon Orchid Cooperative in South Tangerang City in the province of Banten in 2020 exported MSMEs' products to neighboring country, Papua New Guinea with a transaction value of around Rp. 1.5 billion or US$ 100 thousand. The products exported were 50 thousand items consisting of hand sanitizers, masks, hand creams, and 2720 types of perfumes (https://www.antaranews.com/berita/1961448/koperasi-di-tangerang-selatan-ekspor-produk-ukm-ke-papua-nugini).

The Jabung Syariah Agro-Commerce Producer Cooperative (KAN) has successfully entered the international market for animal feed products that have the JABFeed brand through its first export to Brunei Darussalam. This export is the first step in developing the market for feed products. The total volume of exports was 52,500 kg. This cooperative has a core business of dairy cattle and a business unit for animal feed production. Initially, the production of animal feed was only to meet the needs of members. However, along with its development, this cooperative also serves external markets. In addition to providing concentrate, this unit also provides other livestock facilities such as calf milk, milk buckets, milk cans (milk cans), cow carpets, and so on (https://mediaindonesia.com/ekonomi/402366/pakan-ternak-produk-koperasi-diekspor-ke-brunei).

The Green Makmur Farmers Cooperative (THMC) in Tanggamus Regency in the province of Lampung on the southern tip of the Indonesian island of Sumatra in partnership with PT Great Giant Pineapple (GGP) to cultivate more than 400 hectares of banana tree land has succeeded in exporting 64 tons of bananas or 14,266 boxes per month in 2020. Its countries of export destination include China, Malaysia, Singapore, and the Middle East. PT GGP is a large company that is also the largest supplier of canned pineapple in the world. This cooperative has a membership of 820 farmers divided into several groups. Each farmer group consists of dozens of farmers banana farmers/planters with a land area of about 60 hectares per farmer group. In addition to exports, the THMC also supplies the domestic market as much as 20 tons per week to be sent to Jakarta, the Capital city of Indonesia, with variations of Mas Banana, Barangan Banana, and Raja Bulu Banana (https://finance.detik.com/berita-ekonomi-bisnis/d-5475517/ekspor-pisang-64-tonbulan-koperasi-di-lampung-dipuji-menkop-ukm).

Finally, the Pelangi Nusantara Cooperative (Pelanusa) is a community-based social entrepreneur and is engaged in the textile craft by utilizing garment waste in the form of patchwork as its main raw material. This cooperative which was founded in 2012 has been exporting since 2014. In 2021) the number of members is 53 craftsmen, most of whom are women. They make the exported handicrafts in their respective homes, while marketing including exports is carried out by the Pelanusa Cooperative. The regular export is to Japan. In addition, exports have also been to Vietnam and Australia. The goods exported are various kinds of crafts such as various kinds of women's handbags, chair cushions, and various kinds of fabrics. So far, exports have been carried out directly without intermediaries to buyers in these countries.

The biggest problems faced by this cooperative are the products often change according to the buyer's request and human resources. The success of establishing business relationships with those foreign countries cannot be separated from the active participation of the Pelanusa Cooperative in various trade shows both at home and abroad. Participation in many exhibitions is facilitated by, among others, the Ministry of Cooperatives and SMEs, the Ministry of Trade, as well as the local government, especially the East Java provincial cooperative office and regional export development training institutions.

To maintain quality of its export products, the Pelanusa Cooperative has a creative team that does product designs, quality control (QC), and standard operating procedure (SOP) which is a set of step-by-step instructions compiled by an organization to help workers carry out routine operations. SOPs aim to achieve efficiency, quality output and uniformity of performance, while reducing miscommunication and failure to comply with industry regulations.

The mission of the Cooperative is threefold, namely: (i) creating eco-friendly and principled craft and home decoration products to 3R (Reduce, Reuse and Recycle); (ii) creating a creative container for the community in the context of empowering to grow new independent entrepreneurs; and (iii) creating products that have export quality and are able to penetrate the ASEAN, Europe and American markets (https://www.instagram.com/pelanusa_/?hl=en).

References

ADB. (2015). *Asia SME finance monitor 2014*. Asian Development Bank.

Adedayo, S. J., Salau, A. A., Abdulraheem, I., & Zekeri, A. (2020). An assessment of perceptions on entrepreneurship and self-reliance among cooperative societies in Kwara State, Nigeria. *Fuoye Journal of Agriculture and Human Ecology, 3*(1), 14–22.

Adekunle, O. A., Ola, T. O., Ogunrinade, R., & Odebunmi, A. T. (2021). The role of cooperative societies in advancing small and medium scale enterprises in Osun State, Nigeria. *Journal of International Business and Management, 4*(6), 01–13.

Alam, M. S. (2017). Participation of emerging markets in global value chains (GVCs) and factors hindering the operations of small and medium enterprises

(SMEs). *International Journal of Small and Medium Enterprises and Business Sustainability, 2*(3), 1–21.

Amini, A. M., & Ramezani, M. (2008). Investigating the success factors of poultry growers' cooperatives in Iran's Western Provinces. *World Applied Sciences Journal, 5*(1), 81–87.

Amornkitvikai, Y., Harvie, C., & Charoenrat, T. (2012). *Factor affecting the export participation and performance of Thai manufacturing small and medium sized enterprises (SMEs)*. Research Online, Faculty of Commerce, University of Wollongong. http://ro.uow.edu.au/cgi/viewcontent.cgi?art icle=2090&context=commpapers

APEC. (2020, April). *Overview of the SME sector in the APEC Region: Key issues on market access and internationalization*. APEC Policy Support Unit. Asia-Pacific Economic Cooperation Secretariat.

Arteaga-Ortiz, J., & Fernandez-Ortiz, R. (2010). Why don't we use the same export barrier measurement scale? *Journal of Small Business Management, 48*(3), 395–420.

ASEAN. (2015a). ASEAN's external-relations. ASEAN Secretariat.

ASEAN. (2015b, November). ASEAN strategic action plan for SME development 2016–2025. ASEAN Secretariat.

Bakare, A. A., & Akinbode, J. O. (2016). Development financial institutions and SMEs development in Osun State, Nigeria. *Fountain University Osogbo Journal of Management, 1*(2), 6–17.

Belso-Martinez, J. A. (2006). Do industrial districts influence export performance and export intensity? Evidence for Spanish SMEs' internationalization process. *European Planning Studies, 14*(6), 791–810.

Berry, A., & Levy, B. (1999). Technical, financial and marketing support for Indonesia's small and medium industrial exporters. In B. Levy, A. Berry, & J. B. Nugent (Eds.), *Fulfilling the export potential of small and medium firms*. Kluwer Academic Publishers.

Berry, A., Rodriguez, E., & Sandee, H. (2001). Small and medium enterprise dynamics in Indonesia. *Bulletin of Indonesian Economic Studies, 37*(3), 363–384.

BPS. (2020). *Profil Industri Mikro dan Kecil 2019* [2019 Micro and small industry profile]. Badan Pusat Statistik.

Breckova, P. (2018). Export patterns of small and medium sized enterprises. *European Research Studies Journal, XXI*(1), 43–51.

Cardoza, G., Fornes, G., & Xu, N. (2012). *Institutional determinants of Chinese SMEs' internationalization: The case of Jiangsu Province* (Working Paper No. 04-12). School of Sociology. Politics and International Studies. University of Bristol.

Chandra, A., Paul, J., & Chavan, M. (2020). Internationalization barriers of SMEs from developing countries: A review and research agenda. *International Journal of Entrepreneurial Behavior & Research, 26*(6), 1281–1310.

Cole, W. (1998a). Bali's garment export industry. In H. Hill & T. K. Wie (Eds.), *Indonesia's technological challenge*. Research School of Pacific and Asian Studies, Australian National University, and Institute of Southeast Asian Studies.

Cole, W. (1998b). *Bali garment industry: An Indonesian case of successful strategic alliance* (Research paper). The Asia Foundation.

Dabić, M., Maley, J., Dana, L.-P., Novak, I., Pellegrini, M. M., & Caputo, A. (2019). Pathways of SME internationalization: A bibliometric and systematic review. *Small Business Economics, 55*, 705–725.

De Dios, L. C. (2009, May 20–22). *The impact of information technology (IT) in trade facilitation on small and medium enterprises (SMES) in the Philippines*. Paper presented at the Regional Policy Forum on Trade Facilitation and SMEs in Times of Crisis.

Fakih, A., & Ghazalian, P. L. (2014). Which firms export? An empirical analysis for the manufacturing sector in the MENA region. *Journal of Economic Studies, 41*(5), 672–695.

Haddoud, M. Y., Beynon, M. J., Jones, P., & Newbery, R. (2018). SMEs' export propensity in North Africa: A fuzzy c-means cluster analysis. *Journal of Small Business Enterprise Development, 25*(5), 769–790.

Harchegani, E. K., Solati, A., & Fataie, P. (2015). Identifying the factors affecting on SMEs' export performance (Case study: Sports equipment's exporters). *Applied Mathematics in Engineering, Management and Technology, 3*(3), 390–400.

Hessels, J., & Terjesen, S. (2007, October). *SME choice of direct and indirect export modes: Resource dependency and institutional theory perspectives*. Scientific Analysis of Entrepreneurship and SMEs.

Hine, D., & Kelly, S. (1997, April 6–7). *Tickets to Asia: Foreign market entry and sustained competitiveness by SMEs*. Paper presented at the '10th International Conference on SMEs'.

Hoekman, B., & Shepherd, B. (2013, September). *Who profits from trade facilitation initiatives* (ARTNeT Working Paper Series, No. 129). Asia-Pacific Research and Training Network on Trade.

Jones, M. V., & Coviello, N. E. (2005). Internationalisation: Conceptualising an entrepreneurial process of behaviour in time. *Journal of International Business Studies, 36*(3), 284–303.

Julien, P., & Ramangalahy, C. (2003). Competitive strategy and performance of exporting SMEs: An empirical investigation of the impact of their export information search and competencies. *Entrepreneurship: Theory & Practice, 27*(3): 227–245.

Kharel, P., & Dahal, K. (2020). *Small and medium-sized enterprises in Nepal: Examining constraints on exporting* (ADBI Working Paper 1166). Asian Development Bank Institute. https://www.adb.org/publications/sme-nepal-examining-constraints-exporting

Laghzaoui, S. (2007). *Internationalization of SME: A reading in terms of resources and competencies.* Paper presented at the 3rd Iberian International Business Conference.

Leonidou, L. C. (2004). An analysis of the barriers hindering small business export development. *Journal of Small Business Management, 42*(3), 279–302.

Leonidou, L. C., Katsikeas, C. S., Palihawadana, D., & Spyropoulou, S. (2007). An analytical review of the factors stimulating smaller firms to export: Implications for policy-makers. *International Marketing Review, 24*(6), 735–770.

Li, Y., & Wilson, J. S. (2009, June). *Trade facilitation and expanding the benefits of trade: Evidence from firm level data* (Asia-Pacific Research and Training Network on Trade Working Paper Series No. 71). UN-ESCAP.

Mabula, J. B., Dongping, H., & Chivundu-Ngulube, C. D. (2020). SME manager's perceived cooperative support, commitment and trust on learning and entrepreneurship orientation for firm innovation. *Human Systems Management, 39*(2), 233–250.

Madushanka, H., & Sachitra, V. (2021). Factors influencing on export engagement of small and medium-sized enterprises in Sri Lanka: Resource based view. *South Asian Journal of Social Studies and Economics, 9*(3), 38–49.

Mahazril'Aini, Y., Hafizah, H. A. K., & Zuraini, Y. (2012). Factors affecting cooperatives' performance in relation to strategic planning and members' participation. *Procedia-Social and Behavioral Sciences, 65*, 100–105.

Maulana, E. (2015). *Analisis Perkembangan Unit Simpan Pinjam di Koperasi Pegawai Republik Indonesia (KPRI) Dhaya Harta Jombang* [Analysis of the development of the savings and loans unit at the Koperasi Pegawai Republik Indonesia (KPRI) Dhaya Harta Jombang]. Jurusan Pendidikan Ekonomi, Fakultas Ekonomi Universitas Negeri Surabaya.

Mpunga, H. S. (2016). Examining the factors affecting export performance for small and medium enterprises (SMEs) in Tanzania. *Journal of Economics and Sustainable Development, 7*(6), 41–51.

Mupemhi, S., Duve, R., & Mupemhi, R. (2013, October). *Factors affecting the internationalisation of manufacturing SMEs in Zimbabwe.* ICBE-RF Research Report No. 62/13. Investment Climate and Business Environment Research Fund. Midlands State University.

Nembhard, J. G. (2014, February). *The benefits and impacts of cooperatives.* White Paper. Grassroots Economic Organizing (GEO). https://geo.coop/story/benefits-and-impacts-cooperatives

Nyatwongi, L. N. (2015, November). Factors affecting the performance of importing and exporting small and medium enterprises in Mombasa Country, Kenya. School of Business. University of Nairobi. http://erepository.uonbi.ac.ke/bitstream/handle/11295/93235/Nyatwongi,%20Linet%20N

OECD. (2015). *New approaches to SME and entrepreneurship financing: Broadening the range of instruments*. Organisation for Economic Co-operation and Development. https://www.oecd.org/cfe/smes/New-Approaches-SME-fullreport.pdf

Oluyombo, P. (2013). Impact of cooperative societies savings scheme in Rural finance: Some evidence from Nigeria. *Economic Review-Journal of Economics and Business, 11*(1), 22–35.

OSMEP. (2015). *The White Paper on small and medium enterprises of Thailand in 2015 and Trends 2016*. The Office of SME Promotion.

Ottaviano, G., & Martincus, C. V. (2011). SMEs in Argentina: Who are the exporters? *Small Business Economics, 37*(3), 341–361.

Perry, M., & Tambunan, T. T. H. (2009). Re-visiting Indonesian cases for cluster realism. *Journal of Enterprising Communities: People and Places in the Global Economy, 3*(3), 269–290.

Petrit, G., Hashi, I., & Pugh, G. (2012, March). *The small and medium enterprise sector and export performance: Empirical evidence from South-Eastern Europe* (Working Paper No. 002). Centre for Applied Business Research (CABR). Staffordshire University Business School.

Revindo, M. D., & Gan, C. (2016). Export stimuli, export stages and internationalization pathways: The case of Indonesian SMEs. *Economics and Finance in Indonesia, 62*(3), 191–205.

Revindo, M. D., Gan, C., & Massiel, N. W. G. (2019). Factors affecting propensity to export: The case of Indonesian SMEs. *Gadjah Mada International Journal of Business, 21*(3), 263–288.

Ribau, C. P., Moreira, A. C., & Raposo, M. (2018). SME internationalization research: Mapping the state of the art. *Canadian Journal of Administrative Science, 35*(2), 280–303.

Sandee, H., Andadari, R. K., & Sulandjari, S. (2000). Small firm development during good times and bad: The Jepara furniture industry. In C. Manning & P. van Dierman (Eds.), *Indonesia in transition: Social aspects of Reformasi and crisis*. Indonesia Assessment Series, Research School of Pacific and Asian Studies, Australian National University, and Institute of Southeast Asian Studies.

Sandee, H., & Ibrahim, B. (2002, April). *Evaluation of SME trade and export promotion in Indonesia*. Background Report, ADB SME Development Technical Assistance. State Ministry for Cooperatives & SME.

Sari and Susanti. (2010). *Faktor-faktor yang mempengaruhi perkembangan Koperasi* [Factors that influence the development of cooperatives]. http:// isjd.pdii.lipi.go.id/admin/jurnal/39962840.pdf

Siregar, A. P. (2019). Dampak Otonomi Daerah dan Pemekaran Wilayah terhadap Perkembangan Koperasi di Indonesia [The impact of regional autonomy and regional expansion on the development of cooperatives in Indonesia]. *Agridevina, 8*(1), 58–71.

Siregar, A. P., & Jamhari, J. (2013). Analisis Kinerja Koperasi Unit Desa di Daerah Istimewa Yogyakarta [Analysis of the performance of village unit cooperatives in the special region of Yogyakarta]. *Agro Ekonomi, 24*(2), 113–124.

SME Corp Malaysia. (2015, September). *Small and medium enterprise (SME) annual report 2014/2015.* SME Corporation Malaysia.

Susanti, M. I. (2010). Peran Koperasi SerUsaha (KSU) "'Mitra Maju" dalam Meningkatkan Kesejahteraan Anggota di Kampung Sumber Sari Kabupaten [The role of "'Mitra Maju" Multipurpose Cooperative (KSU) in improving members' welfare in Sumber Sari District Village]. *Ejournal Ilmu Pemerintahan, 3*(2), 558–570.

Sushila Devi, R., Nurizah, N., Mohd Shahron, A. S., Rafedah, J., & Farahaini, M. H. (2009). Factors influencing the performance of cooperatives in Malaysia: A tentative framework. *Malaysian Journal of Co-operative Management, 5,* 43–62.

Sushila Devi, R., Nurizah, N., Mohd Shahron, A. S., Rafedah, J., & Farahaini, M. H. (2010). Success factors of cooperatives in Malaysia: An exploratory investigation. *Malaysian Journal of Co-operative Studies, 6,* 1–24.

Suwandi. (2012, November 5). *Model Jaringan Ekspor.* Paper presentation. SEADI seminar.

Tambunan, T. T. H. (2010a). The Indonesian experience with two big economic crises. *Modern Economy, 1*(3), 156–167.

Tambunan, T. T. H. (2010b). *Global economic crisis and ASEAN economy: Theory and empirical findings.* Lambert Academic Publishing.

Tambunan, T. T. H. (2010c). *Trade liberalization and SMEs in ASEAN.* Nova Science Publishers Inc.

Tambunan, T. T. H. (2013, December). *Constraints on Indonesia's export-oriented micro, small, and medium enterprises secondary data analysis and literature survey* (SEADI Working Paper Series No 2). USAID.

Tambunan, T. T. H. (2015a, May). *Utilisation of existing ASEAN-FTAs by local micro-, small- and medium-sized enterprises* (ARTNeT Policy Brief, No. 45). Bangkok: ESCAP (UN).

Tambunan, T. T. H. (2015b). *ASEAN micro, small and medium enterprises toward AEC 2015.* Lambert Academic Publishing (LAP), Saarbrücken.

Tambunan, T. T. H. (2018). Micro, small and medium enterprises in ASEAN Regional Focus. *International Journal of Small and Medium Enterprises and Business Sustainability, 3*(1), 99–132.

Ubaidillah, A. (2021, February). Ekspor Pisang 64 Ton/Bulan, Koperasi di Lampung Dipuji Menkop UKM [Banana exports 64 tons/month, cooperatives in lampung praised by coordinating minister for SMEs]. detik Finance. https://finance.detik.com/berita-ekonomi-bisnis/d-5475517/ekspor-pisang-64-tonbulan-koperasi-di-lampung-dipuji-menkop-ukm

UN-ESCAP. (2010). *The development impact of information technology in trade facilitation.* A Study by the Asia-Pacific Research and Training Network on Trade. Studies in Trade and Investment 69. United Nations Publication.

Urata, S. (2000). *Policy recommendations for SME promotion in Indonesia.* Report to the Coordination Ministry of Economy, Finance and Industry.

Valodia, I., & Velia, M. (2004, October 13–15). *Macro-micro linkages in trade: How are firms adjusting to trade liberalisation, and does trade liberalisation lead to improved productivity in South African manufacturing firms?* Paper presented to the African Development and Poverty Reduction: The Macro-Micro Linkage Conference, Development Policy Research Unit (DPRU) and Trade and Industrial Policy Secretariat (TIPS).

Wattanapruttipaisan, T. (2005, May 19–20). *SME development and internationalization in the knowledge-based and innovation-driven global economy: Mapping the agenda ahead.* Paper presentation, the International Expert Seminar on "Mapping Policy Experience for SMEs".

Wignaraja, G. (2012). *Engaging small and medium enterprises in production networks: Firm level analysis of five ASEAN economies* (ADBI Working Paper 361). Asian Development Bank Institute. http://www.adbi.org/workingpa per/2012/06/01/5076.engaging.small.medium.enterprises/

Yasri. (1996). Unit Usaha Simpan Pinjam Di Koperasi: Beberapa Faktor Yang Mempengaruhi Perkembangannya [Savings and loans business Units in cooperatives: Several factors that affect their development]. http://isjd.pdii.lipi.go. id/admin/jurnal/221971327.pdf

Yean, T. S., & Tambunan, T. T. H. (2018). *Accidental and international exporters: Comparing Indonesian and Malaysian MSMEs.* Trends in Southeast Asia, No. 5. ISEAS Yusof Ishak Institute.

Yoshino, N., & Wignaraja, G. (2015). *SMEs internationalization and finance in Asia.* Paper presented at the IMF-JICA Conference on Frontier and Developing Asia: Supporting Rapid and Inclusive Growth.

Zulhartati, S. (2010). Peranan Koperasi dalam Perekonomian Indonesia [The role of cooperative in the Indonesian economy]. *Guru Membangun, 25*(3), 1–7.

CHAPTER 4

Women Entrepreneurs

4.1 Background

The interest of the public including policymakers, academics, and practitioners to develop women entrepreneurship in Indonesia started to emerge after the Asian financial crisis of 1997/1998 due to at least three main reasons. First, the number of women entrepreneurs increased annually in the country with most of them traditionally found in MSEs while the percentage of those in owning or managing MLEs is relatively small. Moreover, in relation to the economic sector, they are mostly found in trade and services such as small shops, food stalls, beauty salons, boutique/fashions, and catering services stores while most of them in rural areas operate as petty traders in traditional market centers. It was also discovered that those in the industry are concentrated in small-sized handicraft, food and beverages, and clothing industries. Furthermore, the continuous increase in the number of women entrepreneurs leads to their designation as the new engine for economic growth required to bring prosperity and welfare to the country. This is in line with the fact that many global stakeholders have over the past decades recognized them as an important untapped source of economic growth and development for developing countries.

© The Author(s), under exclusive license to Springer Nature
Singapore Pte Ltd. 2022
T. T.H. Tambunan, *Fostering Resilience through Micro,
Small and Medium Enterprises*, Sustainable Development Goals Series,
https://doi.org/10.1007/978-981-16-9435-6_4

Second, the decision of Indonesia to join the UN-initiated Millennium Development Goals (MDGs) which ended in 2015 and followed up by Sustainable Development Goals (SDG) towards 2030 also made the country realize the need to develop women entrepreneurs to achieve Goal 3 of MDG and Goal 5 of the SDG which focuses on gender equality and women empowerment. Third, poverty is still a serious social and political issue in the country and the active involvement of women in economic activities not only as wage-paid workers as they are widely found in labor-intensive industries such as textile and garments, leather products, food and beverages, and tobacco products but also as business owners or entrepreneurs is expected to ensure a significant reduction in the poverty rate.

The Indonesian government is observed to have been making several efforts to develop the potentials of women since the end of the Asian financial crisis by encouraging women's entrepreneurship development through the supports provided to MSEs which are considered an important avenue to test and develop women entrepreneurial ability. Some of the programs used included vocational training, technical assistance, microloans from banks and other formal financial institutions, as well as the financial, technical, marketing, and provision of raw materials by state-owned enterprises through partnership. Most of these were implemented in collaborations with foreign governments such as Australia and Canada, UN organizations through the UN Women, and international non-government organizations such as the Asia Foundation. Moreover, the government launched a public credit guarantee scheme targeting MSEs in 2007 due to the fact that most of these tiny enterprises, especially those in the trade sector, are owned or managed by women.

It is, however, important to note that despite the growing number of women-led businesses or those working as entrepreneurs as well as the significant increase in the initiatives, policies, and resources designed to promote and develop women entrepreneurship, there is still a gender gap in entrepreneurship in Indonesia as observed in other developing countries. It was also discovered that there are limited studies on women entrepreneurs in the country and this is associated with at least two main reasons. First, there is limited national data on the total number of women entrepreneurs and information on their key characteristics in the country. Indonesian Women Entrepreneurs Association (IWAPI) does not also have a comprehensive database on the total number of women entrepreneurs in Indonesia except the list of its members that are mainly owners of medium and large-scale modern businesses in big cities. Second, the public interest in women entrepreneurship only emerged after the 1997/1998 Asian financial crisis mainly due to the introduction of the MDGs as previously explained.

The main objective of this chapter is to examine the development of women entrepreneurs in Indonesia with a focus on personal motivations or reasons for owning businesses and their main constraints in running the businesses. The identification of the personal motivations has the ability to provide an idea on whether the current development of women entrepreneurs in Indonesia is a direct reflection of entrepreneurship spirit among women or, on the contrary, a direct consequence of economic hardships faced by many women in the country. Moreover, the identification of the business constraints also has the ability to indicate the current condition of women's entrepreneurship development and the growth of businesses owned or managed by female in Indonesia.

This research is important from the Indonesian perspective not only because studies on Indonesian female entrepreneurs are rare but none of the existing studies has placed a special focus on the question "why many women are involved in micro or small businesses in Indonesia? Is this a positive sign as regards the perspective of women's entrepreneurship development and government efforts to support them in Indonesia? These questions are important simply because the existing public opinion in Indonesia and probably in many other countries is that the increase in the number of female-led businesses is a positive sign based on the assumption that it reflects the rise of women's entrepreneurship spirit. It is, however, important to note that there are women running low-income generating MSEs, especially those from poor or low-income households, in the form of small food stalls, small traders, and food and beverage stores. Are they engaged in this business due to economic or financial difficulties?

This research focused on women entrepreneurs in MSEs due to three reasons and the first is the fact that entrepreneurship development is usually associated with the growth of MSEs because most people started their businesses on a very small scale. Second, available secondary data suggested that there were more women business owners in MSEs than in MLEs in developing countries of the world. It is, however, important to note that Indonesia does not have official national data on women entrepreneurs in MLEs. Meanwhile, the number of women owning MLEs vary by country based on several local factors such as level of economic development, women access to high education, as well as norms and cultures but the evidence available showed that the number of women operating as business owners or managers in MSEs is much higher than those in MLEs in all countries across the world including OECD and other developed countries (GEM, 2015; WEF, 2015). Third, national policies to promote women's entrepreneurship in Indonesia are an important element of those formulated to develop MSMEs in the country.

The research was, therefore, conducted to specifically answer three questions. First, how has been the development of women entrepreneurs in Indonesia? Second, what are their main motivations or reasons women started their businesses instead of working as employees in established companies, ministries as civil servants, studying in universities, or just staying at home as housewives doing domestic works? Third, what are the main constraints facing women entrepreneurs in Indonesia?

The research was exploratory and the questions were addressed by (i) reviewing selected key literature on the development of women entrepreneurs in developing countries in general and Indonesia in particular, (ii) reviewing official reports and other materials on current national policies to support women entrepreneurship development in Indonesia, (iii) analyzing available secondary data on women entrepreneurs in Indonesia, and (iv) conducting a small field survey on 108 randomly selected MSEs owned or managed by women in the Great Jakarta area. This is due to the fact that the last two research questions require an empirical approach through a field survey in order to closely observe the current situations and obtain direct statements on their motivations as well as the current main constraints experienced by these women in managing their enterprises.

4.2 Some Evidence in Indonesia

A World Bank study conducted by Devadas and Kim (2020) showed that women in the labor force are overrepresented as unpaid workers mostly in family businesses (contributing family workers) and underrepresented as employers. This pattern was based on the observations across income groups despite the high share of female workers with a high level of education in high-income and upper-middle-income groups. It was also discovered that the share of self-employed women without employees (own-account workers) or those owning or managing MSEs decreases and the share in total wage employment increases as a country transit from a low to a higher income level. The findings also showed that women's share of wage employees is nearly half of those with vulnerable employment such as family workers and own-account workers in poor or low-income countries where women with a high level of education make up a smaller share of the workforce. However, the female share of wage employees is almost the same as the share of vulnerable employment in middle-income countries and is estimated to be 1.3 times higher in high-income countries.

The study showed that gender segregation by occupation exists across all income groups and regions with women observed to be overrepresented in clerical, sales, and service roles which are traditionally thought of as women's work and underrepresented in similarly medium-skilled craft and trade work, plant and machinery operation, and assembly. Meanwhile, the proportion of work held by women in high-skilled jobs such as managers, professionals, and technicians are almost the same as their level of educational attainment as reflected by the share of workers with advanced education.

The development of women entrepreneurship in Asian developing countries also has tremendous potential in empowering women and transforming society in the region as observed in other developing countries of the world. However, this potential remains largely untapped in many countries of the region, especially where the level of economic development, reflected by the level of income per capita and the degree of industrialization, is still relatively low. For example, Sinhal (2005) observed that less than 10 percent of the entrepreneurs in South Asia comprising of Bangladesh, Bhutan, India, Maldives, Nepal, Pakistan, and Sri Lanka are women.

The level of women's entrepreneurship development in Indonesia is relatively low, especially in comparison with the developed world, but there is an opportunity for improvement. This is observed from the data available in the Menegkop & UKM that the total number of entrepreneurs was 1.65 percent of the country's total population of 253.61 million people as of January 2015 and this is the lowest in comparison with several other countries in Asia and the United States. Moreover, despite the limited studies and national data on entrepreneurship development by gender in Indonesia, available evidence indicated that the development of women as business owners or managers in the country shared the same features as the trend in several other developing countries.

It was, however, discovered by Tambunan (2009, 2015) that Indonesian women were many times less likely than men to own businesses, especially in large sizes with many employees. This was also confirmed by Shinta Widjaja Kamdani, the founder of Global Entrepreneurship Program Indonesia (GEPI), that the number of women entrepreneurs in Indonesia was much less than men. The statement quoted from ANTARA News.com which was accessed online in 2011 when GEPI was formerly established (http://www.antaranews.com/en/news/89197/gepi-hopes-number-of-indonesian-female-entrepreneurs-up) showed that the gap between male and female entrepreneurs was in the range of 30 percent in the last decade. The gap was observed to reduce slightly in 2000 to 26 percent but increased again to approximately 36 percent in 2002, 37 percent in 2004, 38 percent in 2006, reduced to 32 percent in 2008, and slightly increased again in 2010 to approximately 34 percent. Unfortunately, the GEPI does not provide more recent data on this gap.

The ILO estimates presented in Table 4.1 also showed that the percentage of women employers in Indonesia was very low as indicated by the fact that the number of women entrepreneurs with several workers/employees was very small compared to those working, however, there is a potential for continuous improvement. This was due to the fact

Table 4.1 Indonesian women as employers and own-account workers 2001–2020 (% of total employment by gender)

Year	Employer	Own-account workers
2001	1.1	31.1
2002	1.1	33.9
2003	1.0	29.8
2004	1.1	31.9
2005	1.2	29.9
2006	1.1	32.8
2007	1.4	34.4
2009	1.3	34.5
2014	1.8	28.5
2015	1.8	28.4
2019	1.9	33.3
2020	2.0	33.7

Source ILO (Key Indicators of the Labor Market: http://www.ilo.org/global/statistics-and-databases/research-and-databases/kilm/lang--en/index.htm)

that the percentage in 2001 was estimated at only 1.1 percent and in 2020 was approximately 2 percent with more women found to be self-employed without paid workers such as owners of roadside food stalls or small shops with an average share of 30 percent per year.

The 2016 Economic Census also generally showed that the percentage of women MSE entrepreneurs in all sectors was lower than men with 42.84 percent and 57.16 percent, respectively. However, there were variations between provinces but the highest, approximately 48 percent, was recorded in South Sumatra as indicated in Fig. 4.1. The census also showed that sector or business area where there are more women entrepreneurs than men was the human health and social activities sector with 63.68 percent and they were lowest in transportation and warehousing sector with only 2.22 percent. This indicates the possibility of

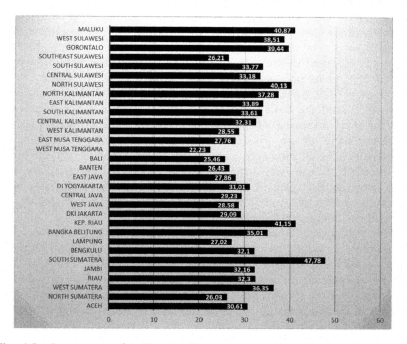

Fig. 4.1 Percentage of MSEs in all sectors owned by female by province, Indonesia, 2016 (%) (*Source* BPS)

different trends in selecting between a woman and man jobs with the women having a higher tendency to avoid too much physical work.

The census also indicated the differences in the turnover generated by MSEs owned by men and those owned or managed by women. It was discovered that the 48.28% owned by men were in the business groups with a turnover between 300 million and 2.5 billion Indonesian IDR while the majority of MSEs owned by women represented by 59.98% were in business groups with a turnover of less than 300 million IDR. Apart from the assumption that business leaders or company managers should be men, several other things lead to the notion that women's ability to lead a business is below the ability possessed by men. One thing often said is that women are considered to have a lesser ability to take risks and are less aggressive in their movements. However, this is still a matter of debate among researchers.

The 2019 National Survey of MSEs in the manufacturing industry (or MSIs) showed that the percentage of businesses in the manufacturing industry owned by women varied by year with most of them observed to mostly engaged in the textile (KBLI 13), other processing industries (KBLI 32), pharmaceutical, traditional medicine, and medicine (KBLI 21), apparel (KBLI 14), rubber and plastic goods (KBLI 22), paper goods (KBLI 17), and the food KBLI 10) industries. Figure 4.2 also indicates that the share increased significantly in 2010 and reached the highest in 2019 but there are no government reports or literature to explain this significant increase. However, one possible explanation is that the absolute number of businesses owned by women increased more rapidly than those managed by men or, alternatively, many men-led businesses were indirectly or directly affected by the 2008/2009 global financial crisis and stopped operating.

The two indices constructed by the United Nations Development Programme (UNDP) to measure gender equity are Gender Inequality Index (GII) and Gender Development Index (GDI). The GII is a composite measure reflecting inequality in achievement between women and men in three dimensions including reproductive health, empowerment, and the labor market. Meanwhile, GDI is the human development index (HDI) adjusted for gender inequality. It is the ratio of female to male HDI values which measure the average achievements of the country in terms of the extent to which people lead a long and healthy life, are educated and knowledgeable, and enjoy a decent standard of living. This index measures achievements in the same basic dimensions as HDI but

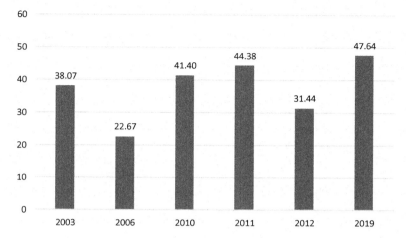

Fig. 4.2 Total MSEs in the manufacturing industry by gender of the owner, 2003–2019 (%) (*Source* BPS, 2020)

also captures inequalities between women and men. It attempts to capture the level of development of women and the extent to which they are free from discrimination in building their capabilities and gaining access to resources and opportunities.

The GDI is not exactly a measure of gender inequalities but rather a reference to the disadvantage (or advantage) of women in the HDI components. In a situation the ratio is closer to 1, it means there is a more balanced situation between men and women, thereby, indicating there are no great variations in the HDI results for both genders while a value closer to 0 represents a more unbalanced HDI between men and women.

Based on the Human Development Report 2020 from UNDP, Table 4.2 shows these two indices for several Asian developing countries. In the category of high human development (based on HDI rank), there were only two Asian developing countries, namely Singapore and South Korea with the highest value of Gender Development Index (GDI).

World Economic Forum (WEF) also publishes an annual report on global gender gap ranking, based on the global gender gap index (GGGI). The index is based on four critical areas of inequalities between men and women:

Table 4.2 Gender Development Index (GDI) and Gender Inequality Index (GII) in selected Asian developing countries, 2020

Country[a]	GDI value	GII value
High human development		
Singapore	0.985	0.065
South Korea	0.936	0.064
Brunei Darussalam	0.981	0.255
Malaysia	0.972	0.253
Thailand	1.008	0.359
China	0.957	0.168
Indonesia	0.940	0.480
Philippines	1.007	0.430
Vietnam	0.997	0.296
Middle human development		
India	0.820	0.488
Bangladesh	0.904	0.537
Lao PDR	0.927	0.459
Nepal	0.933	0.452
Cambodia	0.922	0.474
Pakistan	0.745	0.538
Middle human development		
Afghanistan	0.659	0.655
Yemen	0.488	0.795

[a]Based on HDI rank
Source UNDP (2020)

1. economic participation and opportunity: outcomes on salaries, participation levels, and access to high-skilled employment;
2. educational attainment: outcomes on access to basic and higher level education;
3. political empowerment: outcomes on representation in decision-making structures; and
4. health and survival: outcomes on life expectancy and sex ratio.

The index scores are on a 0–1 scale (0.00 = inequality, 1.00 = equality) but can be roughly interpreted as the percentage of the gender gap that has been closed. The index scores can be interpreted as the percentage of the gap between women and men that has been closed. Table 4.3 shows the ranking of several developing countries in Asia. It shows that, generally, in Southeast Asia, with the Philippines as the highest-ranking country, gender equality was much better than that in South Asia with the

Table 4.3 The Global Gender Gap Index 2007 ranking and 2006 comparisons in selected Asian developing countries

Gender Gap Index			Subindexes			
Country	2007 Rank (among 128 countries)	2006 Rank (out of 115 countries)	Economic participa- tion and opportunity	Educational attainment	Health and survival	Political empowerment
			Rank	Rank	Rank	Rank
Philippines	6	6	2	1	1	14
Sri Lanka	15	13	94	56	1	7
Vietnam	42	–	11	103	91	42
Thailand	52	40	21	81	1	110
China	73	63	60	91	124	59
Singapore	77	65	55	98	115	71
Indonesia	81	68	82	93	81	70
Malaysia	92	72	93	71	97	101
Korea, Rep	97	92	90	94	106	95
Cambodia	98	89	52	112	1	105
Bangladesh	100	91	116	105	122	17
India	114	98	122	116	126	21
Nepal	125	111	114	122	117	83
Pakistan	126	112	126	123	121	43

Source WEF (2007)

exception of Sri Lanka. Further, Table 4.4 presents data from countries in Southeast Asia (ASEAN), based on the recent report of WEF on the GGGI. As can be seen, the Philippines was still in the first rank, while Indonesia was in the fifth place in the region.

4.3   Reason to Open Own Business

Generally, women enter entrepreneurship for many of the same reasons as men, such as wish to become an entrepreneur, to have their own businesses, self-fulfillment, being their own boss, to support themselves and their families, to enrich their lives with careers, to attain financial independence (Hughes, 2006; Kirkwood, 2009a, 2009b; Loscocco & Bird, 2012), or they started their own business in response to the demands of parenthood and spouse/partner roles (Hilbrecht, 2016; Kirkwood, 2009a, 2009b).

Table 4.4 The Global Gender Gap Index rankings in ASEAN by member country, 2020

	Score	Rank	
		ASEAN	*Global*
Singapore	0.724	3	54
Brunei Darussalam	0.686	8	95
Malaysia	0.677	9	104
Thailand	0.708	4	75
Philippines	0.781	1	16
Indonesia	0.700	5	85
Viet Nam	0.700	6	87
Lao People's Democratic Republic	0.731	2	43
Myanmar	0.665	10	114
Cambodia	0.694	7	89

Source WEF (2020)

However, existing literature on the development of women entrepreneurs in South Asia, such as Das (2000), Raju (2000), Sharma and Dhameja (2002), and Sinha (2003) suggested that there were three categories of women entrepreneurs: "chance", "forced", and "created" entrepreneurs. These different categories were based on how their businesses got started, or the main reasons or motivations behind starting their own businesses. Chance entrepreneurs were those who started a business without any clear goals or plans. Their businesses probably evolved from hobbies to economic enterprises over time. Forced entrepreneurs were those who were compelled by circumstances (e.g., death of a spouse, the family facing financial difficulties) to start a business, their primary motivation, and so, tend to be financial. Created entrepreneurs were those who were "located, motivated, encouraged and developed" through, for instance, entrepreneurship development programs. According to one study by Das (2000), the most common reasons given were either financial reasons or to keep busy. He found that only about one-fifth of women were drawn to entrepreneurship by "pull" factors, for instance, the need for a challenge, the urge to try something on their own and to be independent, and to show others that they are capable of doing well in business. It is often stated in the literature that the degree of women entrepreneurship development is closely related to the degree of gender equity, which in developing countries is generally lower than that in developed countries. Although, within the developing countries, the degree varied by country, depending on many factors, including level of economic development, reflected by the level of income per capita, and social, cultural, and political factors. Gender equity has many dimensions, and it is not easy to measure, due to the lack of accurate, gender discriminated social indicators in many countries, especially in the developing world.

Based on his study on women entrepreneurs in Indonesia and many other developing countries in Asia for many years, Tambunan (2009, 2015) found that especially from low-income countries women often showed marked differences from their men counterparts in many characteristics that influenced their decision to run own businesses or to become entrepreneurs. Such like age, work status, education, income, social ties, cultural norms or customs or tradition, family background, marriage status, family obligations, discrimination against women in many aspects of life (which is often the result of gender beliefs inherent in a culture or society), disproportionate bargaining power against men, and public/community perceptions were all significant social, economic, and institutional factors that were among key characteristics which determined a woman's decision to start a business (Tambunan, 2015).

Many other studies (e.g., Hani, 2015; Mahmood et al., 2012; Shah, 2013; Shah & Saurabh, 2015) showed the same evidence that the great variety of women's involvement in economic activities as entrepreneurs across countries reflected distinctions in culture and customs regarding women's participation in the economy (for example, societal views about women's role in the labor force and in business), and in current economic conditions. Basically, individual persons or in this case women open their own business or become producers instead of working as employees in someone else' companies or, for married women, staying at home doing domestic works, could have two different motives. Their decision to conduct own businesses could be purely market orientation reflecting their high spirit of entrepreneurship, i.e., they were "pulled" by market opportunities to conduct their own businesses. Or a means to survive: they were "pushed" to do that because all other options for them to get better jobs outside home were either absent or unsatisfactory, or to support family incomes. Based on her own study on women entrepreneurs in Indonesia, Gunawan (2012) comes with a conclusion that there were two different main motivations that woman decide to run own businesses, i.e., to help the family income or to optimize the talent. The first reason was linked to her family's income condition or poverty, while the second one could be considered as a sign of entrepreneurship.

The relative prevalence of market/business opportunity motivated versus economic necessity-motivated entrepreneurship activity provides useful insights into why women enter entrepreneurship. The former motivation can be considered as "pull" factors driven entrepreneurship, and the latter motivation as "push" factors driven entrepreneurship. In GEM (2015), economic necessity-based is defined as the percentage of those driven by having no better choice for work. Market/business opportunity-based is defined as the percentage of those who are motivated to pursue opportunity. This includes taking advantage of a business opportunity or currently having a job, but still looking for a better opportunity. Table 4.5 shows that in Indonesia there were more males than females as necessity-motivated entrepreneurs in their early stage of entrepreneurship. Other surveyed ASEAN member states also shared the same ratio.

Besides GEM (2015), there are some good studies on female entrepreneurs in developing countries which also discuss women's motivation or reason to conduct their own businesses. These studies are mainly on women entrepreneurs in rural South Asia which included Mahmood et al. (2012), Shah (2013), Saeed et al. (2014), Shah and Saurabh (2015), and Hani (2015) who found that many women did start micro-level businesses to support themselves and their families. By doing a survey on 160 women entrepreneurs in four major cities in Pakistan, Mahmood et al. (2012) aimed to explore the factors responsible for motivation and

Table 4.5 Necessity-motivated entrepreneurship by gender in selected Southeast Asian Countries, 2015

Member states	Female (% of total early-stage female entrepreneurial activities)	Male (% of total early-stage male entrepreneurial activities)
Philippines	60	85
Vietnam	70	71
Indonesia	76	81
Malaysia	80	86
Thailand	81	82

Source GEM (2015)

hindrance in the way of female entrepreneurs and also address the pertinent gender issues in the context of Pakistan. The findings illustrated that the female entrepreneurs were motivated to earn money for personal use, to contribute to family income, personal ambition, and for self-satisfaction. Shah (2013) and Shah and Saurabh (2015) found that many women in India, especially in rural areas, started micro-level businesses to support themselves and their families. Saeed et al. (2014) interviewed 120 female entrepreneurs in Lahore (Pakistan) with the aim to explore social, cultural, and economic implications of female entrepreneurship and identify the causes and motivational factors, obstacles, and gender discrimination. The result revealed that a vast majority of the respondents started their business to contribute to family income and personal interest. Hani (2015) conducted a survey on women entrepreneurs in micro businesses in Sylhet City (Bangladesh). Types of businesses included tailoring, handicrafts, boutique shop, catering, agro-based/ livestock, and clothing businesses. The finding showed that the major reason to start business of 14 out of a total of 50 respondents was generating income for the family, while the main motivation of the remaining respondents ranged from "be self- dependent", "continuation of family businesses", and "gaining economic freedom".

4.4　Constraints

Unfortunately, not so many studies have been made until now on the development of entrepreneurs by gender in Indonesia, especially those focusing on key challenges facing women to become entrepreneurs and main constraints that women-owned businesses must confront. Among very few studies available is from Tambunan (2009, 2015, 2017a, 2017b) who, based on his findings, concluded that the low representative of women as entrepreneurs in Indonesia could be attributed to a range of the following factors:

1. low level of education and lack of training opportunities which made Indonesian women severely disadvantaged in both the economy and society. It was especially true for women living in rural areas or in relatively backward provinces. Many rural women spoke only their native language and never read newspapers and thus they were very restricted to communicate with the outside world. There were also still many social, cultural, and religious taboos that prevented

women who could and should be accessing higher education from doing so. As Suharyo (2005) has found that many parents living in rural areas still have the traditional thinking that (higher) education belongs to men only. Tambunan (2017a, 2017b) also found that enterprises owned by women with only primary school were mainly from the category of MIEs with very low income. By region, better-educated women entrepreneurs were found more in the western and more developed part of the country, i.e., Java, the most populated island, and Sumatera, the second important island in terms of economic activities and population density, than in the eastern part, the least developed area;

2. heavy household chores. Especially in rural areas, women in general have more children, and they were more demanded to do their traditional role as being responsible for housework and childcare than those in urban areas, especially in big cities. According to a 2013 study on access to trade and growth of women's MSMEs in developing economies in the Asia–Pacific region (APEC), cited by Federica Gentile from UBI Business, gender-specific constraints such as childcare responsibilities were also an important issue that women entrepreneurs in Indonesia and other developing economies in the AP region need to deal with in running their businesses (http://www.ubibusiness.com/topics/business-environment/indonesian-women-entrepreneurs-a-catalyst-for-growth-/#.VlOw1F Xotjo);

3. there may be legal, traditions, customs, cultural, or religious constraints on the extent to which women could open their own businesses. Especially in rural areas where a vast majority of population are Muslims and rather isolated from big cities like Jakarta, Islamic-based norms have stronger influences on women's daily life. This made female behavior or attitude in rural areas less open than male (or than urban women) to "doing modern business" culture. In such society, women must fully comply with their primary duty as their husband's partner and housewife, they were not allowed to start their own businesses or to do jobs that involve contact with men, or to manage a company with male employees, or simply they were not allowed to leave the home alone. Marital status also played an important role in the women's choice of job. Older and married women in Indonesia, for instance, were likely to be found in informal enterprises such as trade or other activities which enable

them to combine household work and paid work. On the other hand, young single women who migrated from rural areas are more likely to be found working as wage employees in services and trading enterprises; and

4. limited access to financing from banks or other formal financial institutions. This is indeed a key concern of women business owners in Indonesia. This is found to be more problematic for women in rural areas or outside of major metropolitan areas such as Jakarta and Surabaya. This constraint is related to ownership rights which deprives women of property ownership and, consequently, of the ability to offer the type of collateral normally required for access to bank loans. In Indonesia, men are still perceived as the head of the family, and thus, in general, men are still perceived as the owner or inheritor of family assets such as land, company, and house. A 2013 study on access to trade and growth of women's MSMEs in APEC developing economies, cited by Federica Gentile from UBI Business, reported that in Indonesia, on the one hand, the number of women's-owned MSMEs was growing quickly at around 8 percent annually, but, on the other hand, their growth was potentially hindered by specific challenges, and access to credit was considered in this report as the main challenge for women entrepreneurs, because of complicated loan paperwork and high-interest rates (http://www.ubibusiness.com/topics/business-enviro nment/indonesian-women-entrepreneurs-a-catalyst-for-growth-/#. VlOw1FXotjo). In their study on patterns of Indonesian women entrepreneurship, Hania et al. (2012) found that Indonesian women entrepreneur has a high independent financial aspect in running their business. Only a few women used bank credits.

A good comparable developing region for Indonesia with respect to women entrepreneurs is South Asia. Although in countries in this region the entrepreneurial process is the same for men and women, in practice there were, however, many problems with different dimensions and magnitudes facing women which prevented them from realizing their full potential as entrepreneurs. Entrepreneurship by definition implies being in control of one's life and activities. It is precisely this independence that societies in the region have denied women. According to Sinhal (2005), the situation was more critical in South Asian countries, as compared to other parts of Asia. The business environment for women, which reflected the complex interplay of different factors (e.g., psychological, social/cultural, religion, economic, and educational factors) in the region ultimately resulted in the disadvantaged status of women in society. Women remained far behind men in enjoying freedom and other basic human rights, let alone participating with men on an equal footing in economic activities (e.g., Das, 2000; Dhameja et al., 2002; Ganesan, 2003; Goheer, 2003).

In Bangladesh, many women's enterprises were operating on an informal basis and they were not identified in the country's economy. These enterprises lacked the basic forms and information, marketing opportunities, regulatory and social supports (ADB, 2001). In Nepal, problems faced by women entrepreneurs were mainly low access to credit and marketing networks, lack of access to land and property and reduced risk-taking capacity, lack of access to modern technology, lack of personal security and risk of sexual harassment, severe competition from organized units both in the domestic as well as the international markets, low level of self-confidence, and social and cultural barriers such as exclusive responsibility for household work and restrictions on mobility (ADB, 1999).

In Pakistan, according to Roomi (2006), most of the problems/challenges faced by Pakistani women entrepreneurs were a result of the inferior status of women in society, their underestimation as economic agents as well as the gender bias embedded in the regional, tribal, and/or feudal culture in the name of Islam. Inadequate public transport played also a major role in immobility of women in Pakistan, and this was related to religious and cultural reasons, mainly purdah: the public transport facilities such as buses and vans have separate seating arrangements for men and women. These public buses and vans only have the first two or three rows of seats available for women. All the remaining seats were for men. From reviewing literature on women entrepreneurs in Pakistan, Tambunan (2017a, 2017b) found that the main reasons for the challenges they faced were the notions of "purdah" and "Izzat", which placed severe restrictions on their mobility and they were not allowed to go out and work with men, which might cast doubts on their good reputation and reduce their marriage prospects.

Another study of Roomi in collaboration with Parrot (2008) showed that women entrepreneurs in Pakistan did not enjoy the same opportunities as men due to various deep-rooted discriminatory socio-cultural values and traditions. These restrictions could be observed within the support mechanism that exists to assist such fledgling businesswomen. The economic potential of female entrepreneurs was not being realized as they suffer from a lack of access to capital, land, business premises, information technology, training, and agency assistance. Inherent attitudes of a patriarchal society, that men were superior to women and that women were best suited to be homemakers, create formidable challenges. Women also received little encouragement from some male family members, resulting in limited spatial mobility and a dearth of social capital. Their research suggested that in order to foster development, multi-agency cooperation was required. The media, educational policy-makers, and government agencies could combine to provide women with improved access to business development services and facilitate local, regional, and national networks. This would help the integration of women entrepreneurs into the mainstream economy.

In India, based on their research Yoganandan and Gopalselvam (2018) showed that even though woman entrepreneurship and the formation of woman-owned business networks in India were step-by-step growing, there were still many challenges and barriers that female business owners or marketers faced. One fundamental task that many female marketers faced was the impact that the conventional gender-roles society may still have on women. Accordingly, female entrepreneurs in India were dealing with numerous obstacles related to their organizations. The main important obstacles or challenges were the following. First, the problem of finance. For many women, especially in the rural areas, to raise finance was a huge venture. Generally, women in this country did not have any property and any securities in their personal names. Instead, they were fully relying on men or their husbands either physically and financially and morally. So, they must depend upon their own financial savings or negligible loans from friends and spouse and children. Second is male domination. As in many other developing/low-income countries, women in India were dominated by means of men in her family in addition to enterprise. Indian women still need to get permission from men, e.g., father, brother, or husband to do own businesses.

Third is lack of technology. In India women in general still lack access to advanced technologies including technical training that in fact they need very much for their business to grow or sustain. Fourth is lack of infrastructure development. Women in India may not have enough infrastructure to begin and expand a business. Fifth is lack of education. Especially in rural areas or from poor families, women are low educated, because they were forced by their parents to marry in their very young age. Often evidently, their mother and father made choices for their daughters and after marriage their husband take over decisions what they have to be performed. Sixth is social recognition. Although the pressure for women's emancipation or gender equality is also felt in India, in general, Indian society still considers women to be more appropriate to function as housewives who do domestic work, not to run their own business. Seventh is religion. Certain religions in India do not give preference to women because they are not in accordance with religious norms. Finally, marketing. Women owning small businesses often fully depend on men (i.e., traders or collectors) for selling their goods for many reasons. One of the reasons is that a young girl or a married woman is not allowed by her father or husband to go too far from home. So, she does not have an opportunity to cover the whole marketplace.

4.5 Evidence from a Case Study: Motivation and Constraints

In order to explore the main reason or motivation of women in doing own businesses and to identify their main constraints in running their businesses, a study was conducted with a series of surveys on a total of 108 female-owned/managed-MSEs. The survey used a semi-structured questionnaire and interviews that took place during February–April 2016. There were two main reasons why the selection of respondents was only from the MSE category, not including MLEs. First, based on the fact of the distribution of women entrepreneurs by size of enterprises in Indonesia that (as already explained in previous sections) more women entrepreneurs or women-owned businesses are found in this category of enterprises than in MLEs. Second, it is not easy to identify MLEs managed or owned by female. Annually, BPS issues statistics on MLEs in selected sectors, including the manufacturing industry, with a list of names and addresses of all companies in these sectors. But the list does not have information on the business owner or top executives by gender. To interview owners of big companies also normally require a lot of time as they are usually very busy, and there is also no guarantee that invitation for interviews will be accepted after waiting for weeks.

Most of the respondents were aged above 35 years old and married, and the remaining respondents were much younger, and some were single. Some of them were still studying in the academy (diploma) or university. Most of the respondents lived in Jakarta (the Capital city of Indonesia), although many of them were born outside the city. They came to the city when very young with their parents or already married and followed their husbands as migrants to the city. The remaining respondents were selected from other cities surrounding Jakarta including Tangerang, Bekasi, Cilegon, Depok, and Bogor. The selection of the cities was just a matter of time and cost-efficiency.

More than half of the total respondents were married women (although some of them during the survey period were widows). More than half of the total respondents started their businesses after 2000. Most of the respondents were doing their own businesses in trade and restaurants. The selection of these two sectors was based on the fact (national data) that the majority of MSEs owned by women are found in these sectors. Trade includes such as conventional small shops and market or petty traders. However, few respondents were found in the manufacturing industry making such as simple consumption/household items and food (e.g., bread and snacks), and in "other sectors", which included event organizer, contractors, beauty salon, and catering.

As the aim of this study was not to test any hypotheses but to explore experiences of Indonesian women entrepreneurs regarding their initial motivations or reasons to establish their own businesses, especially married women, all the 108 respondents were selected fully randomly. The finding of this exploration study may add new information to the existing study on women entrepreneurs especially in developing countries.

To meet the main objective of the survey, the respondents were given a variety of alternative answers that they must choose only one, and these answers can be grouped into two categories: "push" and "pull". If a respondent has selected an alternative answer from the "pull" category, then it indicates that she was attracted by, e.g., market opportunities to become an entrepreneur or to establish her own business, although she may have better income/employment opportunities somewhere else. This may suggest that she has an entrepreneurship spirit. Alternative answers open to the respondents from the "pull" category were such as "I want to be an entrepreneur", "I want to have own businesses", or "I want to be financially independent". Whereas alternative answers from the "push" category were "to supplement family income", "I could not find job", or "I have to run/ continue business of my parents/ family businesses".

Although the survey used a deductive approach with pre-determined push and pull questions, during the interviews, the respondents were asked first to tell their initial reasons or motivations in their ow n words, and their social and economic conditions at the time they decided to establish their own businesses. Then, they were asked to choose one of the given alternative answers they think appropriate. When the chosen answers were found inconsistent with their told initial stories, they were asked to elaborate further their stories to get the real picture.

Obviously, based on their answers, a vast majority of the respondents (i.e., 60 persons) could be categorized as the "push" (or "forced") entrepreneurs and the remaining 48 respondents as the "pull" (or "encouraged") entrepreneurs. From the "push" category, 56 respondents said that they run their own businesses just to survive or to supplement their family income, or as the only source of income because they could not find a job elsewhere. Whereas the reason of the remaining 4 respondents was that they must take over their parent's businesses. From these 56 respondents whose motivation was to "supplement family income", most of them have only senior high school or lower education, and they were married. For married respondents, the status of employment of their husbands was found to vary, e.g., regular employees in a private company, small trader, civil servant, office boy, driver, self-employment, and some were unemployed.

The respondents said that they have never dreamed before to have their own businesses. Most of them claimed that one day after finishing school they will get married and, if allowed by their husband, they will look for work as an employee in a company or become a housewife. They said frankly that the salary of their husband was not enough to support their family, and so, if they could not find jobs elsewhere, opening own small businesses according to their ability was their only option.

Finally, the respondents from both categories were asked about their constraints in running their businesses. As with other issues investigated, here too they were given some alternative answers in which each of them had to choose only one that they considered as the main constraint they faced. The alternative answers w ere: (I) limited access to finance, (II) no support from family or husband; (III) difficult to manage time for family/ household and business; (IV) difficult to get a business license; (V) difficult to get market access (heavy competition); (VI) difficult to get raw materials (no stock available or prices are too expensive); (VII) difficult to find workers (in many cases in Indonesia as in other "Muslim" countries, many women-owned businesses are allowed by their husbands to have only female employees); and (VIII) others (e.g., market demand declines, inflation, and difficult to find location).

As shown by Fig. 4.3, the most interesting finding was that almost all the "push" respondents said that lack of access to finance (problem I) was their most serious constraint; while only very few of the "pull" respondents said the same. There is no precise theoretical explanation for this, as for banks they do not make or cannot see the difference between the "push" and the "pull" entrepreneurs. For banks or financial institutions in general, only business visibility and bankability of an applicant are their most concern. Another interesting finding was that problem II (no support from family or husband) only found in the "pull" category, although only few of them said this as their main constraint. The same for problem IV (difficult to get business license), only found by (though only few) the "pull" respondents.

Overall, it revealed that limited access to finance was the most serious constraint. There was no evidence that banks in Indonesia discriminate against women in providing credit. Officially, there is no specially designed credit application procedure that differentiated between men and women or between single women and married women in the credit application procedure. In the past, for married women applicants, banks used to require a signature of their husband, but not anymore (although it may happen occasionally in some villages).

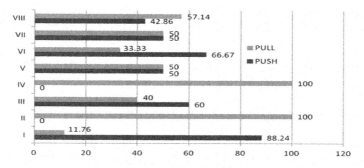

Fig. 4.3 Respondents from both categories by main constraints (*Source* Field survey: February–April 2016)

References

ADB. (1999). *Women in Sri Lanka*. Asian Development Bank.

ADB. (2001). *Women in Bangladesh*. Asian Development Bank.

BPS. (2020). *Profil Industri Mikro dan Kecil 2019* [2019 Micro and small industry profile]. Badan Pusat Statistik.

Das, D. J. (2000). Problems faced by women entrepreneurs. In K. Sasikumar (Ed.), *Women entrepreneurship*. Vikas Publishing House.

Devadas, S., & Young E. K. (2020, October). *Exploring the potential of gender parity to promote economic growth* (Research & Policy Briefs No. 39). The World Bank Malaysia Hub, The World Bank Group.

Dhameja, S. K., Bhatia, B. S., & Saini, J. S. (2002). Problems and constraints of women entrepreneurship. In D. D. Sharma & S. K. Dhameja (Eds.), *Women and rural entrepreneurship*. Abhishek Publications.

Ganesan, S. (2003). *Status of women entrepreneurs in India*. Kanishka Publications.

GEM. (2015). *Women's entrepreneurship*. Special Report, Global Entrepreneurship Monitor, The Center for Women's Leadership at Babson College.

Goheer, N. A. (2003). *Women entrepreneurs in Pakistan—How to improve their bargaining power*. ILO/SEED.

Gunawan, J. (2012). *Woman entrepreneurs in Indonesia: Challenging roles of an economic and social actor*. Riwani Globe.

Hani, F. F. (2015). Entrepreneurial motivation and challenges: A study on women entrepreneurs in Sylhet City. *Global Disclosure of Economics and Business, 4*(2), 111–122.

Hania, U., Rachmaniaa, I. N., Setyaningsiha, S., & Putria, R. C. (2012). Patterns of Indonesian women entrepreneurship. *Economics and Finance, 4*, 274–285.

Hilbrecht, M. (2016). Self -employment and experiences of support in a work–family context. *Journal of Small Business & Entrepreneurship, 28*(1), 75–96.

Hughes, K. (2006). Exploring motivation and success among Canadian women entrepreneurs. *Journal of Small Business and Entrepreneurship, 19*(2), 83–94.

Kirkwood, J. (2009a). Spousal roles on motivations for entrepreneurship: A qualitative study in New Zealand. *Journal of Family and Economic Issues, 30*(4), 372–385.

Kirkwood, J. (2009b). Motivational factors in a push-pull theory of entrepreneurship. *Gender in Management: an International Journal, 24*(5), 346–364.

Loscocco, K., & Bird, S. R. (2012). Gendered paths: Why women lag behind men in small business success. *Work and Occupations, 39*(2), 183–219.

Mahmood, B., Khalid, S., Sohail, M. M., & Babak, I. (2012). Exploring the motivation and barriers in way of Pakistani female entrepreneurs. *British Journal of Education, Society & Behavioural Science, 2*(4), 353–368.

Raju, G. (2000). Women entrepreneurship development through DWCRA. In K. Sasikumar (Ed.), *Women entrepreneurship*. Vikas Publishing House.

Roomi, M. A. (2006). *Women entrepreneurs in Pakistan: Profile, challenges and practical recommendations*. School of Management Royal Holloway, University of London, London.

Roomi, M. A., & Parrott, G. (2008). Barriers to development and progression of women entrepreneurs in Pakistan. *Journal of Entrepreneurship, 17*(1), 59–72.

Saeed, S., Malik, N., Sohail, M. M., Tabassum, A., & Anwar, H. N. (2014). Factors motivating female entrepreneurs: A study conducted in major urban area of Punjab. *Mediterranean Journal of Social Sciences, 5*(4), 669–675.

Shah, H. (2013). *Creating an enabling environment for women's entrepreneurship in India* (South and South-West Asia Office Development Papers 1304). South and South-West Asia Office, United Nations Economic and Social Commission for Asia and the Pacific (UN ESCAP).

Shah, H., & Saurabh, P. (2015). Women entrepreneurs in developing nations: Growth and replication strategies and their impact on poverty alleviation. *Technology Innovation Management Review, 5*(8), 34–43.

Sharma, D. D., & Dhameja, S. K. (2002). *Women and rural entrepreneurship*. Abhishek Publications.

Sinha, A. (2003). *Experience of SMEs in South and South-East Asia*. SEDF and World Bank.

Sinhal, S. (2005). *Developing women entrepreneurs in South Asia: Issues, initiatives and experiences* (ST/ESCAP/2401). Trade and Investment Division. UNESCAP.

Suharyo, W. I. (2005, April–June). *Gender and poverty* (Gender and Poverty No. 14). SMERU Research Institute.

Tambunan, T. T. H. (2009). Women entrepreneurs in Indonesia: Their main constraints and reasons. *Journal of Asia Entrepreneurship and Sustainability, V*(3), 37–51.

Tambunan, T. T. H. (2015). *ASEAN micro, small and medium enterprises toward AEC 2015*. Lambert Academic Publishing (LAP).

Tambunan, T. T. H. (2017a). Women entrepreneurs in MSEs in Indonesia: Their motivations and constraints. *International Journal of Gender and Women's Studies, 5*(1), 88–100.

Tambunan, T. T. H. (2017b). Women entrepreneurs in MSEs in Indonesia: Their motivations and main constraints. *Journal of Women's Entrepreneurship and Education, 1–2*, 56–86.

UNDP. (2020, April). *The social and economic impact of Covis-19 in the Asia-Pacific region*. United Nations Development Programme. file:///C:/Users/USER/Downloads/UNDP-RBAP-Position-Note-Social-Economic-Impact-of-COVID-19-in-Asia-Pacific-2020.pdf

WEF. (2007). *The global gender gap report 2007*. World Economic Forum.

WEF. (2015). *The global gender gap report 2015*. World Economic Forum.

WEF. (2020). *The global gender gap report 2020*. World Economic Forum.

Yoganandan, G., & Gopalselvam, G. (2018). A study on challenges of women entrepreneurs in India. *International Journal of Innovative Research & Studies, 8*(III), 491–500.

CHAPTER 5

MSMEs in Times of Economic Crisis

5.1 Introduction

Indonesia now is much more vulnerable to any economic shocks than, say, 30 years ago, for the following reasons. First, since economic reforms started in the 1980s towards trade, banking, investment, and capital account liberalizations, the Indonesian economy has become more integrated with the world economy. Second, at a decreasing rate, Indonesia is still dependent on exports of many primary commodities, i.e., mining and agriculture which means that the economy is still sensitive to any world price/demand instability for those commodities. Third, Indonesia has become increasingly dependent on imports of a number of food items such as rice, food grains, cereals, wheat, corn, meat, dairy, vegetables and fruits, or even oil. Any increase or instability of world prices or the world production failures of these commodities will have big effects on domestic consumption and food security in Indonesia. Fourth, more Indonesian working population, including women, went abroad as migrant workers, and hence livelihoods in many villages in Indonesia have become increasingly dependent on remittances from abroad. Any economic crisis that hit the host countries (such as that happened in Dubai during its financial crisis in 2009) will hit the Indonesian economy too. Finally, as a huge populated country with increasing income per capita, domestic food consumption is not only high but also keeps increasing. Accelerating

---

© The Author(s), under exclusive license to Springer Nature
Singapore Pte Ltd. 2022
T. T.H. Tambunan, *Fostering Resilience through Micro,*
Small and Medium Enterprises, Sustainable Development Goals Series,
https://doi.org/10.1007/978-981-16-9435-6_5

101

output growth in agriculture is therefore a must for Indonesia, and this depends on various factors, including climate, an exogenous factor. As Indonesia is located between the Pacific ocean and the Indian ocean in the line of equator, the country is always vulnerable to El Nino/La Nina phenomenon which may cause failures in rice (and other commodities) harvest and therefore will generate a hyperinflation.

Indeed, in the past 25 years, Indonesia has experienced two big external originated financial crises, the Asian financial crisis started by mid 1997 and reached its peak in 1998, the global financial crisis in 2008 and 2009, and the outbreak of coronavirus disease (COVID-19) in 2020. During these crises, the most concern was their impacts on employment, poverty, and MSMEs.

This chapter examines the Indonesian experiences with these two crises and their impacts on MSMEs. It addresses two key questions. First, what were the main transmission channels through which the three crises affected MSMEs? Second, were the impacts on MSMEs different between these three crises, and if yes, what factors made them different? Third, how did the affected MSMEs deal with the crises or what were their crisis mitigation measures?

5.2   Types and Transmission Channels of Economic Crises

Economic crisis can be defined as the wild fluctuations, outside the acceptable limits of change, in the prices or supplies of commodities. An economic crisis is usually seen as a situation in which the economy of a country experiences a sudden downturn in its aggregate output or gross domestic product (GDP). There are many early triggers of an economic crisis, for instance, the sudden weakening of the exchange rate of a currency (commonly called the currency crisis) or the sudden collapse of the financial sector in a country (called the financial or banking crisis) or the COVID-19 pandemic.

Judging from the process of occurrence, the economic crisis has two different characteristics. First, an economic crisis that occurs suddenly or appears without any previous signs commonly called an unexpected economic shock, for example, the very large increase in the price of crude oil in the international market in 1974 by the organization of the oil-producing countries or OPEC as a strong reaction from crude oil producing countries in the Middle East region against the siding of

Western countries, especially the United States and Western Europe to Israel, which was involved in a major war with Arab countries, particularly Egypt, Syria, Iraq, and Jordan. For the world or especially oil-importing countries, included the United States, EU (European Union), Japan, and China, the increased oil price was considered the first oil crisis (the second was in 1979). Meanwhile, for Indonesia, which at that time was still one of the world's oil exporters, that first oil crisis was a huge advantage (oil boom) providing a very large (unexpected) income for the Indonesian government. The Asian financial crisis in the period 1997–1998 which also hit Indonesia could also be included in this category, although for Indonesia, that 1997/1998 crisis did not really come as a surprise compared to the 1974 first oil crisis, because before the Indonesian economy was hit, Thailand's economy had already been shaken by it. A few months later after Thailand's currency, bath, experienced a big depreciation, then the Indonesian rupiah (IDR) began to shake, around mid-1997, and continued until it reached the climax in the first half of 1998 when the exchange rate of the IDR against the USD had reached above 10,000 IDR per one USD, compared to only around 2000 IDR per one USD in early 1997.

Meanwhile, the economic crisis which is not sudden but goes through a long accumulation process is like the global financial crisis 2008–2009. This crisis was preceded by the most serious financial crisis ever to occur in the United States after the Great Depression in the 30s, which eventually spread to other developed countries such as Japan and Europe through global financial linkages. It was only after a few months that the world economy began to experience a recession marked by a decline in global income and demand which also affected the economy of Indonesia and many other countries in the world.

Apart from being distinguished according to the process as discussed earlier, economic crises can also be distinguished according to their type or source. This section provides a theoretical discussion of how different types of sources of economic crises have different transmission channels of impacts on economic sectors, households, and communities. Understanding this very well is important, especially for policymakers or economic development planners. They must have sufficient knowledge of a particular type of economic crisis, what are its main transmission channels, what sectors will be directly affected, and so on. This understanding will assist policymakers in preparing economic policies or appropriate actions in anticipating the arrival of an economic crisis, and with adequate information they can also minimize its negative effects, especially on the rate of income growth (in total and in real per capita) and poverty.

An economic crisis can originate from outside or from within a country/region. From within a country/region, for instance, a sudden drop in the production of a commodity. In the agricultural sector, for example, crop failure due to changes in extreme weather that were not anticipated, or because of natural disasters such as large floods that inundate rice fields. External sources like the 2008–2009 global financial crisis (except for the United States, this crisis came from within), or the first oil crisis in 1974 or the second in 1979 for oil-importing countries. Economic crises originating from various sources also have different processes or transmission channels of impact, and the sectors of the economy directly affected are also different. Depending on the nature and magnitude of the production, consumption, and investment relationships of these sectors with the rest of the domestic economy, economic crises from various sources ultimately form a different total impact on a country's economy. The following sections of this chapter discuss various types of economic crises that many countries have ever experienced in the last 50 years, or which are likely to occur again in the future.

5.3   Literature Review

The Crises and Their Impacts on MSMEs

There are plenty of literature on the impact of the 1997/1998 Asian financial crisis and the 2008/2009 global financial crisis such as economic growth, export, import, foreign loans, employment/unemployment, poverty, migrant workers, child labor, farm household incomes, education, and health (e.g., Bello, 1999; Hartono, 2011; Kane, 2009; Pearson & Sweetman, 2011; Priyambada et al., 2005; Shin, 2015; Tambunan, 1998, 2010a, 2010b, 2011a, 2011b; Tambunan & Busneti, 2016; UNICEF, 2009; World Bank, 2009). Literature on the impact of COVID-19 on the economy has also started to grow (e.g., ADB, 2020; Chesbrough, 2020; Kim et al., 2020; ILO, 2020a, 2020b, 2020c, 2020d; Shakil et al., 2020; Suryahadi et al., 2020; UNCTAD, 2020a, 2020b; UNDP, 2020a, 2020b).

In Indonesia, the Asian financial crisis began with the depreciation of its national currency, the IDR, against the USD by more than 200 percent between 1997 and 1998. As a result, many domestic companies that relied heavily on foreign loans and imports of processed raw materials, semi-finished products, components, machinery, production equipment and tools, and other inputs were forced to stop their activities. The impact of the first crisis was so severe that the country's economy slumped into a deep recession with an overall negative growth of about 13 percent. Whereas the second crisis was generally regarded as an international trade or export crisis as global demand for exports from many countries including Indonesia declined significantly (Griffith-Jones & Ocampo, 2009; Khor & Sebastian, 2009; Hartono, 2011). The impact of the second crisis, however, was not as severe as the first one, and Indonesia maintained positive rates of economic growth during the period 2008 and 2009.

The 2020 COVID-19 crisis was generally considered as domestic supply and demand crisis due to the declined consumption and production as a direct consequence of policies on social/physical distance, work and schools from home, and the necessity for companies in non-strategic sectors to stop their activities. Suryahadi et al. (2020) estimated that COVID-19 would reduce Indonesia's economic growth between 1 and 4 percent. Even, it was estimated that the Indonesian economy would experience a recession of minus 5.4 percent (OECD Eurostat).

With respect to MSMEs, it is often stated in the literature that one comparative advantage of MSMEs relative to LEs is their flexibility and capacity to move from one product to another when market demand changes, and expand easily when the economy grows, and contract easily in case of economic crises (Tambunan, 2019). Berry et al. (2001) added that MSMEs are very important in industries or economies that face rapid market or economic condition changes, such as a sharp macro-economic downturn because they work as a shock absorber in the business cycle. In Sandee et al. (2000), it is stated that MSMEs can be expected to perform better under volatile macro-economic conditions than LEs that produce more standardized products, where the reorganization of the assembly line takes time.

However, some authors argued that MSMEs, as with their larger counterparts, can also be severely affected by the economic crisis. It depends, among other factors, on the type of the crisis and thus its main transmission channels through which the crisis affects the MSMEs. Experiences in many countries in Southeast Asia showed that credit, import, and domestic demand were the most important transmission channels through which the 1997/1998 Asian financial crisis affected local MSMEs. For instance, in Thailand, findings from Chantrasawang (1999), Berry et al. (2001), Bakiewicz (2004), and Régnier (2005) showed that many Thai MSMEs were forced to discontinue their production activities mainly because credit from banks was not available, interest rate was extremely high, and domestic demand for their products dropped significantly. The same happened too in Malaysia where many MSMEs were affected because of (i) domestic demand declined, (ii) no credit was available while they relied heavily on loans from banks and other formal financial institutions, (iii) they were highly dependent on imported raw materials and other inputs that became very expensive, and (iv) many MSMEs were key suppliers to multinational corporations that were also affected by the crisis that led to less orders or order cancelations (Abdullah, 2002; Mustafa & Mansor, 1999). In the Philippines, many local MSMEs in certain industries such as the auto parts and electronic goods industries had to stop production as domestic demand for new cars and electronic goods dropped significantly during the crisis (Berry & Rodriguez, 2001; Tecson, 1999).

With respect to the 2008/2009 global financial crisis, it revealed from many developing countries that the most important transmission channel was the decline in world demand which also affected export-oriented MSMEs as well as MSMEs acted as subcontractors to large-sized exporting companies in labor-intensive manufacturing (e.g., textile, garment, footwear, seafood processing, and electronic) and MSMEs producing items for tourism (Griffith-Jones & Ocampo, 2009; Khor & Sebastian, 2009; Nguanbanchong, 2009; Hartono, 2011).

Another important transmission channel was the banking sector which caused the loss of international confidence in the local banking system and thus the letter of credit could not be issued, and no domestic bank and trade credits were available (Humphrey, 2009). ADB (2009) also reported that the shrinking of trade finance due to the 2008/2009 crisis was one of the major transmission channels through which the crisis affected many MSMEs. However, based on evidence in Central Asia during the crisis, Pasadilla (2010) conjectured that LEs were going to be harder hit by the shrinking of trade finance than MSMEs because of the former's heavier reliance on foreign bank borrowing and global capital markets. The possible adverse impact on MSMEs would include weakness in demand, both domestic and foreign, which could affect their sales and profits, and thus their capacity to raise financing which these enterprises relied upon heavily.

Chakraborty (2012) analyzed the channels through which the 2008/2009 crisis-affected export-oriented firms in India by using income statement and balance sheet indicators for around 5000 manufacturing firms. His findings showed that the worse export performance of Indian firms was mostly explained by the negative demand shock from India's major trading partners, with the impact being higher for the United States than the EU. On the other hand, domestic financial conditions, accompanied by loose monetary policy, acted as a supporting factor to export-oriented firms.

By using the firm-level data provided by the Central Register of the Republic of Macedonia (CRM), Jovanovikj and Georgievska (2015) investigated the impact of the crisis on the country's economy by evaluating the relative importance of three transmission channels, i.e., the domestic demand, the export/trade, and the financial channels. The results showed that firms domestically producing and selling had relatively weaker performance. The trade channel appeared important only for exporting companies, whereas the financial channel did not play a significant role during the crisis.

Claessens et al. (2011) examined the impact of the crisis on firm performance and the role of different transmission channels on a sample of 42 advanced emerging economies. Using accounting data for 7722 non-financial firms, they investigated the role of the same three channels through which the crisis may have affected the firms, which findings indicated that export and demand channels were the most important in transmitting the crisis. With respect to country specifics, the results pointed to trade linkages as the prime propagator of shocks, while financial linkages were found to play a considerably weaker role.

With respect to the COVID-19, OECD, in its updated report on SME policy response to the crisis (OECD, 2020a, 2020b), explained that the COVID-19 crisis affected MSMEs through both the supply and demand sides. On the supply side, MSMEs faced a shortage of labor, as workers were unwell or needed to look after their children while schools were closed, and movements of people were restricted. Measures to contain the disease by lockdowns and quarantines led to further and more severe drops in capacity utilization. As supply chains were also interrupted by the crisis, many MSMEs also experienced shortages of parts, intermediate goods, or processed raw materials. On the demand side, MSMEs also suffered from a cash shortage due to a dramatic decline in demand and revenue. All these effects were compounded because workers were laid off and firms were not able to pay salaries. More generally, MSMEs were likely to be more vulnerable to "social distancing" than LEs. The impact of the virus could have potential spill-overs into financial markets which would make MSMEs suffer even more. These various impacts have affected both MSMEs and LEs. However, according to the report, the effect on MSMEs was especially severe, particularly because of higher levels of vulnerability and lower resilience related to their size.

Shafi et al. (2020) collected data from 184 Pakistani MSMEs by administering an online questionnaire, and the data were analyzed through descriptive statistics. The results indicated that most of the participating enterprises have been severely affected by the significant drop in demand and they were facing several issues such as financial problems, supply chain disruptions, decrease in demand, reduction in sales and profit, among others. Further, more than two-thirds of participating enterprises reported that they could not survive if the lockdown lasts more than two months.

Results of the ILO SCORE Programme Survey showed that enterprises in many affected countries were struggling to survive the effects of COVID-19 (ILO, 2020a, 2020b, 2020c, 2020d). Of the 1000 MSMEs surveyed from eight countries across four continents, 70 percent have had to shut down operations. Half (50%) have temporarily closed their business by following direct instructions from the authorities, while the other 50 percent have closed temporarily due to a reduction in orders, cases of staff COVID-19 infection, or more sadly, permanently. More than 75 percent of MSMEs were experiencing or expecting a reduction in revenues through 2020. In some cases, the reductions in revenues were very high. One-third (33%) of businesses anticipated losing more than half of their revenues. About 75 percent of companies suffering from reduced demand and one-third (33%) experiencing a more than 50 percent drop in customer orders. Nearly 9 out of 10 businesses were experiencing a shortage in cash flow.

Crisis Mitigating Measures (CMMs)

The ILO Survey showed that MSMEs were responding to the economic fall-out from COVID-19 in several ways (ILO, 2020d). Half of the MSMEs surveyed have reduced their production of goods and services to match demand reductions and constraints on their production. Over one-third (38%) of MSMEs were negotiating wage modifications with workers or revised payment terms with banks and suppliers. Less frequently, some MSMEs were trying to diversify their sales channels or products to try to reduce the effects of the crisis on their business.

From their research in Pakistan, Shafi et al. (2020) also provided evidence on CMMs adopted by affected MSMEs. The enterprises surveyed have chosen a different variety of strategies to curb the crisis. Particularly, 31 percent of the sampled enterprises have shut down the business completely, while 19 percent have partially closed their businesses, whereas 18 percent of enterprises were planning to apply for a loan, and 12 percent of enterprises were continuing to operate their business. Only 4 percent of participating enterprises expressed that they were planning to change the business line to address the COVID-19 challenge. Additionally, 2 percent were struggling to work remotely. Working remotely as much as possible is one of the best ways to stay safe and minimize the exposure to get infected. Nevertheless, not all MSMEs, especially MSEs in the rural or backward regions have the required resources to adopt such a strategy.

5.4 Empirical Evidence

The 1997/1998 Asian Financial Crisis

Macroeconomic Impacts

In August 1997 Indonesia's currency, rupiah, began to slide in what at first appeared to be only the spillover from the financial crisis in Thailand. In the following months, Bank Indonesia (BI), the central bank of Indonesia, had tried several times with little success to stop the depreciation of rupiah against the US dollar through open market operations. By May 1998 Indonesia was suffering from the combined effects of a currency, financial, economic, and political crisis. Rupiah collapsed in waves, from its level in mid 1997 at around Rp 2200 per one US dollar to Rp 5000 by October 1997, to Rp 6000 by December 1997, to a free fall in January 1998 which took the currency as low as Rp 17,000 per US dollar (Bello, 1999; Tambunan, 2010a, 2010b, 2011a).

Economies of Indonesia and South Korea were among the most severely affected by this crisis. The Indonesian economy had plunged into a deep recession in 1998 with overall growth at minus around 13 percent (Fig. 5.1). Aggregating all economic sectors into three key sectors shows that industry was the most severely affected which led output of the

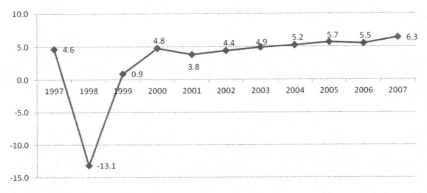

Fig. 5.1 Indonesian GDP growth rates during the Asian Financial Crisis and the Recovery Periods, 1997–2007 (%) (*Sources* BPS [*Berita Resmi Statistik: Pertumbuhan Ekonomi Indonesia; Laporan Bulanan Data Sosial-Ekonomi; Statistik Indonesia*], various issues)

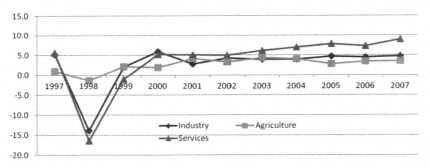

Fig. 5.2 Output growth rates of the three key sectors in Indonesia during the Asian Financial Crisis and the Recovery Periods, 1997–2007 (%) (*Sources* BPS [*Berita Resmi Statistik: Pertumbuhan Ekonomi Indonesia; Laporan Bulanan Data Sosial-Ekonomi; Statistik Indonesia*], various issues)

sector dropped at around 14 percent in 1998, followed by services at 16.5 percent, and agriculture experienced a decline of 1.3 percent (Fig. 5.2).

The crisis also led to a significant drop in income per capita to drop reaching the lowest level at around US$ 600 in 1999 from the highest level ever reached since the beginning of the new order era at almost US$ 1200 in 1996 (Fig. 5.3). As many companies got affected directly

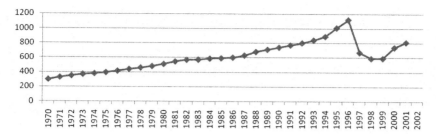

Fig. 5.3 Development of Indonesian Income per Capita, 1970–2002 (US dollar) (*Sources* BPS [*Statistik Indonesia*] various issues; ADB [*Key Indicators Asia and the Pacific*], various issues)

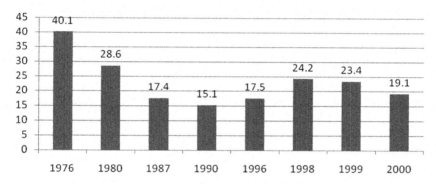

Fig. 5.4 Poverty rate in Indonesia, 1976–2000 (%) (*Source* BPS [*Statistik Indonesia*], various issues)

or indirectly by the crisis, especially in the industrial sectors, stopped their operations or reduced their production volumes which led to the increase in unemployment, poverty rate also increased during the crisis period (Fig. 5.4).

Domestic prices (including prices of food and other basic needs) also rocketed significantly, which resulted in inflation rate at 78 percent in 1998, caused by money supply expansion and rupiah depreciation. In response to this development, students in many universities in various cities, including Jakarta, started to demonstrate in early 1998, followed soon by riots in the capital Jakarta and several other cities in May 1998, leading to the resignation of Soeharto who had been in power since 1966.

In fact, before the crisis in Indonesia became worst, in October 1997, the International Monetary Fund (IMF) announced that, in conjunction with the World Bank and the Asian Development Bank, it had put together a US$ 37 billion rescue deal for Indonesia. In return, the Indonesian government agreed to close several troubled banks, to reduce public spending, balance the budget, and unravel the crony capitalism that was so widespread in Indonesia. The initial response to the IMF deal was favorable, with the rupiah strengthening to around Rp 3200 per US$. However, the recovery was short-lived. In November 1997, the rupiah resumed its decline in response to growing skepticism about President Suharto's willingness to take the tough steps required by the IMF. Moreover, currency traders wondered how the Indonesian government was going to be able to deal with its dollar denominated private sector debt, which stood at US$ 80 billion (Hill, 1999).

However, with the improvement of macroeconomic management where Indonesia had implemented a program of wide-ranging policy reforms since the crisis, in combination with a prudent monetary and fiscal policy, a sound banking system, a large stock of international reserves, and a more flexible exchange rate, Indonesian economy started to recover in 1999. Since that year up to 2007, the pattern of Indonesian economic growth shows a positive trend.

Impacts on MSMEs

The impact of the crisis or, more specifically, the depreciation of IDR against USD by more than 200 percent per August 1998 on local MSMEs can be examined empirically from two different approaches, namely international trade, and finance (Fig. 5.5) and the demand side and supply side of the economy (Fig. 5.6). With respect to the first approach, the key channels were export, import, and foreign loans. At least theoretically, *ceteris paribus*, the depreciation of IDR against USD will have a positive effect on Indonesian exports, i.e., it will increase the price competitiveness of Indonesian made goods and services in the international market, and export of MSMEs will also increase. While the fall in the IDR exchange rate will reduce Indonesia's imports because import prices become expensive and increase the cost of foreign borrowing.

With respect to the second approach (Fig. 5.6), the supply-side (SS) effects occurred through the inputs market (i.e., factors of production, including labor and finance, and other inputs), and the demand-side (DS)

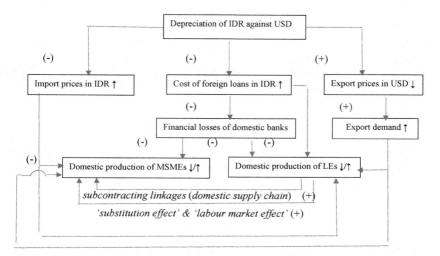

Fig. 5.5 Examining empirically the effects of the 1997/1998 crisis on MSMEs in Indonesia with the first approach

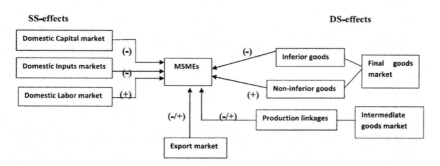

Fig. 5.6 Examining empirically the effects of the 1997/1998 crisis on MSMEs in Indonesia with the second approach

effects happened through the output market (i.e., finished and semi-finished goods and components). The SS effects of the depreciation of IDR have had both positive and negative effects. The negative effects came from two sources. First, the financial market: the significant increase in interest rate due to tight national liquidity as a direct monetary policy response to the depreciation combined with the collapse of domestic banks due to their financial losses in their transactions with foreign banks and increased non-performing loans of many domestic private companies. As a result, many local MSMEs (as also LEs) faced financial difficulties because bank credit was no longer available or too expensive. Second, the inputs market: all import prices in IDR of processed raw materials, components, and other inputs increased significantly, and this hit severely local MSMEs that relied heavily on import for their inputs (Tambunan, 2019).

The positive SS effect happened through the labor market. Many domestic companies have gone bankrupt due to the weakening of the IDR, and so many people became unemployed. In a country like Indonesia where there are no unemployment benefits, those without formal jobs were forced to seek jobs in the informal sector dominated by micro and small business activities or to run their own micro or small businesses.

Related to the DS effects, there are four main sources of demand for MSMEs' products: (a) individuals/households, (b) business communities (companies), (c) national governments (e.g., departments), and (d) exports. The first source is domestic final demand, whereas the second and third comprise domestic demand for semi-finished or intermediate goods or components. The last source represents both final and intermediate demand from abroad.

With respect to the first source of demand, whether the DS effect will be negative or positive, theoretically, it depends on the relationship between the type of goods/services purchased from MSMEs and the level of consumer income. If the purchased goods/services are inferior (or noninferior), which have a negative (positive) income elasticity of demand, then when consumer income declines, the DS effect will be positive (negative) for MSMEs. Conversely, if consumer income increases, the DS effect will be negative (positive). To examine this effect empirically is however a difficult task because there is no data on consumed goods or services produced by MSMEs (Table 5.1).

Discussing the second and third sources of demand, the stability of demand for MSMEs' products during the crisis will depend strongly on the performance or ability to survive the crisis of LEs that used to purchase goods or services from MSMEs (e.g., via subcontracting arrangements) prior to the crisis. Theoretically, the DS effect on MSMEs is negative when LEs reduce their purchases due to the crisis. But the

Table 5.1 The hypotheses of the DS effects on MSMEs of the income declines in the final

Income group	Type of products usually purchased	The nature of MSMEs' products from their perspective	The income Elasticity of demand for MSMEs' products	Changes in demand for MSMEs' products
High	Luxury/very expensive	Very inferior	Very negative	Large increase
Middle	Less expensive	Less inferior	Less negative/ more positive	Moderate increase/decrease
Low	Cheap	Noninferior	Very positive	Large decrease

deprecation of IDR can have a substitution effect that generates market demand opportunities for MSMEs: many LEs that used to buy inputs from abroad before the depreciation had to buy cheaper inputs produced by MSMEs in the local market during the crisis period. Local consumers must also change their consumption behavior from buying imported goods when the IDR was still cheap to domestic goods produced by local MSMEs at much cheaper prices.

Finally, with respect to export, the DS effect can also be positive or negative (or even no effect at all). Theoretically, the depreciation of the IDR will increase the world price competitiveness of Indonesian exporting companies, *ceteris paribus*, other price determinants are constant. But Indonesia relied heavily on the import of many goods, including processed raw materials, machinery, equipment, production tools, and other industrial goods. So, if exporting MSMEs use many imported inputs to produce their export goods, the depreciation of the IDR can even suppress their exports.

Thus, the net effect of the IDR depreciation on local MSMEs during the Asian financial crisis could be positive or negative, depending on whether the total positive "substitution effect (SE)", "export effect (EE)", and "labor market effect (LME)" were stronger or weaker than the total negative "import effect (IE)" and "financial market effect (FME)". As can be seen in Fig. 5.7, secondary data provided by the Menegkop and UKM showed obviously that the number of MSMEs declined from nearly 39.8 million units in 1997 to 36.8 million in 1998. So, this may

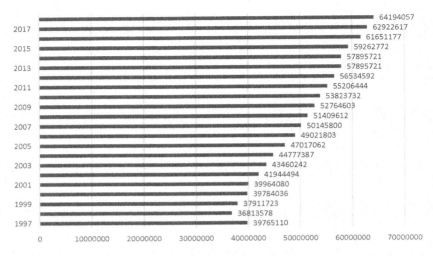

Fig. 5.7 Total number of MSMEs in Indonesia (units) (*Source* Menegkop and UKM [www.depkop.go.id])

suggest that the total positive SE, EE, and LME were weaker than the IE and FME.

In 1999, the number of MSMEs began to increase again and continued even during the 2008/2009 crisis. This may have suggested that the first crisis was more severe than the second crisis for MSMEs. To support this view, Fig. 5.8 illustrates the percentage changes in real GDP and the number of MSMEs in Indonesia during the two crises. As seen, the change pattern of the two variables was the same, and in 1998, both percentages of changes were both negative, whereas in the second crisis, both variables continued to grow positively.

Few studies were conducted based on field surveys and direct observations of MSMEs in various industries during this crisis period (Table 5.2), whereas empirical studies after 1999 were mostly based on secondary data analysis. In general, the findings of these studies support the general notion that the 1997/1998 crisis had a negative impact on MSMEs. Jellinek and Rustanto (1999) provided interesting facts. They found that the crisis has also created greater domestic market opportunities for many MSMEs in several industries as many individuals or households affected by the crisis changed their consumption behavior from purchasing imported

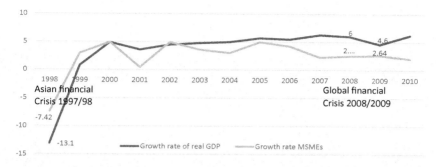

Fig. 5.8 Percentage changes of real GDP and total number of MSMEs in Indonesia (*Source* Indonesian State Ministry of Cooperative and SME [www.depkop.go.id])

Table 5.2 Studies on the impact of the 1997/1998 crisis on MSMEs in Indonesia

Author	Methodology	Industry/sector	Main transmission channels
Tambunan (1998), Dierman et al. (1998), Jellinek and Rustanto (1999), Musa (1998), Wiradi (1998), AKATIGA and the Asia Foundation (1999), Sandee et al. (2000), Berry et al. (2001), Hill (1999, 2001), Sato (2000), Wie (2000), and Wengel and Rodriguez (2006)	• Field surveys • Direct observations • Secondary data analyses	E.g., footwear, furniture, batik (Indonesian traditional cloth), bricks, tofu, cigarette (*kretek*), metal industry, and agriculture	• Expensive imported raw materials • No credit available • Low domestic demand

goods prior to the IDR depreciation to domestic goods at much cheaper prices. This change in people's consumption behavior has an impact on increasing demand for local MSMEs.

118   T. T.H. TAMBUNAN

Global Financial Crisis 2008/2009

Impacts on Some Sectors

The 2008/2009 crisis was generally regarded as an international trade or export crisis, as the export market was the main important DS channel through which the crisis had caused exports of many developing countries in Southeast Asia to decline significantly (e.g., ADB, 2009; Griffith-Jones & Ocampo, 2009; Hartono, 2011; Hurst et al., 2010; Khor & Sebastian, 2009; Nguanbanchong, 2009; SMERU, 2009). Griffith-Jones and Ocampo (2009) assessed the impact of the 2008/2009 crisis in some developing countries, including Southeast Asia, and with their findings, they argue that the main transmission channel of the crisis to exporters of these countries was through the decline in world demand.

In summary, from the available literature with the evidence of the impact of the 2008/2009 crisis on MSMEs, Table 5.3 shows exports most affected by the crisis in some other developing countries in Southeast Asia. Some of these goods, for example, textile, clothing, leather, and food and beverages, are important products of MSMEs in these countries,

Table 5.3 Most affected exports by the 2008/2009 crisis in some other Southeast Asian Countries

Country	Commodities
Malaysia	Industrial equipment, processed and preserved meat, fish, fruit, vegetables, oils and fats, basic chemicals, rubber and plastics products, metal manufacturers and general industrial nonelectrical machinery, telecom, sound recording and reproducing apparatus, office accounting and computing machinery
Philippines	Electrical machinery and apparatus, office accounting and computing machinery, road vehicles and components, clothing, leather products and footwear, processed and preserved meat, fish, fruit, vegetables, oils/fats, and beverages
Singapore	Basic chemicals, rubber and plastic products, food products, tobacco products, electrical machinery and apparatus, office accounting and computing machinery, metal manufacturers, general industrial nonelectrical
Vietnam	Machinery and equipment, food and beverages, leather, leather products and footwear, textiles, rubber and plastics products, wood products (excl. furniture)

Sources ADB (2009), Khor and Sebastian (2009), Griffith-Jones and Ocampo (2009), Nguanbanchong (2009), SMERU (2009), Hurst et al. (2010), database from the ASEAN Secretariat, and national data on trade from some individual countries either as subcontractors or as final producers for domestic and export markets.

The most affected exports in Indonesia were wood-and rattan-based furniture, textile and clothing, and leather products including footwear. These industries have traditionally been among the major industries of MSMEs (Tambunan, 2019). However, compared to the 1997/1998 crisis, Indonesia was much better in dealing with 2008/2009.

Impacts on MSMEs

ADB (2009) and Hurst et al. (2010) stated that the 2008/2009 crisis would affect not only "direct" export oriented MSMEs but also "indirect" ones that produced or supplied inputs or components to the first ones or exporting LEs through domestic subcontracting or to multinational companies in foreign countries through regional or global supply chain processes. Nguanbanchong (2009) shows that in some countries in the region, export-oriented MSMEs in labor-intensive manufacturing (e.g., textile, garment, footwear, seafood processing, and electronic) and MSMEs producing items for tourism were most affected. Many workers in these companies, especially women, were affected by a number of ways such as dismissal of permanent as well as contract workers, reduction of days or hours of work, and freezes at minimum wage.

Figure 5.9 illustrates how the 2008/2009 crisis could affect MSMEs in Indonesia. There were two main transmission channels: (a) decreasing

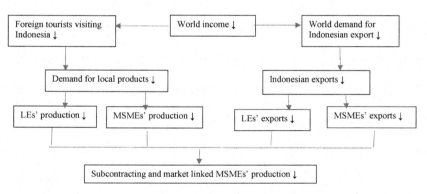

Fig. 5.9 Theoretical framework of the effects of the 2008/2009 crisis on MSMEs in Indonesia

world demand for Indonesian MSME products, and (b) decreasing number of foreign tourists visiting Indonesia which resulted in a decline in local market demand for MSME products.

Figures 5.7 and 5.8 shown before may give the impression that MSMEs were not severely affected by the 2008/2009 crisis as the total number of MSMEs in that period increased, instead of declining as happened in 1998. This is not saying, however, that not even one firm had been negatively affected. There must be many MSMEs experienced decline in their sales during this global financial crisis. For example, SMERU Research Institute provided evidence that many MSMEs in the textile and garment industry in Bandung and Cimahi in the West Java province were affected. It was found that 150 MSMEs were threatened with bankruptcy due to rising prices of imported raw materials, which caused production costs to rise by about 20 percent, whereas on the demand side, they faced less orders especially from foreign buyers (SMERU, 2009). However, it is possible that the affected MSMEs could continue operating, or if there were several MSMEs that stopped producing, but the number of new MSMEs that started operating in 2008/2009 was more than the number that closed.

Tourism-related handicraft industries were also affected by the crisis. According to this SMERU's (2009) report, in the second half of 2008, there were several handicraft industries in Bali that began to ask their workers to stay at home. The most important handicraft in this province is silversmith. In Celuk village, for example, it was found that 30 of them have been temporarily suspended. In Tegallalang village in Ubud, Bali, many of the craftsmen who made wooden masks had to stop their production. Many *songket* (a traditional fabric of West Sumatra) weavers in Palembang and Ogan Ilir in Sumatra ceased production because some of their overseas buyers, especially from Singapore and the United States, no longer buy their products since October 2008. In the eastern province of Java, production in the brass handicraft industry fell by 50 percent due to lower demand from many countries (including the United States) and it was estimated that number of workers who lost their jobs increased by 50 percent.

Wood-and rattan-based furniture, one of Indonesia's major export goods, was also heavily affected by the crisis. This industry has traditionally been among the major industries of MSMEs. As foreign demand for Indonesian furniture decreased due to the crisis, the industry had to lay off nearly 35,000 workers in early 2009. In the first and second quarters of 2009, compared with the first and second quarters of 2008, the value of Indonesian furniture exports fell by, respectively, 35 percent and 30 percent. Timber exports also fell by 28 percent in the first quarter of 2009 compared with the same quarter of 2008, and 23.2 percent drop in export volume of wooden furniture, doors, and windowsills (Tambunan, 2019).

There are three possible reasons why the total number of MSMEs in Indonesia continued to increase during the crisis. First, many (if not all) export-oriented MSMEs were still able to operate because they shifted their marketing from the export market to the domestic market. Second, MSMEs in the tourism industry also survived even with low turnover. Third, workers laid off from large-scale exporting companies affected by the crisis started their own businesses as their means to survive because Indonesia has no unemployment benefits, as explained earlier.

COVID-19 Pandemic Crisis 2020–2021

Macroeconomic Impacts

As shown before, since the end of the Asian financial crisis 1997–1998, which caused Indonesia's economy to drop by 13 percent, Indonesia's economic growth has continued to be positive until 2020 when the COVID-19 pandemic broke out (Fig. 5.10). BPS data shows that as a direct consequence of the "anti-COVID-19 impact" policy which resulted in a drastic reduction in domestic economic activities, the country's economy in 2020 experienced a growth contraction of 2.07 percent. As in other affected countries, the anti-COVID-19 impact policy has brought business activities to a standstill in many sectors or drastically reduced their activities. Business fields that experienced the deepest growth contraction were transportation and warehousing with 15.04 percent, and provision of accommodation and food and drink amounted to 10.22 percent. The anti-COVID-19 impact policy resulted in a drastic reduction in the mobilization of people including tourists so that the use of transportation such as trains, airplanes, and buses between cities, hotel reservations, and visits to restaurants were drastically reduced. Other sectors with negative growth were company services by 5.44 percent; other services by 4.10 percent; and large trade and retail; car and motorcycle repair by 3.72 percent. According to the Ministry of Manpower, approximately 96 percent of companies in all affected sectors in Indonesia

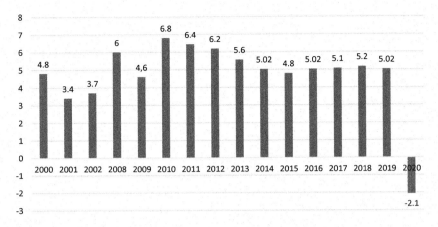

Fig. 5.10 Annual growth of Indonesian real GDP, 2000–2021 (%) (*Source* BPS [https://www.bps.go.id/])

were affected directly or indirectly by this policy (Bayu, 2021). However, there are some sectors still experiencing positive growth, including health services and social activities 11.60 percent; information and communication 10.58 percent; procurement water, waste management, waste, and recycling by 4.94 percent; real estate of 2.32 percent; and agriculture, forestry, and fisheries 1.75 percent.

The sector hardest hit by the pandemic is the tourism sector. Judging based on those who entered through all international airports in the country, the number of foreign tourists visited Indonesia in January 2021 dropped significantly by 99.79 percent compared to the number of those visited in January 2020. All international airports in Indonesia experienced a decline, even at most airports the decline reached 100 percent. Meanwhile, the main international airport in Indonesia, Soekarno-Hatta, experienced a decrease at 99.34 percent. Figure 5.11 shows number of foreign tourists visited Indonesia per month for the period January 2020–January 2021.

The large number of companies that closed or reduced their activities during the COVID-19 pandemic automatically resulted in an increase in the number of unemployed. According to official data from the government, the open unemployment rate in August 2020 was 7.07 percent of total labour force, which means from 100 people in the workforce, there

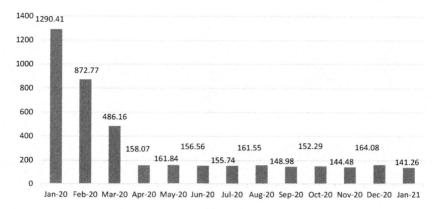

Fig. 5.11 Number of visiting foreign tourists in Indonesia during the Period January 2020–January 2021 (thousand visitors) (*Source* BPS [https://www.bps.go.id/])

were about seven unemployed. In August 2020, the open unemployment rate experienced a sizable increase of 1.84 percentage points compared to August 2019 (Fig. 5.12). By gender, the figure shows that in August 2020, the total unemployed male was 7.46 percent of total male labor force, higher than the employment rate for women which amounted to 6.46 percent. Compared to August 2019, men's unemployment rate rose 2.22 percentage points, while that of women increased 1.24 percentage points.

Next, Fig. 5.13 shows the development in the number of underemployments during the same period. Workers included in this underemployment category are those who work hours below normal working hours (i.e., less than 35 hours per week), and are still looking for or accepting other jobs. As seen from the figure, the underemployment rate in August 2020 was 10.19 percent. This means, of 100 people working there were 10 people half unemployed. The underemployment rate for August 2020 has increased quite significantly, namely 3.77 percentage points compared to August 2019. In August 2020, the male underemployment rate was 10.77 percent, while the underemployment rate for women was 9.30 percent. The unemployment rates for men and women have increased, respectively, by 4.25 and 3.05 percentage points during the period past year.

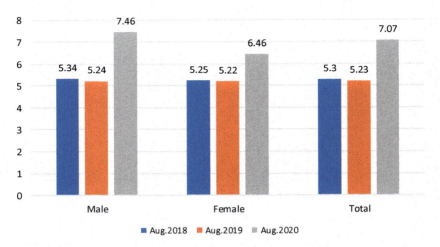

Fig. 5.12 Trend of open unemployment rate by gender in Indonesia between August 2018 and August 2020 (percent) (*Source* BPS [https://www.bps.go.id/])

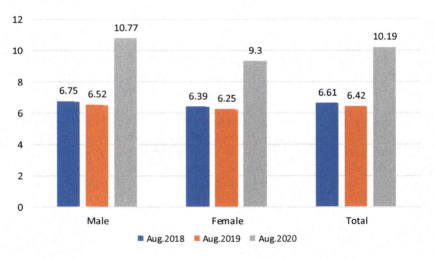

Fig. 5.13 Trend of underemployment rate by gender in Indonesia, August 2018–August 2020 (percent) (*Source* BPS [https://www.bps.go.id/])

According to official data, the working-age population affected by COVID-19 is grouped into four components, namely (a) unemployed; (b) not included in the labor force that has stopped working in the period February–August 2020; (c) residents who worked before COVID-19 with temporary status: currently not working; and (d) working residents who experienced a reduction in working hours. Conditions (c) and (d) are the impact of the COVID-19 pandemic felt by those who are currently still working, while conditions (a) and (b) are the impact of the COVID-19 pandemic on those who have stopped working.

In Table 5.4 the number of people with working-age affected by COVID-19 is recorded as much as 29.12 million people, consisting of 2.56 million people unemployed (A), 0.76 million people not in the labor force (B), 1.77 million people do not work temporarily (C), and 24.03 million people in the category of working population who experienced a reduction in working hours (D). Judging from gender, the male working-age population affected by COVID-19 reached 17.75 million people, which is bigger than female working-age population, i.e., 11.37 million people. Meanwhile, when viewed from the area of residence, the population of working-age in urban areas affected by COVID-19 is as many as 20.56 million people, while in rural areas is as many as 8.56 million people.

The anti-COVID-19 impact policy has also affected the mobility of commuter workers. Commuter workers are residents who work outside the district/city where they live and routinely go and return to their place

Table 5.4 Impact of COVID-19 on the working-age population by sex and region of place live, August 2020 (million people)

Description	Sex		Location		Total
	Male	Female	Urban	Rural	
a) A due to COVID-19	1.66	0.90	1.94	0.62	2.56
b) B due to COVID-19	0.24	0.52	0.53	0.23	0.76
c) C due to COVID-19	1.09	0.68	1.27	0.50	1.77
d) D due to COVID-19	14.76	9.27	16.82	7.21	24.03
Total	17.75	11.37	20.56	8.56	29.12
Working population (E)	101.96	102.02	115.82	88.15	203.97
Percentage of E	17.41	11.15	17.75	9.71	14.28

Source BPS (https://www.bps.go.id/)

of residence on the same day. In August 2020, the number of commuter workers in Indonesia was 7.01 million people or down 21.07 percent when compared to the conditions in August 2019 (8.89 million people). The phenomenon of commuting workers is usually found in big cities. Current commuter workers' entry to big cities has generally decreased. The biggest percentage drop occurred in the city of Bandung amounting to 32.91 percent. DKI Jakarta Province, as the capital, too experienced a significant decrease in commuter workers in five city areas, around 19–32 percent (Table 5.5).

In Indonesia, high and sustained economic growth during the New Order era (1966–1998) made a major contribution to poverty reduction (as measured by the number of people living below the poverty line as a percentage of the population). The percentage of poverty continued to decline during the period 1970–1997. In 1998 the poverty rate went up again when the country was hit by the Asian financial crisis, and in 1999 started to decline again as the Indonesian economy began to recover. In 2020, however, the percentage of poor people increased slightly caused by the COVID-19 pandemic (Fig. 5.14).

Based on the area of residence, in the period of March 2020–September 2020, the number of urban poor people increased by 876.5 thousand people, while in rural areas it increased by 249.1 thousand

Table 5.5 Percentage of change in commuter workers entering big cities August 2019–August 2020

City	% Decline
Bandung city	−32.91
North Jakarta	−31.76
South Jakarta	−31.46
Central Jakarta	−28.05
Denpasar	−27.57
Menado	−27.46
Surabaya	−24.58
Medan	−20.27
East Jakarta	−20.22
West Jakarta	−19.26
Semarang city	−11.72
Makassar	−10.56
Palembang	−7.06
Banjarmasin	−1.41

Source BPS (https://www.bps.go.id/)

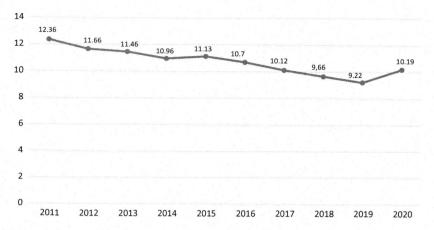

Fig. 5.14 Poverty rate in Indonesia, 2011–2020 (%)* (*Note* *September. *Source* BPS [http://www.bps.go.id])

Table 5.6 Number and percentage of poor population by region September 2019–September 2020

Region/year	Total poor population (million people)	Percentage of poor population
Urban		
September 2019	9.86	6.56
September 2020	12.04	7.88
Rural		
September 2019	14.93	12.60
September 2020	15.51	13.20
National		
September 2019	24.79	9.22
September 2020	27.55	10.19

Source BPS (http://www.bps.go.id)

people. The percentage of poverty in urban areas increased from 7.38 percent to 7.88 percent. Meanwhile, in rural areas, it increased from 12.82 percent to 13.20 percent (Table 5.6). This difference can be easily understood given the fact that agriculture, which dominates the rural economy, has been much less affected by the COVID-19 pandemic compared to the secondary and tertiary sectors, especially the processing

Table 5.7 Percentage and number of poor population by Island in Indonesia, September 2020

	Percentage of poor people			Number of poor people (000 men)		
	Urban	Rural	Total	Urban	Rural	Total
Sumatera	8.80	11.34	10.22	2.306.81	3.759.37	6.066.18
Java	8.03	13.03	9.71	8.105.76	6.646.27	14.752.03
Bali and Nusa Tenggara	8.99	18.18	13.92	633.96	1.482.53	2.116.49
Kalimantan	4.72	7.51	6.16	375.55	640.56	1.016.11
Sulawesi	5.95	13.45	10.41	477.07	1.584.44	2.061.51
Maluku and Papua	5.49	28.51	20.65	139.34	1.398.02	1.537.36
Indonesia	7.88	13.20	10.19	12.038.50	15.511.19	27.549.69

Source BPS (http://www.bps.go.id)

industry, tourism (especially entertainment, accommodation, and recreation areas), and trade (especially offline trade activities).

As shown in Table 5.7, the largest percentage of poor people are in the Island region Maluku and Papua, amounting to 20.65 percent. Meanwhile, the lowest was on the island of Kalimantan amounting to 6.16 percent. In terms of numbers, mostly the poor are still on the island of Java (14.75 million people), while the total population, the lowest poor were on the island of Kalimantan (1.02 million people).

Since the end of the 1998–1999 Asian financial crisis, several provinces have experienced a decline in poverty, while in other provinces it remained high or even gotten worse. This difference in changes in poverty rates between provinces or islands is caused by the differences between provinces/islands in many respects, such as the rate of economic growth (low or high) and its nature (whether it is labor-intensive meaning that economic growth creates many new job opportunities or capital intensive meaning the rate of employment growth lower than the rate of economic growth), the structure of the economy (whether the economy is still agrarian or dominated by non-primary sectors, especially the manufacturing industry which is the largest sector in contributing added value to the economy), the condition of infrastructure (quantitative or qualitative), and the size of the impact of the crisis on the province concerned (which is largely determined by, among other things, the economic openness of the province to the wider regional or international economy, and the province's readiness to an economic shock). Apart from these factors,

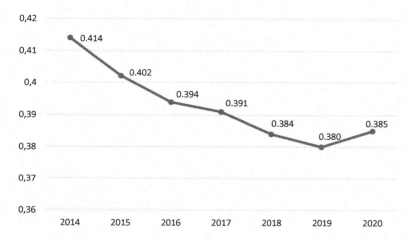

Fig. 5.15 Development of the Gini Ratio, September 2014–September 2020 (*Source* BPS [http://www.bps.go.id])

the implementation at the provincial level of anti-poverty programs, especially during times of crisis, from the central and local governments also greatly determines the success of a province in reducing poverty.

With respect to inequality in income distribution, because of the COVID-19 pandemic, the Gini Ratio value experienced an increase in March 2020 and September 2020 (Fig. 5.15). Based on the area of residence, the urban Gini Ratio in September 2020 is 0.399. This shows an increase of 0.006 points compared to March 2020 which amounted to 0.393 and increased 0.008 points compared to September 2019 which amounted to 0.391. For rural areas, the Gini Ratio is in September 2020 was recorded at 0.319, an increase of 0.002 points compared to the conditions in March 2020 and an increase of 0.004 points. Compared to conditions in September 2019. Rural Gini Ratio in March 2020 and September 2019 was recorded as 0.317 and 0.315, respectively.

Impacts on MSMEs
So far in the past few months the COVID-19 pandemic has severely affected many MSMEs as well as LEs in Indonesia through four main channels (Fig. 5.16). The first channel was the result of the "anti-COVID-19 impact" policy which consisted of three main elements: (i)

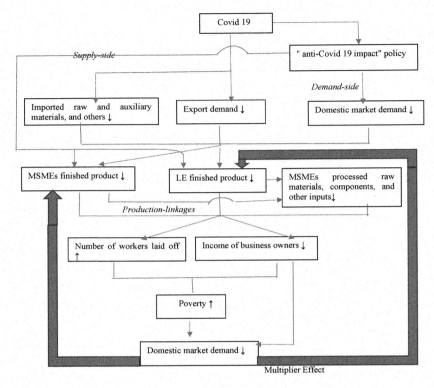

Fig. 5.16 Impact of COVID-19 pandemic on MSMEs in Indonesia

social/physical distancing, (ii) learn and work from home, and (iii) the temporary suspension of business activities in non-strategic sectors. The second element obviously has caused the number of buyers in the local market to decrease dramatically (↓). Thus, this policy element has affected MSME activities on the demand side ("demand effect"). Whereas the third element of the policy has affected MSMEs on the supply side ("supply effect"). These demand side and supply-side effects did not happen only in MSMEs manufacturing finished products but also in those that supply processed raw materials, components, spare parts, auxiliary goods, semi-finished goods, and other inputs. The second channel was the decrease in world demand, especially from China, for Indonesian products which caused Indonesia's exports to decrease (ADB, 2020). The third channel was the decline in imports of processed raw materials and auxiliary materials, especially from China, which forced many companies, including MSMEs, in Indonesia which were highly dependent on imports from China to reduce/stop their productions (Kompas, 2020a, 2020b). The fourth channel was the increase in the number of poor people as many employees have been laid off, or their wages were cut, which further led local market demand to decline that hit the MSME business.

As shown before, the sector hardest hit by the pandemic was the tourism sector. As illustrated in Fig. 5.17, the negative impact of COVID-19 on the tourism sector in turn has a negative impact on MSMEs, both directly and indirectly through several transmission channels. The direct impact was through the reduction of MSME activities in the tourism sector, such as restaurants, cafes, travel agencies, local transportation, rentals, cheap accommodation/hotels, and various kinds of entertainment. Meanwhile, the indirect impact was a decrease in orders received by small-sized suppliers (e.g., catering, provision of food and beverages, cleaning services, repair services, rental of musical instruments, rental of sports equipment, and laundry) from companies directly related to tourism as mentioned previously. In addition, the decrease in the number of tourists in Indonesia during 2020 both from abroad and domestic

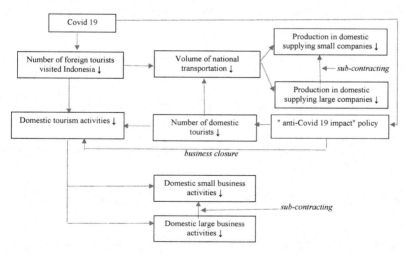

Fig. 5.17 The impact of COVID-19 on MSMEs through its effects on tourism

(due to the "anti-COVID-19 impact" regulations) has an impact on the volume of transportation activities both at home and on national airlines serving international routes such as Garuda and Lion Air. In turn, this decline also resulted in the reduction of orders for suppliers in the country, many of which were from the MSME category.

Since March 2020 stories or news about the impact of COVID-19 pandemic on MSMEs in many parts of the country from various sources began to emerge. MSMEs in the tourism sector were the hardest hit, followed by MSMEs in business lines which were heavily affected by the "anti-COVID-19 impact" policies such as small shops, restaurants, cafes, and transportation. Table 5.8 summarizes these stories and news for the period of March and April 2020.

To have more recent evidence about the impact of the crisis on MSMEs, the author of this book has conducted a survey on 137 MSMEs during May–September 2020 with respondents randomly selected from various cities and sectors in Indonesia and most of them were from the food and beverage business including restaurants, food processing, and catering. The others were from such as small shops, clothing, café and coffee shop, photocopy services, haircut and washing services, mini-markets, transportation services, craft industries, music studio, creative content production workshops, groceries, printing, and laundry. With terms of marketing, most of them marketed their products in a conventional way (offline).

Initially, there were 143 owners of MSMEs selected for the survey. However, six of them were found at that time to no longer operate. They admitted that they were bankrupt because their sales had decreased too much, which made it impossible for them to maintain their business. So, these six MSMEs were excluded from the sample.

From the survey, it revealed that some of them only experienced a decrease in turnover, others only experienced an increase in production costs, but their turnover was not interrupted, and there were also some who experienced both. In terms of rising costs, Fig. 5.18 shows the number of respondents according to the cost increase category. The categories with the highest number of respondents experiencing it were the cost increases, up to 10 and beyond 10 and up to 20 percent. However, the number of respondents who did not experience an increase in costs was much higher, 36 people. While in terms of declining sales, Fig. 5.19 shows the number of respondents according to the sales decline category. The category with the greatest number of respondents is the decline in

5 MSMES IN TIMES OF ECONOMIC CRISIS 133

Table 5.8 Evidence on the impact of COVID-19 on MSMEs, March–April 2020

Source	Impact
Rahman (2020), Santoso (2020), Tambunan (2020)	Since mid-March 2020, 163,713 MSMEs have been seriously affected. As many as 56% due to a decrease in sales, 22% difficulty in capital, 15% difficulty in the distribution of products, and 4% difficulty finding raw materials
Hermansah (2020)	Based on a survey of MSMEs, 96% claimed to have been negatively impacted. As many as 75% experienced a significant decrease in sales; 51% believed that their business would only last one month to the next three months
Anwar (2020)	Of the 14,238 MSMEs in Serang City, 10,238 were affected. Only 4000 MSMEs have survived this epidemic
Kompas (2020a)	The decrease in demand for MSME products was expected to decrease by around 60–80%. This decrease was caused by a decrease in the number of buyers visiting shops
Sundari (2020)	Many MSMEs in the Cimahi City have experienced a decline in sales of up to 80%. Even many MSMEs were forced to lay off their employees. Especially those that their businesses rely heavily on daily production activities were severely affected. Also export-oriented MSMEs were also affected
Nurzaman (2020)	Ms. Tarli Sutarli is the manager of the Bueuk stamp coffee plant located in Golempang Hamlet, Ciliang Village, Parigi District, Pangandaran Regency. According to her, at normal times her turnover can reach 7–12 million IDR per month. Recently, hit by the corona pandemic crisis, she almost closed her business because her turnover has dropped dramatically from day-to-day
Burhan (2020)	MSME revenues in the culinary, fashion retail, and beauty services sectors fell during the corona pandemic. The culinary sector experienced a decline in daily income of up to 37%, the fashion retail by 35%, and beauty services by 43% percent. Also food orders at restaurants decreased very significantly by up to 60%. The negative impact of the pandemic was felt most significantly by MSMEs that still ran their businesses offline

(continued)

Table 5.8 (continued)

Source	Impact
Kompas (2020b, 2020c)	By April 2020, there were 212,394 laid-off workers and 1,205,191 workers who were sent home but still paid (not full) from 74,430 companies. From the informal sector, the number of workers affected and losing their jobs reached 282,000 people from 34,453 enterprises, mostly from the micro and small enterprise category

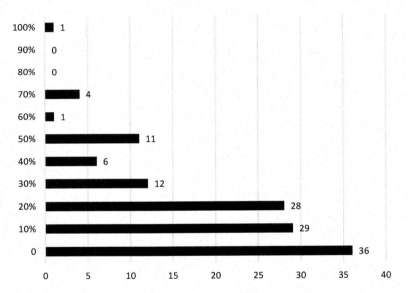

Fig. 5.18 Number of respondents by category of cost increases (*Source* Field survey 2020)

sales above 40 and up to 50 percent, only four respondents admitted that their turnover had not decreased.

Types of Business Risks and Crisis Mitigating Measures (CMMs)
It is said that when a company is facing an unexpected fall in market demand for its products, especially if the decline is not expected to be a

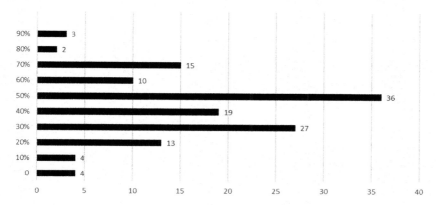

Fig. 5.19 Number of respondents by category of sales decline (*Source* Field survey 2020)

short-term phenomenon, it will take some adjustment measures to reduce the pressure on its profit. Or, if the price of a raw material has increased significantly due to interference in its supply or distribution, or because of a depreciation of national currency, companies highly dependent on that raw material will take several adjustment steps to maintain production. CMMs can in various forms such as fewer production volumes, less working days or hours per day, laid-off workers, substitution of raw materials, and change the way of marketing. The choice of forms taken will depend largely on the type of crisis and hence the type of business risks, the apparent impact of the crisis, and, perhaps more importantly, the owner's own expectation about the prospect of the current condition his or her business is facing.

Experiences with the three crises discussed earlier have shown that different types of crises with different transmission channels pose different types of business risks, such as production risk, credit risk, or market risk. Therefore, different types of business risks require different alternative forms of CMMs. Table 5.9 describes the type of business risks faced by MSMEs and the forms of CMMs recommended.

With respect to the 1997/1998 Asian financial crisis, there was only one research done by Dierman et al. (1998) who tried to look at CMMs adopted by affected MSMEs in the furniture and batik industries in various locations in Central Java. In the second crisis, Tambunan (2019)

136   T. T.H. TAMBUNAN

Table 5.9 Different types of business risks and different appropriate forms of CMMs by type of crisis, 1997/1998, 2008/2009, and 2020

Type of crisis	Transmission channels	Type of business risk	Forms of CMMs recommended
1998/98 crisis (currency crisis)	• Import • Credit • Export • Domestic supply chain	(1) Production risk: • high production costs due to high prices of imported raw materials (2) Credit risk: • high loan interest rate (3) Market risk: • less or no demand from LEs (stop subcontracting linkages)	• Substitution of raw material • Efficiency in using raw materials • Reducing number of workers/labor costs • Reducing other non-labor and non-raw material costs • Looking for alternative sources of funding • Finding alternative sources for subcontracting arrangements at home and abroad
2008/09 crisis (world demand crisis)	• Foreign tourists • Export	Market risk: • less export demand • less domestic demand related to less foreign tourists visiting Indonesia	• Exploration of domestic market • Finding new markets (export market diversification) • Reducing production cost, e.g., lay off some workers or reducing working time Cutting back on production

(continued)

Table 5.9 (continued)

Type of crisis	Transmission channels	Type of business risk	Forms of CMMs recommended
2020 COVID-19 crisis (production and market demand crisis)	• Import • Export • Domestic demand	(1) Market risk: • less domestic demand (2) Production risk: • stop production (due to "anti-Covid-19 impact" policy)	• Change business line • Change the way of marketing • Reducing production cost, e.g., lay off some workers or reducing working time • Cutting back on production

conducted a field survey over the period July–August 2009 on MSMEs in three furniture production centers in Java. Whereas during the COVID-19 crisis, there are many stories in newspapers and the internet about how MSMEs handled the crisis. As seen in Table 5.10, obviously, during the 1998/1999 crisis, the adopted CMMs were mainly to cope with the increased production cost, whereas during the 2008/2009 and the COVID-19 crisis, the adopted CMMs were to cope with the declined market demand.

From the survey on 137 MSMEs conducted by the author during May–September 2020 it was revealed that quite a number of respondents chose more than one form of CMMs. Most of them experienced a decrease in turnover or an increase in costs large enough to force them to take a number of adjustment steps. Figure 5.20 shows the number of respondents according to the chosen form of CMMs. As can be seen, the most popular CMMs were reducing production volume and changing conventional or offline marketing systems to online marketing systems or e-commerce. With respect to the latter, this was indeed highly recommended by the government that all MSMEs should switch to an online marketing system so that their sales can remain smooth or at least not to fall too much in this COVID-19 period.

From the survey on 137 MSMEs conducted by the author during May–September 2020, it was revealed that quite a number of respondents chose more than one form of CMMs. Most of them experienced a

138 T. T.H. TAMBUNAN

Table 5.10 Evidence on CMMs adopted by affected MSMEs during the three crises

Type of crisis	Adopted CMMs	Source
1998/98 crisis (currency crisis)	Replaced imported raw materials with local raw materials	Dierman et al. (1998)
2008/09 crisis (world demand crisis)	• Finding new markets (export market diversification) in less or not affected countries • Exploration of domestic market • Halting new recruitment • Reducing non-labor cost or labor cost • Canceling/delaying facilities upgrading • Reducing working time • Cutting back on production • Lay off some workers	Tambunan (2019)
2020 COVID-19 crisis (production and market demand crisis)	• change business line to those which are not too affected by the crisis or have a chance of survival or even growth, • turn to the business of making masks and other personal protective equipment that were most sought during the Covid pandemic • change the way of marketing from offline to online or e-commerce by using existing trading platforms, • switch from waiting for buyers to visit the shop to the home delivery via telephone call, SMS, or WhatsApp	Afifiyah (2020), Ciremaitoday (2020), KB (2020), Kompas (2020b), Setyowati (2020), Tambunan (2020)

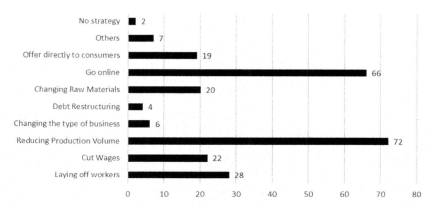

Fig. 5.20 Number of respondents by form of CMM (*Source* Field survey 2020)

decrease in turnover or an increase in costs large enough to force them to take a number of adjustment steps. Figure 5.20 shows the number of respondents according to the chosen form of CMMs. The most popular CMMs were reducing production volume and changing conventional or offline marketing systems to online marketing systems or e-commerce. With respect to the latter, this was indeed highly recommended by the government that all MSMEs should switch to an online marketing system so that their sales can remain smooth or at least not to fall too much in this COVID-19 period.

References

Abdullah, M. A. (2002). An overview of the macroeconomic contribution of small and medium enterprises in Malaysia. In C. Harvie & B.-C. Lee (Eds.), *The role of SMEs in national economies in East Asia*. Edward Elgar.

ADB. (2009). *Key indicators for Asia and the Pacific 2009*. Asian Development Bank.

ADB. (2020, March 6). *The economic impact of the COVID-19 outbreak on developing Asia* (ADB Briefs, No.128). Asian Development Bank.

Afifiyah, S. (2020, April 11). *Jenis Usaha yang Justru Melejit Saat Wabah Covid-19* [The type of business that actually skyrocketed during the Covid-19 outbreak]. Tagar.id. https://www.tagar.id/jenis-usaha-yang-justru-melejit-saat-wabah-covid19

AKATIGA and the Asia Foundation. (1999, August). *The impact of economic crisis on Indonesian small and medium enterprises*. Study prepared for the United States Agency for International Development, Jakarta.

Anwar, K. (2020, April). *10.238 UMKM di Kota Serang Terdampak Wabah COVID-19* [10,238 MSMEs in Serang city affected by the COVID-19 outbreak]. https://banten.idntimes.com/business/economy/khaerul-anwar-2/10238-umkm-di-kota-serang-terdampak-wabah-covid

Bakiewicz, A. (2004). Small and medium enterprises in Thailand: Following the leader. *Asia & Pacific Studies, 2*, 131–151.

Bayu, D. J. (2021). *Kemnaker Catat 96% Perusahaan Terkena Dampak Pandemi Corona* [Ministry of manpower records 96% of companies affected by the Corona pandemic]. Katadata.co.id. https://katadata.co.id/agungjatmiko/berita/5efc879e27b5b/kemnaker-catat-96-perusahaan-terkena-dampak-pandemi-corona

Bello, W. (1999). The Asian financial crisis: Causes, dynamics, prospects. *Journal of the Asia Pacific Economy, 4*(1), 33–55.

Berry, A., & Rodriguez, E. (2001). *Dynamics of small and medium enterprises in a slow-growth economy: The Philippines in the 1990s*. Research paper, June (Stock No. 37181), The International Bank for Reconstruction and Development/The World Bank, Washington, DC.

Berry, A., Rodriguez, E., & Sandee, H. (2001). Small and medium enterprise dynamics in Indonesia. *Bulletin of Indonesian Economic Studies, 37*(3), 363–384.

Burhan, F. A. (2020, April). *Bisnis Anjlok akibat Pandemi Corona, UMKM Bisa Ubah Strategi Usaha* [Business drops due to Corona pandemic, MSMEs can change business strategy]. Katadata.co.id. https://katadata.co.id/berita/2020/04/15/bisnis-anjlok-akibat-pandemi-corona-umkm-bisa-ubah-strategi-usaha

Chakraborty, P. (2012). *The great trade collapse and Indian firms* [Ph.D. dissertation, Graduate Institute of International and Development Studies, Geneva].

Chantrasawang, N. (1999, September). *Current issues of SMEs in Thailand: Its linkages with FDI and the impact of the financial crisis* (pp. 28–3). Paper presentation, the International Conference on Small and Medium Enterprises at New Crossroads: Challenges and Prospects, Universiti Sains Malaysia.

Chesbrough, H. (2020). To recover faster from Covid-19, open up: Managerial implications from an open innovation perspective. *Industrial Marketing Management, 88*, 410–413. https://doi.org/10.1016/j.indmarman.2020.04.010

Ciremaitoday. (2020, April 21). Kisah Perajin Batik Perempuan di Cirebon, Bangkit Ditengah Pandemi COVID-19 [The story of a female batik craftsman in Cirebon, Rising amid the COVID-19 pandemic]. *News*. https://kum

paran.com/ciremaitoday/kisah-perajin-batik-perempuan-di-cirebon-bangkit-ditengahpandemi-covid-19-1tGcuTSTNoV/full

Claessens, S., Tong, H., & Shang-Jin, W. (2011). *From the financial crisis to the real economy: Using firm-level data to identify transmission channels* (NBER Working Paper No.17360).

Dierman, van, P., Tambunan, T., Tambunan, M., & Wie, T. K. (1998, May). *The IMF 50-point program: Evaluating the likely impact on SMEs.* Draft report for the Asia Foundation.

Griffith-Jones, S., & Ocampo, J. A. (2009, April). *The financial crisis and its impacts on developing countries* (Working Paper No. 53). International Policy Center for Inclusive Growth.

Hartono, D. (2011). *Assessing policy effectiveness during the crisis: The case of Indonesia.* International Labour Organization (International Institute for Labour Studies).

Hermansah. (2020, April). *Simak strategi bertahan bagi UKM hadapi krisis akibat Covid-19 Pastikan bisnis Anda tetap berjalan dan mampu bertahan pada saat kondisi pandemi saat ini* [Check out the survival strategy for SMEs to face the crisis due to Covid-19 Make sure your business continues to run and is able to survive during the current pandemic conditions]. Alinea.id. https://www.alinea.id/bisnis/strategi-bertahan-bagi-ukm-hadapi-krisis-akibat-covid-19-b1ZLs9tpp

Hill, H. (1999). *Indonesia in crisis.* Unpublished draft postscript for the second edition of The Indonesian Economy since 1966, Cambridge University Press.

Hill, H. (2001). Small and medium enterprises in Indonesia: Old policy challenges for a new administration. *Asian Survey, 41*(2), 248–270.

Humphrey, J. (2009, March). *Are exporters in Africa facing reduced availability of trade finance.* Research paper, Institute of Development Studies Brighton.

Hurst, R., Buttle, M., & Sandars, J. (2010). The impact of the global economic slowdown on value chain labor markets in Asia. In A. Bauer & M. Thant (Eds.), *Poverty and sustainable development in Asia: Impacts and responses to the global economic crisis.* Asian Development Bank (ADB) and ADB Institute.

ILO. (2020a). *COVID-19 and the world of work: Impact and policy responses, ILO Monitor* (1st ed.). International Labour Organization.

ILO. (2020b). *COVID-19 and the world of work: Updated estimates and analysis, ILO Monitor* (2nd ed.). International Labour Organization.

ILO. (2020c). *COVID-19: Protecting workers in the workplace.* International Labour Organization. https://www.ilo.org/global/about-the-ilo/new sroom/news/WCMS_738742/lang-en/index.htm

ILO. (2020d). *MSME day 2020: The COVID-19 pandemic and its impact on small business.* International Labor Office. https://www.ilo.org/empent/wha tsnew/WCMS_749275/lang--en/index.htm

Jellinek, L., & Rustanto, B. (1999, July). *Survival strategies of the Javanese during the economic crisis*. Consultancy Report to the World Bank.

Jovanovikj, B., & Georgievska, L. (2015). Transmission channels of the global economic crisis: Micro evidence for Macedonia. *Journal of Contemporary Economic and Business Issues, 2*(1), 5–20.

Kane, J. (2009). What the economic crisis means for child labour. *Global Social Policy, 9*(Suppl.), 175–196.

KB. (2020, April 14). *Daftar Usaha yang Bisa Jadi Pilihan di Tengah Pandemi Virus Corona* [List of businesses that can be an choice in the middle of the corona virus pandemic]. Kumparan BISNIS, Bisnis. https://kumparan.com/kumparanbisnis/daftar-usaha-yang-bisa-jadi-pilihan-di-tengah-pandemi-virus-corona-1tDiIgDLASf/full

Khor, N., & Sebastian I. (2009, December). *Exports and the global crisis: Still alive, though not quite kicking yet: ADB Economics* (Working Paper Series No. 190). Asian Development Bank.

Kim, J., Kim, J., Lee, S. K., & Tang, L. (2020). Effects of epidemic disease outbreaks on financial performance of restaurants: Event study method approach. *Journal of Hospitality and Tourism Management, 43*, 32–41.

Kompas. (2020a, May 9). Peluang Memanfaatkan Lonjakan Pengunjung Laman E-dagang [Opportunity to take advantage of e-commerce site visitor surges]. *Kompas Newspaper*, p. 9.

Kompas. (2020b, April 9). Jumlah Korban PHK Terus Bertambah [The number of layoff victims continues to increase]. *Kompas Newspaper*, p. 9.

Kompas (2020c, April 17), Stabilitas Sosial Dijaga [Social stability is maintained]. *Kompas Newspaper*, p. 1.

Musa, A. (1998). *A study on access to credit for small and medium enterprises (SMEs) in Indonesia before and during the economic crisis (1997–1998)*. Study prepared for the Asia Foundation and the United States Agency for International Development, Jakarta.

Mustafa, R., & Mansor, S. A. (1999, October 30–31). *Malaysia's financial crisis and contraction of human resource: Policies and lessons for SMIs*. Paper presentation, the APEC Human Resource Management Symposium on SMEs.

Nguanbanchong, A. (2009, September 15–16). *Feminized recession impact of global economic crisis on women in Southeast Asia*. Paper presented at the seminar on Gender and the Economic Crisis: Impact and Responses.

Nurzaman. (2020, April). *Dampak Wabah Covid-19 UMKM (Usaha Micro Kecil Menengah) Banyak Gulung Tikar* [The impact of the Covid-19 outbreak MSMEs (Micro, small and medium enterprises) Many have been out of business]. KICAUNews.com. https://kicaunews.com/2020/04/07/dampak-wabah-covid-19-umkm-usaha-micro-kecil-menengah-banyak-gulung-tikar/

OECD. (2020a). *Coronavirus (COVID-19): SME policy responses*. Updated 15 July. Organisation for Economic Co-operation and Development.

OECD. (2020b, April). *Evaluating the initial impact of COVID-19 containment measures on economic activity. OECD Policy Responses to Coronavirus (Covid-19)*. Organisation for Economic Co-operation and Development. https://www.oecd.org/coronavirus/policyresponses/evaluating-the-initial-impact-of-covid-19-containment-measures-on-economic-activity/

Pasadilla, G. O. (2010, January). *Financial crisis, trade finance, and SMEs: Case of Central Asia* (ADBI Working Paper Series, No. 187). ADB Institute.

Pearson, R., & Sweetman, C. (Eds.). (2011). *Gender and the economic crisis*. Practical Action Publishing in association with Oxfam GB.

Priyambada, A., Suryhadi, A., & Sumarto, S. (2005). *What happened to child labor in Indonesia during the economic crisis? The trade-off between school and work*. SMERU Research Institute.

Rahman, R. (2020, April 16). 37,000 SMEs hit by COVID-19 crisis as government prepares aid. *The Jakarta Post*. https://www.thejakartapost.com/news/2020/04/16/37000-smes-hit-by-covid-19-crisis-asgovernment_prepares-aid.html

Régnier, P. (2005). The East Asian financial crisis in Thailand: Distress and resilience of local SMEs. In C. Harvie & B.-C. Lee (Eds.), *Sustaining growth and performance in East Asia*. Edward Elgar.

Sandee, H., Andadari, R. K., & Sulandjari, S. (2000). Small firm development during good times and bad: The Jepara furniture industry. In C. Manning & P. van Dierman (Eds.), *Indonesia in transition: Social aspects of reformasi and crisis*. Indonesia Assessment Series, Research School of Pacific and Asian Studies, Australian National University, and Institute of Southeast Asian Studies.

Santoso, Y. I. (2020). *Menghitung dampak Covid19 terhadap dunia usaha hingga UMKM* [Calculating the impact of Covid19 on the business world to MSMEs]. https://nasional.kontan.co.id/news/menghitungdampak-covid-19-terhadap-dunia-usaha-hinggaumkm?page=all

Sato, Y. (2000). How did the crisis affect small and medium-sized enterprises? From a field study of the metal working industry in Java. *The Developing Economies, XXXVIII*(4), 572–595.

Shafi, M., Liu, J., & Ren, W. (2020). Impact of COVID-19 pandemic on micro, small, and medium-sized enterprises operating in Pakistan. *Research in Globalization, 2*, 1–14. https://www.sciencedirect.com/science/article/pii/S25900 51X20300071?via%3Dihub

Shakil, M. H., Munim, Z. H., Tasnia, M., & Sarowar, S. (2020). COVID-19 and the environment: A critical review and research agenda. *Journal of Science of the Total Environment, 745*(9). https://openarchive.usn.no/usn-xmlui/bitstream/handle/11250/2675634/COVID-19%2band%2bthe%2benviron ment%2bA%2bcritical%2breview%2band%2bresearch%2bagenda.pdf?sequence= 2&isAllowed=y

Setyowati, D. (2020, April). *Siasat Empat UMKM Bertahan di Tengah Pandemi Corona* [Four MSMEs' tactics to survive in the midst of the Corona pandemic]. https://katadata.co.id/berita/2020/04/20/siasat-empat-umkm-bertahan-di-tengah-pandemi-corona

Shin, K.-Y. (2015). The two crises and inequality in the labour market. *International Union Rights, 22*(1), 3–5.

SMERU. (2009, November). *Monitoring the socioeconomic impact of the 2008/2009 global financial crisis in Indonesia* (Media Monitoring No. 04/FS/2009). SMERU Research Institute.

Sundari, L. S. (2020, April). *Dampak Pandemi Covid-19, Omzet UMKM di Kota Cimahi Turun 80 Persen* [The impact of the Covid-19 pandemic, MSME turnover in Cimahi City dropped 80 percent]. Galamedianews.com. https://www.galamedianews.com/?arsip=254042&judul=dampak-pandemi-covid-19-omzet-umkm-di-kota-cimahi-turun-80-persen

Suryahadi, A., Al Izzati, R., & Suryadarma, D. (2020). *The impact of COVID-19 outbreak on poverty: An estimation for Indonesia* (SMERU Working Paper). SMERU Research Institute.

Tambunan, T. T. H. (1998, March 20–21). *Impact of East Asia currency crisis and economic development on Indonesia's SMEs and priorities for adjustment.* Paper prepared for the SME Resourcing Conference, ASEAN Chamber of Commerce and Industry.

Tambunan, T. T. H. (2010a). The Indonesian experience with two big economic crises. *Modern Economy, 1*, 156–167.

Tambunan, T. T. H. (2010b). *Global economic crisis and ASEAN economy.* Lambert Academic Publishing.

Tambunan, T. T. H. (2011a). *Economic crisis and vulnerability: The story from Southeast Asia.* Nova Science Publishers Inc.

Tambunan, T. T. H. (2011b). The impact of the 2008–2009 global economic crisis on a developing country's economy: Studiesfrom Indonesia. *Journal of Business and Economics, 2*(3), 175–197.

Tambunan, T. T. H. (2019). The impact of the economic crisis on micro, small, and medium enterprises and their crisis mitigation measures in Southeast Asia with reference to Indonesia. *Asia Pacific Policy Study, 6*(1), 1–21.

Tambunan, T. T. H. (2020, Mei 20). *Dampak dari Covid-19 Terhadap UMKM.* Focus Group Discussion.

Tambunan, T. T. H., & Busneti, I. (2016). The Indonesian experience with two big financial crisis and their impacts on micro, small and medium enterprises. *Asian Research Journal of Business Management, 3*(4), 83–100.

Tecson, G. (1999). Present status and prospects of supporting industries in the Philippines. In *Present status and prospects of supporting industries in ASEAN (I): Philippines-Indonesia.* Institute of Developing Economies, Japan External Trade Organization.

UNCTAD. (2020a). *The Covid-19 shock to developing countries: Towards a "whatever it takes" programme for the two-thirds of the world's population being left behind.* United Nations Conference on Trade and Development.

UNCTAD. (2020b). *Investment trends monitor: Impact of the coronavirus outbreak on global FDI.* https://unctad.org/en/PublicationsLibrary/diaein f2020d2_en.pdf?user=1653

UNDP. (2020a). *Assessment report on impact of COVID-19 pandemic on Chinese enterprises.* United Nations Development Programme.

UNDP. (2020b). *COVID-19: Looming crisis in developing countries threatens to devastate economies and ramp up inequality.* United Nations Development Programme. https://www.undp.org/content/undp/en/home/newscentre/news/2020/COVID19_Crisis_in_developing_countries_threatens_devastate_economies.html

UNICEF. (2009). *Impact of the economic crisis on children: What the crisis means for child labour.* United Nations International Children's Emergency Fund.

Wengel, ter J., & Rodriguez, E. (2006). SME export performance in Indonesia after the crisis. *Small Business Economics, 26,* 25–37.

Wie, T. K. (2000). The impact of the economic crisis on Indonesia's manufacturing sector. *The Developing Economies, XXXVIII*(4), 420–453.

Wiradi, G. (1998). *Rural Java in a time of crisis: With special reference to Curug village, Cirebon, West Java.* Paper presentation, the Economic Crisis and Social Security in Indonesia, Berg-en-Dal.

World Bank. (2009). *The global economic crisis: Assessing vulnerability with a poverty lens.*

CHAPTER 6

Development of Financial Technology with Reference to Peer-to-Peer (P2P) Lending

6.1 Introduction

Now in the digital area, banks are making more non-face-to-face financial transactions. Twenty years ago, the organizations in the business ecosystem were banks and/or lenders, consumers and/or companies, e-commerce merchants, or credit reporting agencies; and the ecosystem of business funding was not so complex. But today, the ecosystem is changing. There are more organizations involved in the ecosystem and information from social media becomes more important. In Indonesia, the appearance of financial technology (FinTech)-based companies that have been grown rapidly since the past few years has made the business funding ecosystem in the country also more complex.

FinTech is an innovation in the financial services industry that utilizes the use of technology. Its products are usually in the form of a system built to carry out specific financial transaction mechanisms, including payments, funding or lending, banking (digital banking), capital market, insurance, supporting services, and many others.

According to a FinTech global market report issued in 2020 by the Business Research Company, the global FinTech market was valued at about $127.66 billion in 2018 and is expected to grow to $309.98 billion at an annual growth rate of 24.8 percent through 2022, with the United Kingdom (UK) as one of the most advanced fintech markets. Growth in

© The Author(s), under exclusive license to Springer Nature
Singapore Pte Ltd. 2022
T. T.H. Tambunan, *Fostering Resilience through Micro,*
Small and Medium Enterprises, Sustainable Development Goals Series,
https://doi.org/10.1007/978-981-16-9435-6_6

147

the digital payments sector is driving the market for global FinTech, and the growth in the digital commerce market and proliferation of mobile technology has contributed to the growth of the digital payments sector. For instance, companies such as Square and Stripe provide portable Point-of-Sale (POS) systems which can instantly read and process touchless payments like Apple Pay, along with credit cards. The report states that as an increasing number of businesses are adopting digital payment systems, the demand for FinTech solutions is increasing and driving the growth of the market. The main players in the arena of are FinTech government entities, which can range widely from regulators, central banks, sovereign wealth funds, and all the authorities that grant licenses and can actively influence the financial sector; traditional financial services firms; FinTech companies that provide financial services alongside their core products like Uber and Amazon which have dedicated internal teams of engineers and experts making a strong push towards increasing their presence in the sector; companies that provide technology for financial transactions such as Bloomberg, Thomson Reuters, American Express, Visa, etc.; professional/individual investors; and new, disruptive companies operating in several different sectors (BRC, 2020).

Among FinTech-based products, peer-to-peer (P2P) lending is the most popular and also important for funding MSEs that have difficulty accessing bank credit without collateral or financial records. Banks often consider these businesses as less profitable. P2P lending is one of the innovations in the financial services sector with the use of technology that enables lenders and loan recipients to conduct loan lending transactions without having to meet in person. The lending and borrowing transaction mechanism are carried out through an online system that has been provided by P2P lending provider, both through the application and on the website page. P2P lending only acts as a meeting mediator lenders and loan recipients. Lenders and loan recipients must first register and fill out the required personal data before they can apply for loans or loan applications. P2P lending is different from FinTech. FinTech is general and is not limited to one particular financial services industry. Whereas P2P lending is limited to financial service innovation in lending and borrowing transactions only. Hence, given the widely discussed failure of banks or other formal sources of funds in providing adequate loans to small businesses, the emergence of FinTech-based P2P lending offers significant opportunities.

According to a recent report entitled *Peer-to-peer Lending—Global Market Trajectory & Analytics*, issued by Research and Markets in 2020, the global P2P lending market grew at a compound annual growth rate of around 25 percent during 2014–2019. Increasing digitization in the banking industry is one of the key factors driving the growth of the market. Furthermore, the emergence of small businesses, especially in developing countries, is stimulating the market growth. These small businesses require financing alternatives with no collateral, minimal charging fees, and convenient repayment options. Apart from this, as stated in the report, P2P lending platforms also eliminate the cost of establishing physical branches, staffing, and maintenance, thereby gaining preference among the masses (RM, 2020a).

Whereas in another report on ASEAN, it is stated that in the region P2P lending industry is disrupting the loan market for small businesses that are primarily served by banks. P2P lenders are launching products that use technologies such as machine learning and artificial intelligence (AI) to shorten the entire lending process from more than 4 weeks to 1 week or less. According to this report, P2P lending platform providers are especially needed in Indonesia, the Philippines, and Vietnam because there are so many especially MSEs that cannot obtain loans from mainstream commercial banks (including government-assisted loans), which forces them to struggle with day-to-day business (RM, 2020b).

Banks are expected to be the main investor. Initially, banks felt that FinTech was a threat to their business. According to a report from EYGM Limited (2017), the growth of FinTech strengthened the general belief that it would disrupt the banking sector. Yet, as the report emphasized, collaboration rather than competition will eliminate the disruption. The report further confirms that the biggest short-term threat to most banks comes from fellow banks rather than FinTech because fellow banks may be better at utilizing FinTech.

On the other hand, FinTech did not intend to cooperate with formal financial institutions. FinTech companies had better skills and agility, as well as third-party funding. However, they realized that it would be difficult to break the dominance of incumbent banks. Therefore, the banking sector and FinTech companies began to see that their futures existed in their collaboration.

Based on the above background, the objective of this chapter is twofold: (1) to examine the development of FinTech, particularly P2P lending in Indonesia, and (2) to explore the importance of P2P lending as an alternative source of funding for MSEs in Indonesia. This Indonesian case is very important for two main reasons. First, most small businesses in Indonesia do not have access to bank financing. Second, P2P lenders have grown rapidly in recent years, which are expected to become an alternative funding for small businesses in the country. It is also confirmed by a 2020 report on development of FinTech companies in ASEAN which emphasized that P2P lending platform providers are especially needed in Indonesia (and the Philippines and Vietnam) because there are so many MSEs that cannot obtain loans from mainstream commercial banks (including government-assisted loans), which forces them to struggle with day-to-day business (RM, 2020b). However, until now there has been no published data either at the macro (national) level or micro-level (from individual P2P lending companies) regarding the number of MSEs that have ever received loans from P2P lenders and how this has affected the performance of this business group.

More specifically, this research addresses the following three research questions:

    i. How is the development of P2P lending companies in Indonesia?
   ii. Has the emergence of P2P lending companies benefited MSEs?
  iii. How is the ecosystem of MSEs funding in Indonesia with the emergence of P2P lending?

The first question is important because after all the presence of P2P lenders in Indonesia is a new phenomenon not only that has significantly changed the ecosystem of funding in general but also is disrupting the loan market for small businesses that is primarily or traditionally served by banks. The second question is important because as said before there are still many MSEs in Indonesia that cannot obtain loans from mainstream banks. Therefore, the presence of P2P lending platform providers is expected to fill this gap by extending services to the un- or under-banked small business segment of the market. In this study, the benefits obtained by small businesses or MSEs are measured by growth in their production/turnover or business expansion. Whereas the success of P2P lending is measured by the large number of financed small businesses spreading across many regions in the country and have not experienced non-performing loans. The third question is important because with the presence of P2P lending companies, the number of external sources of funding or credit suppliers for small businesses in Indonesia has increased, which in itself has changed the ecosystem of MSEs funding in Indonesia.

6.2 Literature Review

In a simple way, FinTech can be defined as any technology that helps companies in financial services to operate or deliver their products and services, or that helps companies or individuals to manage their financial affairs. Among FinTech-based products, P2P lending is the most popular. It is one of the innovations in the financial services sector that enables lenders and loan recipients to conduct loan lending transactions via online or a website interface.

The formal financing ecosystem has significantly changed with the digital era's emergence of FinTech. In fact, it has become more complex. Today, there are many nonface-to-face financial transactions. Twenty years ago, players in the financing ecosystem included banks and non-bank financial institutions, consumers, business owners, and credit reporting agencies. There are more players in today's ecosystem, including FinTech-based lending providers that offer loans to customers without using data from credit bureaus. The process can be done easily and efficiently through mobile devices.

There are many studies, seminar papers, and reports on fintech, including Bruton et al. (2015), Feng et al. (2015), Government Office for Science (2015), Lin and Viswanathan (2015), Serrano-Cinca et al. (2015), Buckley and Webster (2016), Computer Business Review (2016), Cumming and Schwienbacher (2016), Haddad and Hornuf (2016), Iyer et al. (2016), Milne and Parboteeah (2016), BIS and FSB (2017), Toronto Centre (2017), Eugenia (2018), Han et al. (2018), Jagtiani and Lemieux (2018), Lukonga (2018), Bavoso (2019), Hendriyani and Raharja (2019), Morgan and Trinh (2019), Nemoto et al. (2019), Thakora (2019), Frost (2020), and Iman (2020). One shared conclusion from the literature is that the growth rate of FinTech will become more rapid, including in developing countries. First, businesses and the economy will grow, resulting in an increase in funding. Second, it can be difficult to obtain loans from banks, especially for small or start-up businesses.

Unfortunately, empirical evidence on the role of P2P lending companies in funding small businesses is limited. Most studies on P2P lending, such as Bruton et al. (2015), Milne and Parboteeah (2016), Jagtiani and Lemieux (2018), Han et al. (2018), Creehan (2019), Nemoto et al. (2019), and Oh and Rosenkranz (2020), do not focus on small businesses. Nemoto et al. (2019), for instance, found that P2P lending was found in the world's biggest markets: People's Republic of China (PRC) and the United States. As shown in their study, in 2015, US$100 billion and US$34 billion of new FinTech credit were issued in the PRC and the United States, respectively. As a comparison, fintech lending in Asia and the Pacific (excluding the PRC) was only US$1.1 billion. It was less than US$1 billion in the Eurozone. However, their study does not provide detailed information about P2P lending to small businesses. This may be because it does not differentiate according to business size in countries where data on FinTech lending is available.

With respect to Indonesia, so far, there is very little research on the importance of P2P lending on MSEs funding, including that ever done by the author of this book and his team. Based on their finding, Tambunan et al. (2021) concluded that at least in theory with the presence of P2P lending companies, the number of MSMEs, especially MSEs, in Indonesia, including those located in rural areas (of course, villages that have access to the Internet or Wi-fi) to obtain funds from formal sources will increase. Other available studies include Pranata (2019) who focused on the role of digital payments and FinTech in accelerating the development of small businesses in two provinces in Indonesia, Nusa Tenggara Barat (NTB) and Bali. The study also concludes that inclusive FinTech can benefit small businesses, especially those marginalized in terms of geographical and technological capability as long as they have Internet access.

Digitalization and FinTech offer many opportunities to address small business constraints by providing better access to finance. Examples include branchless banking technologies like Internet banking, P2P lending, or crowdfunding. These, in turn, can enhance productivity and competitiveness. Nemoto et al. (2019) stressed a need to encourage the growth of P2P lending to support small businesses, especially those with growth potential. With P2P or FinTech, several constraints to financing (i.e., lack of credit information and relatively high cost of servicing small business financing needs) could be reduced (IMF, 2019).

However, digitalization's ability to unlock productivity and growth for small businesses in developing countries, including Indonesia, is far from being fully exploited. Therefore, empirical studies, especially on P2P lending, are needed. Findings from such studies may help policymakers create a conducive environment in which FinTech could thrive by redesigning regulatory policies to induce further innovation.

Banks are expected to be the main investor of funds for FinTech companies. Initially, banks felt that FinTech was a threat to their business. A study of 45 major global banks conducted by EYGM Limited (2017) shows that these banks were involved with FinTech. However, only a quarter of the banks were extensively involved due to obstacles in collaborating with FinTech companies. Obstacles included navigating procurement, vendor risk management, technical implementation, and the handling of this issue by banks and FinTech companies. On the other hand, FinTech did not intend to cooperate with formal financial institutions. FinTech companies had better skills and agility, as well as third-party funding. However, they realized that it would be difficult to break the dominance of incumbent banks. Therefore, the banking sector and FinTech companies began to see that their futures existed in their collaboration.

Hatami (2018) has also observed that worldwide sometime around the tail-end of 2010 the banks started realizing that something called a FinTech could be a threat to their business. This is a time when some senior executives in the bigger banks were asking the digital leaders if it would be possible to slow down internet adoption by their customers. The banks' natural reaction was initially of disbelief and denial. As the likes of Transferwise, Zopa, SoFi, and Fidor started gaining momentum, this was followed by fear with boards buzzing with stories about a Blockbuster moment. Bank "Innovation teams" were hurriedly set up to fight the FinTech wave. Then, investment by the banks in internal digital development started growing fast. The banks were going to beat the FinTech at their own game. But things did not go as expected. The big spend in innovation by the banks did not stop the FinTech from being disruptive and from growing their customer bases. The banks have realized that they didn't have what it took to succeed. At the same time the FinTech companies have realized that even though they had better skills, were more agile and were becoming increasingly better funded, breaking the domination of the incumbent banks was going to be hard. So, banks and FinTech providers started realizing that the future of both lies in collaboration.

So, in the past few years, many reports and media coverage have shown increased cooperation between banks and FinTech. According to Ghanem (2018), a growing number of traditional banks are collaborating with FinTech companies, with 91 percent of bank executives wanting to work with FinTech firms. Eighty-six percent voiced concerns that a lack of collaboration could damage businesses in the fast–growing digital ecosystem. Additionally, 42 percent of bank executives said that a collaboration between banks and FinTech companies would help banks lower their cost base. Regulations involving the sharing of customer data, such as the European Revised Payment Services Directive (PSD2) Europe and Open Banking Standards in the UK, also encourage bank and fintech partnerships.

Oleg Boyko, chair and founder of Finstar Financial Group (a private equity company operating in Europe, United States, Asia, Latin America, and the Commonwealth of Independent States [CIS]), believes that changes in consumer behavior, advancements in cloud-based technology, increased power and availability of mobile devices, and the emergence of data science are challenging the business models of traditional financial institutions. Boyko also believes that the partnership between FinTech companies and banks will bring strategic value, insight, and management capability to both parties (Mathews, 2018).

The main findings from research by Deloitte Development LLC (2018) showed that financial institutions are more likely to collaborate than compete with FinTech companies. However, traditional banks find it difficult to interact effectively with FinTech companies because they move faster and are less structured. The banking sector lacks a clear path to developing a cooperative relationship with FinTech companies. It is also difficult to set benchmarks to measure success. According to this study, consolidation can occur as FinTech companies seek to be more attractive in an increasingly competitive market and financial institutions seek more sophisticated partners.

Mathews (2018) stated that partnering with FinTech companies gives banks an opportunity to increase their revenue and enhance services or customer experience while taking fewer risks or adding staff. FinTech companies, on the other hand, gain access to a loyal customer base and have opportunities to take advantage of the bank's extensive financial service experiences while navigating the regulatory environment. According to Mathews (2018), there are three ways to partner:

1. Software-as-a-Service: In this common approach, a FinTech company licenses or sells the technology that underlies its activities to the bank. This may be an offering where banks place their branding on products to promote end-to-end solutions. The bank does not have to invest in infrastructure or development costs for internal solutions as they begin to offer a variety of modern and innovative products under their brand while maintaining control over the customer relationship cycle. On the other hand, FinTech companies, especially new ones (startups), get access to low-cost funding through trusted partnerships while knowing that regulatory requirements will be addressed through the bank infrastructure.
2. Referrals: In this approach, banks refer clients to a relevant FinTech to eliminate gaps in their service offerings. This process provides financial service offerings to individuals without bank accounts. This process, which usually happens in the lending sector, allows FinTech to offer faster customer onboarding, processing, and approval times, cheaper loans, and alternative methods of funding and credit lines.
3. Outright Purchase: In this approach, the bank buys the rights to technology or buys the company. This model is not common. Banks gain exclusive rights to technology, which gives them a competitive advantage, rapid expansion into new markets, and a new customer base. FinTech companies join an established bank ecosystem. This offers additional funding for product development and direct financial market expertise to guide a product launch. This can also be a profitable choice for founders who want to get out of the market while ensuring existing customers still benefit from products and services.

According to Hatami (2018), there are four groups/models of collaboration between FinTech companies and banks:

1. Channel: Banks use FinTech companies as a channel to sell their products to bank customers. Benefits for banks include offering new products or services to customers while expending little time, effort, or capital. The bank also gains valuable insight about whether customers like propositions. This, in turn, assists in creating strategic plans. On the other hand, fintech companies benefit from access to

new customers and sales, improvement of their brand through relationships with banks, and market insight to perfect their products. Customers receive new, attractive offers from their banks. They also get guarantees from banks that FinTech can be trusted with their money.

2. Supplier: In this collaboration, the bank acts as a supplier to the fintech company. A proposition is made by integrating the capabilities of FinTech companies in bank offerings. For customers, the offer looks like a bank that provides services (even if there are statements about a FinTech's contributions to the terms and conditions of the offer).

3. Satellite: This collaboration is a further development of the supplier model. Although the bank acquires a FinTech company, the FinTech remains relatively independent. The FinTech company receives capital injections, implicit validation of its business models through the bank, and access to bank customers. Banks see this investment as a means of experimenting in specific business areas without affecting their existing operations. With this approach, the bank gains market intelligence and ensures exclusivity and control of new propositions.

4. Merger: In this traditional acquisition model, a FinTech company is integrated and renamed in the bank. This benefits the bank by bringing innovation to its brand. This also increases customer goodwill and rigidity.

6.3   METHOD

This research adopted a descriptive approach that analyzes secondary and primary data. It utilized a survey method by using a semistructured questionnaire to collect the primary data from two groups of respondents (30 owners of MSEs who received P2P loans and 30 managers/heads of registered P2P lending companies). Of these respondents, a total of 40 were deemed usable (10 MSEs and 30 P2P lending companies). The survey was conducted from October 2019 to November 2019 in Jakarta. The majority of registered FinTech companies with the Financial Services Authority (OJK) are in this area.

The survey implementation process went through several stages as follows. By September 30, 2019, 127 FinTech companies were registered with the OJK. Initially, all registered fintech companies were included in the research sample. However, not all were P2P lending companies that provided microfinance needed by small businesses. Many provided other types of financing, such as supply chain finance, invoice finance, cofinancing, inventory financing, and payday loan. From the P2P category, most did not distinguish their customers between individuals or households (e.g., home renovations, buying a new car, and paying school fees) and entrepreneurs or owners of small businesses to expand their businesses. At that time, 30 P2P companies recorded their customers according to these two categories. Therefore, only they were included in the sample.

Most of the 30 companies refused to provide data on their small business customers. Thus, for the survey, in total there was only information from 50 MSEs obtained from a few companies. Then, a semi-structured questionnaire was sent to them via email. Of this number, 30 completed the questionnaire. But only ten were deemed usable. Most were not open to providing information, especially regarding financial figures like income, revenue, and the amount of P2P credit received, or maybe because they didn't have a good financial record, as commonly found in small businesses (especially microenterprises) in Indonesia.

In the second stage, all of these 10 respondents were contacted again via email or telephone to clarify their answers and to have further and broader discussions with them, especially to have their opinions about the existence of P2P lending providers.

This survey was needed to answer questions 2 and 3. For question 2 (benefits for MSEs), the owners of these 10 MSEs were asked about their main constraints, sources of funds (formal and informal), the size of loan they obtained, the benefits they experienced if any (e.g., whether their turnover or production capacity has increased), and if they have any plan in the future to borrow again and from what sources (P2P again or other sources) and their main reason for choosing a certain source of funds.

A semi-structured interview was adopted in this survey to gather qualitative and quantitative information from the respondents. Quantitative information is such as the percentage growth of production/turnover and the amount of loans obtained from P2P lending providers, and qualitative information is their opinion regarding the existence of an online funding system and their main reason for (also) borrowing money from P2P lending companies.

For question 3 (ecosystem of MSEs funding with the presence of P2P lending providers), the owners/managers of these 30 P2P lending companies were asked with questions regarding, e.g., the number of MSEs they funded, difficulties they may have faced in channeling funds, their channeling system (directly to MSEs or indirectly via intermediaries such as cooperative or supplier of raw material), and their suppliers of funds.

To validate and deepen the survey findings, a series of focus group discussions (FGD) were conducted with selected respondents from the 30 FinTech-based P2P lending companies.

Secondary data was collected from three sources: (1) data on small business credit from Bank Indonesia (BI); (2) data on small businesses in the manufacturing industry from the Central Statistics Agency (BPS); and (3) data on registered FinTech companies from the OJK. This secondary data especially from the OJK was needed to answer question 1.

Because there is no national data on MSEs that obtained loans from P2P lending providers, a case study like this is an appropriate alternative. Of course, findings from a survey with very few respondents like this case study will not provide a general picture of the importance of P2P lending for small businesses in Indonesia. However, as the first exploratory study conducted in Indonesia, the findings can serve as preliminary information for future studies with a larger sample.

6.4 Findings and Discussion

The First Question: Development of P2P Lending

In Indonesia, the existence of FinTech-based companies is regulated by the government (OJK) through two regulations, namely Regulation No. 77, 2016 Concerning Loan Service to Loan Money Based on Information Technology, and Regulation No. 13, 2018 Concerning Digital Financial Innovations in the Financial Services Sector.

Regulated in POJK 77/2016 are general provisions, implementation, loan service users for money loans based on information technology (IT), agreements, risk mitigation, IT system governance, education, and protection of loan service users for money loans based on IT, electronic signatures, principles and technical introduction of customers, prohibitions, periodic reports, sanctions, other provisions, transitional provisions, and closing provisions.

All FinTech companies must be registered and licensed by the OJK. At least they must obtain a registered mark before carrying out their operational activities. Then, after a maximum of 1 (one) year of obtaining a registered mark, they are required to submit a permit application to the

OJK. Both registered and licensed companies can carry out operational activities in accordance with applicable regulations. If the company that has been registered and has been operating for 1 (one) year does not submit a request for licensing, it must return the registration mark to the OJK. While licensed companies do not have an expiry period on their licensed mark.

FinTech companies or providers that are not registered are considered illegal. According to the OJK definition, illegal FinTech companies are those that have carried out their business activities but have not yet registered or not licensed after one year of operation. One of the biggest risks for the public with the presence of illegal FinTech companies is the misuse of digital personal data, where illegal FinTech companies will access and retrieve all users' personal digital data that are on their mobile phones including contact lists, contact history, galleries, photos, and short message service (SMS). On the access and acquisition of such data, digital personal data obtained by illegal FinTech providers is misused, generally in many billing cases where the user's personal data is used to (i) disseminate or neutralize various negative user information to all contact lists on the user's handphone and/or do billing to all parties in the contact list. In this regard, the OJK has coordinated with the State Ministry of Communication and Information (Kemenkominfo RI) and the Investment Alert Task Force (KPK) in tackling illegal FinTech providers.

The number of P2P lending providers in Indonesia continues to increase every year. As of April 2020, the number reached 161 companies. The profiles of all FinTech lending companies registered in Indonesia between December 2019 and April 2020 are shown in Table 6.1. FinTech-based P2P lending companies in Indonesia receive various types of financing, including invoice financing, supply chain financing, merchant financing, microfinancing, property financing, house renovation financing, and bailouts for rent. Financing targets of P2P lending companies also vary from financing MSMEs, financial inclusion, village development/improvement, and women empowerment.

Of this total, 151 companies were in the great Jakarta (i.e., Depok, Bogor, Bekasi, and South Tangerang). The rest were in other cities, namely Bandung in West Java Province, Lampung in Lampung Province (Sumatera), Surabaya in East Java Province, Makassar in South Sulawesi Province, and Bali in Province Bali.

Regarding status, 110 companies were local and 51 were financed with foreign capital. Many had borrowers from outside Java. Thirteen were

Table 6.1 Company profile of P2P lending providers in Indonesia, December 2019 and April 2020

No.	Description	December 2019	January 2020	February 2020	March 2020	April 2020	% Δ April 2020
1	Number of Accumulated Lender Accounts (Entity Unit)						
	Java	500,030	508,014	520,172	528,441	534,504	6.89
	Outside Java	102,149	104,205	106,021	107,966	109,652	7.35
	Abroad	3756	3781	3810	3826	3837	2.16
	Total	605,935	616,000	630,003	640,233	647,993	6.94
2	Number of Accumulated Borrower Accounts (Entity Unit)						
	Java	15,397,251	16,943,440	18,403,371	19,865,254	20,364,998	32.26
	Outside Java	3,171,872	3,553,727	3,907,082	4,292,313	4,405,307	38.89
	Total	18,569,123	20,497,167	22,327,795	24,157,567	24,770,305	33.40
3	Total Accumulated Transaction of Lenders (No. of Accounts)						
	Java	41,126,937	45,722,659	50,815,670	56,445,722	59,427,438	44.50
	Outside Java	1,459,580	1,499,916	1,547,266	1,598,056	1,626,896	11.46
	Abroad	17,831,694	18,856,725	19,774,227	20,713,236	21,156,430	18.65
	Total	60,418,211	66,079,300	72,137,163	78,75,014	82,210,764	36.07
4	Total Accumulated Transaction of Borrowers (No. of Accounts)						
	Java	68,215,545	75,408,358	84,604,087	95,342,352	105,523,181	54.69
	Outside Java	13,660,488	15,092,986	16,919,628	18,941,003	20,280,674	48.46
	Total	81,876,033	90,501,344	101,523,715	114,283,355	125,803,855	53.65

No.	Description	December 2019	January 2020	February 2020	March 2020	April 2020	% Δ April 2020
5	Accumulated total credits (Rp)						
	Java	69,823,521.5	75,708,121.7	81,633,839.0	87,723,569.8	90,879,451.1	30.16
	Outside Java	1,673,989.3	12,665,934.3	13,760,729.6	14,810,823.8	15,179,791.0	30.03
	Total	81,497,510.8	88,374,056.0	95,394,568.6	102,534,393.5	106,059,242.2	30.14
6	Outstanding Loan (Rp)						
		13,157,156.0	13,516,951.4	14,495,545.3	14,792,048.9	13,749,972.8	4.51
7	The lowest average loan value (Rp)						
		34,130,705	43,599,318	35,324,868	42,950,127	50,355,200	47.54
8	Average value of loans disbursed (Rp)						
		99,708,028	118,068,844	126,928,152	22,481,756	111,438,147	11.76

Source OJK (https://www.ojk.go.id/id/kanal/iknb/data-dan-statistik/fintech/Pages/Statistik-Fintech-Lending-Periode-Bulan-April-2020.aspx) licensed. They were still allowed to operate if they were registered in the OJK (fulfilled the OJK requirements) but had not been granted licenses. However, within one year since they started operation, they must apply for a license and attach their annual financial statements.

Illegal P2P lenders also increased. They have mushroomed in recent times, especially during the COVID-19. pandemic period. They took advantage of the weakening of the household economy due to the pandemic. They especially targeted households or individuals who were experiencing economic difficulties and were in dire need of money to meet their daily needs. According to that story, from 2018 until June 2020 the total illegal P2P lending providers had been frozen by the OJK was 2591 entities.

There are three main fintech models operating in Indonesia, namely (i) P2P lending; (ii) equity crowdfunding; and (iii) working capital related, i.e., merchant and e-commerce finance, invoice finance (factoring), supply chain finance, and trade finance. P2P lending companies do not only finance business (productive loans) but also non-business (consumptive loans) such as property and furniture, home renovation, education, women's empowerment activities, healthcare, bailouts for rent, and other general lending. Consumptive loans are given in the form of direct cash disbursement or online credit card, whereas productive loans are provided in the form of direct cash disbursement or non-cash disbursement through a partnership with a product provider. For example, in agriculture lending, P2P lending to farmers through a partnership with, e.g., a fertilizer producer.

With respect to risk management, for different types of loan or different market potentials, P2P lending providers adopt different approaches. For productive loans, there are three different loans for different market potentials. First, general lending for large number of businesses, especially MSEs, i.e., around 62 million units in 2018 and examples of risk management are: (i) utilize invoices as collateral and analyze the credibility of anchor suppliers and/or (ii) develop and delegate agents to acquire MSEs, with a group lending model as the guarantor. Second, online merchant lending for growing number of online merchants, along with rising e-commerce and social media users (130 million in 2018) and adopted risk management is utilizing third-party data (for instance, e-commerce transactions) to determine the credit scores of potential borrowers. Third, industry-specific lending for, e.g., the agriculture sector which contributed around 13.14 percent of Indonesia's total GDP in 2017, and employed at least 31 percent of Indonesians, and for this there are two choices of risk management approached available, namely provide non-cash support (e.g., farming raw materials) and training in order to increase the production, or provide an O2O business model (PwC, 2019).

For consumptive loans, there are four different loans for different market potentials. First, education lending for more than 190 thousand university students' dropped out in 2017, as a result of a lack of financial capability, and large opportunity to tap borrowers with higher customer lifetime values. The risk management approach adopted by P2P lending companies for this loan category is to leverage partnerships with universities to obtain student data and conduct direct transfers to universities. Second, healthcare lending for the increase in healthcare spending of 14.9 percent between 2012 and 2018 which indicates the increasing concern regarding healthcare services. Two approaches for risk management are to conduct partnerships with hospitals to allow specific medical loan applications for potential borrowers, and/or conduct direct transfers to avoid the misuse of disbursed loans. Third, lending for financing property and furniture for increasing housing backlog (5.8 million in 2019), and no financing available for down payments, with one example of risk management is conducting direct transfers to landlords to ensure the proper usage of disbursed loans. Finally, general lending for large numbers of the underserved population (more than 71 percent of the population) with limited access to financing. For this category, the risk management measure utilizes multiple personal data points (e.g., personal IDs and selfies with IDs) and transaction histories (e.g., frequency and average order value) to determine creditworthiness (PwC, 2019).

The Second Question: Benefit for MSEs

Although MSMEs are widely recognized to have a vital role in economic development in Indonesia, these enterprises, especially MSEs face many obstacles that make them difficult to expand or even to survive, and limited access to funding from formal sources is the most serious. The Indonesian government has long been aware of this problem, and therefore since the "New Order" era (1970) until now the emphasis of MSMEs policy is on MSME funding. The first time the government launched a

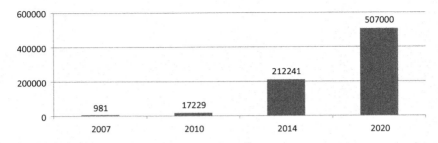

Fig. 6.1 Total accumulated KUR distribution, 2007–2020 (Rp billion) (*Source* Bank Indonesia [BI] [http://www.bi.go.id/id/umkm/kredit/data/Default.aspx])

specially designed credit scheme for MSMEs was in 1971, followed by many other credit schemes in the 1980s and 1990s (Tambunan, 2018a, 2018b). In 2007, the government launched a public guarantee credit scheme, known as People's Business Credit (or KUR), specifically for MSEs that do not have access to commercial banks due to lack of valuable assets as collateral (Fig. 6.1).

It is not easy to know exactly how many of the approximately 62 million MSMEs in Indonesia need funds from outside sources, or who have ever applied for loans to banks or other formal financial institutions. However, the 2017 national survey of manufacturing MSEs may provide a clue. Regarding the source of capital, it reveals three categories of MSEs, namely (a) fully financed by own money (i.e., 3,679,592 respondents or 82.42 percent of the total MSEs surveyed); (b) partially funded by external sources (i.e., 608,352 respondents or 13.63 percent); and (c) the rest (i.e., 176,744 respondents or 3.99 percent) who are wholly dependent on capital from external sources. Those who wholly or partly used money from external sources, only a small percentage of them fully used bank loans. More respondents used funds from non-bank such as savings and loan cooperatives (credit unions), pawnshops, multifinance/leasing companies, microfinance institutions, or from informal sources such as friends, relatives, money lenders, payments in advance from consumers, or debt to the suppliers of raw materials (i.e., payment of raw materials after goods had been sold). Many MSEs' owners prefer informal sources of funding because they can get the money immediately with no administration costs, although interest rate that they pay is often much higher than commercial banks' rates (BPS, 2018).

Further, Fig. 6.2 describes the MSME funding ecosystem in Indonesia. The financial service providers can be grouped into two categories, namely banks and non-banks. The bank category can be divided further into two sub-categories, namely rural banks (i.e., Bank Perkreditan Rakyat or BPR) and commercial banks. Then, each sub-category can be distinguished between Islamic or Sharia banks and conventional banks. A Sharia bank is a banking system based on the principles of Islamic or Sharia law and guided by Islamic economics. Islamic law prohibits collecting interest or "riba". That is why sharia banking is also known as non-interest banking. Whereas, non-banks include microfinance institutions, venture capital companies, saving and loan cooperatives, pawnshops, and also recently P2P lending companies.

To expand MSMEs' access to bank funding, in 2018, the Indonesian central bank, Bank Indonesia required all banks to allocate at least 20 percent of their total credits to MSMEs. Since then, banking attention to MSMEs has been getting better each year. Based on the credit balance value, the total MSME outstanding loans from commercial banks

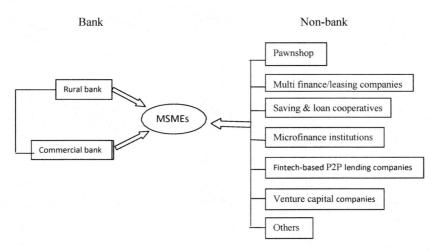

Fig. 6.2 The MSME funding ecosystem in Indonesia

increased annually, from almost 640 trillion IDR in 2013 to 1024.9 trillion IDR in August 2018. Likewise, the number of bank accounts owned by MSMEs also increased to more than 16 million in August 2018 from below 10 million in 2013. However, as shown in Fig. 6.3, the percentage of total loans of these enterprises in total commercial bank loans is still very low. Likewise, the number of bank accounts owned by MSMEs (Fig. 6.4). Although the number continues to increase, compared to the number of MSMEs in Indonesia which reached nearly 63 million units, it is obvious that most MSMEs still do not have access to banks.

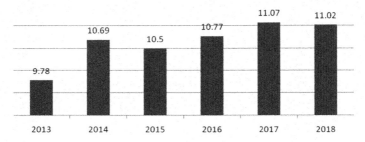

Fig. 6.3 MSMEs' outstanding commercial loans of MSMEs in Indonesia, 2013–2018 (percent of total commercial loans) (*Source* Bank Indonesia [https://www.bi.go.id/id/pencarian/Default.aspx?k=kredit%20UMKM])

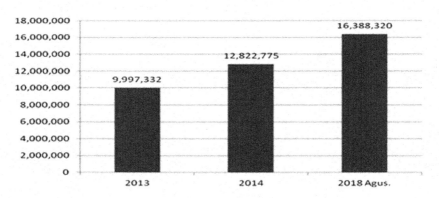

Fig. 6.4 Total number of MSME bank credit accounts 2013–2018 (*Source* Bank Indonesia [https://www.bi.go.id/id/pencarian/Default.aspx?k=kredit%20UMKM])

Therefore, the existence of FinTech companies that have been grown rapidly in Indonesia since the last few years is very welcome, as this new way of financing via online is considered a good alternative source of funding for MSMEs, especially MSEs. The limitations of conventional lending providers, both formal as well as informal, leave room for FinTech lending players such as P2P lending companies to provide an alternative source of funding for MSEs. There are three main limitations of access to underserved markets of formal conventional lending providers, such banks, multifinance companies, cooperatives, pawnshops, and microfinancial institutions, namely: (i) requirement for physical verification and high cost to scale, (ii) the underwriting process requires a credit history or proof of a steady income, which means that asset-based collateral is required, and (iii) for cooperatives, the ticket size is relatively small, and there is a lack of competitiveness in terms of attracting money suppliers to the market. Whereas the limitation of informal conventional lending providers such as loan sharks is that irrational credit risk assessment with limited funding (Jagtiani & Lemieux, 2018).

From findings of the survey and FGDs, as also supported by national data 2017 on manufacturing MSEs (BPS, 2018), it reveal several reasons why most MSEs find it difficult to get funds from banks. Among them are lack of valuable assets for collateral, no financial records, the proposal is rejected, the type of business is considered not promising, and the business is operated traditionally without a good management system.

How FinTech or P2P lending providers overcome the above mentioned limitations are the followings: (i) they utilize digital footprints as substitutes for physical documents for verification purposes, and/or third-party data (e.g., e-commerce) in order to define eligibility, which results in a lower operational cost as compared to conventional lending; (ii) they process the underwriting assessment using a digital processing platform, with various data points, to identify the typical attributes for interest rate charges without prior collateral; (iii) they have developed a simple and convenient platform for investment, as most of the process are conducted through the digital platform, which attracts a large number of potential lenders; and they have also developed customized credit assessment models, which utilize behavioral data to identify the typical attributes for interest rate charges, supported by large amounts of funding from retail and institutional lenders (Nemoto & Yoshino, 2019; Pranata, 2019; PwC, 2019).

P2P loan disbursement to businesses (productive loans) such as MSEs can be in the form of cash loans or non-cash (e.g., raw materials). Whereas other borrowers such as individuals or households (consumptive loans) are in the form of cash loans or installments.

For MSEs P2P loans have advantages over other financing alternatives, especially in aspects of loan interest rates, conditions, length of the loan disbursement process, and loan size. P2P loan interest rates, as required by the OJK, are small (7 percent). As noted, P2P loans do not require collateral (depending on the loan size). In addition, the loan application process is short (some having one working day) and completely online (CFI, 2018). Overall, P2P loans have advantages as an alternative financing for small businesses compared to conventional banks (including People's Credit Banks), pawnshops, microfinance institutions, and cooperatives.

Among these P2P lending companies is PT Amartha Mikro Fintek. By the end of 2018, the company had distributed loans of more than IDR 635 billion to 152,000 small businesses (most of those owned by women and agricultural sectors). The company increased to IDR 1.7 trillion by the end of 2019. Other P2P lending companies with small businesses as their main target include Drrupiah.com, Cekaya.com, Taralite.com, Credy.co.id, DuitPintar.com, and Modal.co.id.

Table 6.2 shows the profiles of the 10 small business owners who received loans from P2P lending companies. The businesses include small shop owners who sell cell phones, cat food, children's toys, and camping equipment, producers of shoes and furniture, and laundry business owners. In terms of sources of capital, they use their own money or borrow from their suppliers or other informal sources. They also rely on loans from formal sources like P2P lending. Some of this sample received loans from microfinance institutions or a government-designed credit scheme with low interest rates for small businesses, called People Business Credit (or KUR).

Although the 10 respondents received P2P lending, findings from the in-depth interviews show that their own money still plays a crucial role in financing their businesses (see Table 6.2). They all considered P2P loans as an additional fund when their own money and loans from other sources (if any) were not enough to cover their expenditures. A respondent said … *I borrowed this online because the KUR I got was not enough*…On average, P2P loans are between 20 and 30 percent of total needed capital. Only one respondent borrowed money from P2P lending

6 DEVELOPMENT OF FINANCIAL TECHNOLOGY ... 169

Table 6.2 Profile of the surveyed ten small business' owners

Respondents	Profile				
	First year of business	Type of business	Sources of fund		Reason not borrow from bank
			Formal	Non-informal	
I	1990	Billboards	3	4	a
II	2008	Furniture	1,2,3	4,5,6	a
III	2009	Toys	1,2,3	4	a
IV	2017	Cat food	1,3	4	b
V	2001	Handphone	1,3	4	b
VI	2010	Laundry	3	4	a
VII	2009	Snack	1,3	4	a
VIII	2010	Camping equip.	1,3	4,7	a
IX	2009	Fashion	3	4	a
X	2013	Footwear	3	4	b

Note 1: KUR; 2: MFIs; 3: fintech; 4: own money; 5: suppliers; 6: customers; 7: relatives; a: collateral; b: complicated

up to 50 percent of their needed capital. *I need additional capital to expand my business ... Asking for additional credit from banks is not easy and from KUR is very limited,,,,* he said.

The respondents said that P2P lending does not require collateral and the application process is not complicated. Some claimed they could get loans within 24 h. *Even in the middle of the night I can apply for a loan ... just contact* via *the internet or email ...* a respondent admitted. Funds also arrive quickly provided that the requirements (i.e., identification card, family card of the applicant, business license, financial reports, or data about the business) can be fulfilled quickly and the business is considered feasible. However, the P2P loan interest rate is slightly higher than the bank's interest rate. Like most small businesses, especially traders and shop owners who need cash daily or weekly as they deal with suppliers, being able to get a loan at any time without complicated administration and assets as collateral is more important than paying a slightly higher interest rate.

Only five respondents claimed that P2P loans greatly benefited their business. Two said that P2P loans allowed them to expand their business from micro (without workers) to large scale (with several workers). The other respondents said their business scale was relatively the same.

However, they noted that the average turnover per month increased because their working capital increased. With respect to the second five respondents, their business volume did not experience a significant increase. However, due to P2P loans, their business could sustain itself. A respondent even admitted ... *even though I got a loan online, there were many other factors that influenced my business* ...

The above findings do not represent all small businesses in Indonesia that obtained P2P loans. The sample represents 10 customers due to the difficulty of identifying P2P loan-granted small businesses. However, this discovery provides preliminary evidence of the role of P2P lending as an alternative source of funding for small businesses.

The Third Question: The Way P2P Companies Operate and the Ecosystem of MSEs Funding

The 30 P2P lending companies are located in Jakarta, with some customers outside of Jakarta. Others are small businesses in distant districts like West Nusa Tenggara and South Sulawesi Provinces. Types of financing for the sampled companies vary from invoice financing, supply chain financing, merchant financing, microfinancing, and seller financing. The main financing target of most companies is small businesses with legal status. Some provide loans to women empowerment in rural areas, education, property, consumption expenditures, and multifunction. Many of the companies have more than one type of financing; others focus on financing small businesses. Findings from the interviews with randomly selected 8 P2P lending providers who have well recorded their MSE debtors show that many of them since they started their business up to 2019 have continued to expand lending to MSEs (Table 6.3).

Some of the 30 companies surveyed focused on MSE funding. Other companies extended loans to individuals for consumption, education, property, women empowerment, and others. Although the companies are in Jakarta, few have customers outside Jakarta or Java. They channel their funds through branches outside Java.

All of the companies are dependent on outside investors for the provision of funds, such as banks, wealthy people, multifinance companies, venture capital companies, state-owned companies, and other institutions, including from abroad. Of the 30 companies interviewed, 17 admitted that banks are their largest source of funds. For some, banks are the only source of funds. Some companies collaborate with more than one bank.

Table 6.3 Number of MSEs granted loans by the interviewed P2P lending providers

Respondent	First year of business	Indicator	Changes	
			First year	2019
1	2018	No of MSEs (unit)	349	480
		Total credit (IDR million)	51	81
2	2017	No of MSEs	113	113
		Total credit (IDR million)	111	111
3	2018	No of MSEs	2428	2428
		Total credit (IDR million)	19,642.5	19,642.5
4	2018	No of MSEs	3321	3472
		Total credit (IDR million)	52,673.8	114,453.9
5	2017	No of MSEs	0	8
		Total credit (IDR million)	0	39,965.6
6	2018	No of MSEs	2788	5180
		Total credit (IDR trillion)	1.17	2.94
7	2017	No of MSEs	0	1967
		Total credit (IDR million)	0	601,664.3
8	2016	No of MSEs	32	11,470
		Total credit (IDR million)	6058	26,073.6

Source Interviews

They prefer to collaborate with banks to obtain more funds. Of course, they must submit the names of prospective borrowers and their creditworthiness to the bank. The bank assesses the information before approving the funding. The number of MSEs funded by the bank, although indirectly, can increase at a relatively lower cost. From the government's perspective, this is a positive assessment for the bank as it relates its policies to require all banks in Indonesia to extend credit to MSMEs.

Although at first the banks felt the presence of FinTech as a threat to their business, banks are expected to be the main investor for FinTech companies in Indonesia.

FinTech is a new phenomenon. Not all banks in Indonesia are familiar with the system and culture of P2P lending companies (cooperation between banks and P2P lending companies). Therefore, both parties may face obstacles. Based on the results of several FGDs, Table 6.4 presents the obstacles faced by the surveyed P2P lending companies collaborated with banks.

As discussed before in the literature review, according to Mathews (2018), there are three types of collaboration between banks and P2P lending companies, namely software-as-a-service, referrals, and outright purchase. While according to Hatami (2018), there are four models of collaboration, namely channel, supplier, satellite, and merger. From the survey and FGDs' results, it turns out that the most adopted type of collaboration is referrals and at the same time banks act as the main suppliers of funds. This type provides financial service offerings to individuals without bank accounts, and it allows P2P lending providers to offer faster customer onboarding, processing, and approval times, cheaper loans, and alternative methods of funding and credit lines. A proposition is made by integrating the capabilities of fintech companies in bank offerings. For customers, the offer looks like a bank that provides services

Table 6.4 Constraints faced by P2P lending companies when collaborating with banks

- The bank requires face-to-face customer verification. The fintech system is online
- The bank lacks real-time transaction technology. Requests for transactions must be made via email and tellers, which takes a long time. There is no connection to send or exchange real-time data between the bank and P2P lending companies
- There are no restrictions by the authority (OJK). Yet many banks are hesitant to cooperate with P2P lending companies because they are unclear on existing regulations
- The way the bank calculates loans installments, as well as interest and penalties, is often different from the method applied by the P2P lending company
- Risk perception in conservative-classified banks can become an obstacle for the distribution of funds to P2P lending companies, especially for the agricultural sector where risk tends to be high. P2P lending companies serve businesses in all sectors if all requirements are met
- Bureaucracy in the banking sector is often long and complicated. This makes lending from P2P companies take a long time. However, one of the characteristics that is also one of the advantages of fintech compared to banks is that credit is fast and easy
- Many banks still consider collaboration with P2P lending companies as a high-risk business. This hampers many banks' cooperation in funding and customer references

(even if there are statements about a fintech's contributions to the terms and conditions of the offer).

Regarding channeling funds, some companies go directly to MSE. Others channel through intermediary institutions like cooperatives, distributors, suppliers, multifinance companies, and others. The main reason they pass through intermediary institutions is that it is easier or more efficient in reaching many prospective borrowers. In addition, there is more certainty that the loan plus the interest will be paid according to the agreement. In other words, intermediary institutions act as guarantors. For example, a shoe-making cooperative whose members are shoe craftsmen. To increase the volume of production which requires additional capital, the cooperative applies for a loan to a P2P lending company, and the funds raised are given to members who really need it. Thus, in this case the cooperative guarantees the credit to the P2P lending provider, while the members who used the funds are responsible to the cooperative. Meanwhile, lending to a small business through a supplier of raw materials is in the form of purchasing raw materials. The payment will be made within a certain time by the small business owner to the supplier as agreed, and then the supplier will repay back the loan to the P2P lending provider.

Overall, Fig. 6.5 describes the ecosystem of MSE funding by FinTech-based P2P lending companies in Indonesia. It can be seen that, although for many P2P lending providers banks are their main suppliers of funds, many P2P lending providers have more than one source of funds, such as individual investors, mutual finance companies, and venture capital

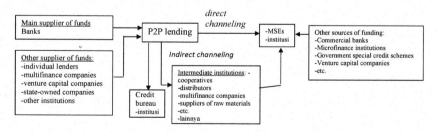

Fig. 6.5 Ecosystem of MSEs funding with the emergence of P2P lending provider in Indonesia

companies. The latter channel a lot of funds to start-up companies but through P2P lending companies that act as guarantors. In addition, many state-owned companies act as investors in many P2P lending companies. This is in line with the policy in Indonesia which requires every state-owned companies to set aside a percentage of their profits to help small businesses in various forms, including funding.

REFERENCES

Bavoso, V. (2019). The promise and perils of alternative market-based finance: The case of P2P lending in the UK. *Journal of Banking Regulation, 21*, 395–409. https://doi.org/10.1057/s41261-019-00118-9

BIS & FSB. (2017). *FinTech credit: Market structure, business models and financial stability implications.* Bank for International Settlements. https://www.bis.org/publ/cgfs_fsb1.htm

BPS. (2018, June). *Profil Industri Mikro dan Kecil 2017* [2017 Micro and small industry profile]. Badan Pusat Statistik.

BRC. (2020). *Fintech global market opportunities and strategies.* The Business Research Company. https://www.thebusinessresearchcompany.com/report/fintech-global-market-report

Bruton, G. D., Khavul, S., Siegel, D. S., & Write, M. (2015). New financial alternatives in seeding entrepreneurship: Microfinance, crowdfunding, and peer to peer innovations. *Entrepreneurship Theory and Practice, 39*(1), 9–26.

Buckley, R. P., & Webster, S. (2016). *Fintech in developing countries: Charting new customer journeys* (UNSW Law Research Paper No. 2016–73). University of New South Wales. Retrieved February 11, 2018, from https://ssrn.com/abstract=2850091

CFI. (2018). *Accelerating Financial Inclusion with New Data.* May, Washington, DC: Center for Financial Inclusion. https://www.centerforfinancialinclusion.org/accelerating-financial-inclusion-with-new-data-2

Computer Business Review. (2016). *UK fintech VC investment booms to almost $1bn.* http://www.cbronline.com/news/verticals/finance/uk-fintech-vc-investmentbooms-to-almost-1b4820702

Creehan, S. (2019). How digital innovation can increase small business access to finance in Asia. In N. Nemoto & N. Yoshino (Eds.), *Fintech for Asian SMEs* (1–17). Asian Development Bank Institute.

Cumming, D., & Schwienbacher, A. (2016). *Fintech venture capital* (SSRN Working Paper). http://ssrn.com/abstract=2784797

DDLLC. (2018). *Closing the gap in fintech collaboration: Overcoming obstacles to a symbiotic relationship.* https://www2.deloitte.com/content/dam/Deloitte/global/Documents/Financial-Services/gx-fsi-dcfs-fintech-collaboration.pdf

6 DEVELOPMENT OF FINANCIAL TECHNOLOGY ... 175

Eugenia, O. A. (2018). Peer-to-peer lending: Business model analysis and the platform dilemma. *International Journal of Finance, Economics and Trade, 2*(3), 31–41.

EYGM Limited. (2017). *Unleashing the potential of FinTech in banking*. https://www.ey.com/en_gl/banking-capital-markets/five-challenges-for-banks-as-they-evolve-risk-management

Feng, Y., Fan, X., & Yoon, Y. (2015). Lenders and borrowers' strategies in online peer-to-peer lending market: An empirical analysis of ppdai.com. *Journal of Electronic Commerce Research, 16*(3), 242–260.

Frost, J. (2020). *The economic forces driving fintech adoption across countries* (BIS Working Papers No. 838). Monetary and Economic Department, Bank for International Settlements. https://www.bis.org/publ/work838.pdf

Ghanem, E. (2018). *Banks and FinTech collaborate via different engagement approaches*. Capgemini Financial Services Analysis. https://www.capgemini.com/2018/08/banks-and-fintechs-collaboration-by-engagement/#_ftn

Government Office for Science. (2015). *Fintech futures: The UK as a world leader in financial technologies*. UK Government Chief Scientific Adviser. https://www.gov.uk/government/uploads/system/uploads/att achment_data/file/413095/gs-15-3-fintech-futures.pdf

Haddad, C., & Hornuf, L. (2016). *The emergence of the global fintech market: Economic and technological determinants*. https://www.researchgate.net/pub lication/307957382

Han, L., Xiao, J. J., & Zhi, S. (2018). Financing knowledge, risk attitude and P2P borrowing in China. *International Journal of Consumer Studies, 43*(2), 166–177.

Hatami, A. (2018). *Bank & FinTech collaboration models*. https://medium.com/@ahatami/bank-fintech-collaborations-how-big-banks-plan-to-stand-up-to-the-big-tech-challenge-24eea57db095

Hendriyani, C., & Sam'un J. R. (2019). Business agility strategy: Peer-to-peer lending of Fintech startup in the era of digital finance in Indonesia. *Review of Integrative Business and Economics Research, 8*(4), 239–246.

Iman, N. (2020). The rise and rise of financial technology: The good, the bad, and the verdict. *Cogent Business & Management, 7*(1). https://doi.org/10.1080/23311975.2020.1725309

IMF. (2019). *Financial inclusion of small and medium-sized enterprises in the Middle East and Central Asia*. International Monetary Fund. https://www.imf.org/en/Publications/Departmental-Papers-Policy-Papers/Issues/2019/02/11/Financial-Inclusion-of-Small-and-Medium-Sized-Enterprises-in-the-Middle-East-and-Central-Asia-46335

Iyer, R., Khwaja, A. I., Luttmer, E. F. P., & Shue, K. (2016). Screening peers softly: Inferring the quality of small borrowers. *Management Science, 62*, 1554–1577.

Jagtiani, J., & Lemieux, C. (2018). Do Fintech lenders penetrate areas that are underserved by traditional banks? *Journal of Economics and Business, 100*, 43–54.

Lin, M., & Viswanathan, S. (2015). Home bias in online investments: An empirical study of an online crowdfunding market. *Management Science, 62*, 1393–1414.

Lukonga, I. (2018). *Fintech, inclusive growth and cyber risks: A focus on the MENAP and CCA regions* (IMF Working Paper No. 18/201). International Monetary Fund. www.imf.org/en/Publications/WP/Issues/2018/09/11/Fintech-Inclusive-Growth-and-Cyber-Risks-Focus-on-the-MENAP-and-CCA-Regions-46190

Mathews, A. (2018). *Mutually beneficial bank-FinTech collaboration models.* https://gomedici.com/mutually-beneficial-bank-fintech-collaboration-models/

Milne, A., & Parboteeah, P. (2016). *The business models and economics of peer-to-peer lending.* The European Credit Research Institute (ECRI). https://www.ceps.eu/ceps-publications/business-models-and-economics-peer-peer-lending/

Morgan, P. J., & Trinh, L. Q. (2019). *Fintech and financial literacy in the LAO PDR* (ADBI Working Paper Series No. 933). Asian Development Bank Institute.

Nemoto, N., & Yoshino, N. (Eds.) (2019). *Fintech for Asian SMEs.* ADBi.

Nemoto, N., Storey, D., & Huang, B. (2019). Optimal regulation of peer-to-peer lending for SMEs. In N. Nemoto & N. Yoshino (Eds.), *Fintech for Asian SMEs.* Asian Development Bank Institute (ADBi).

Oh, E. Y., & Rosenkranz, P. (2020). *Determinants of peer-to-peer lending expansion: The roles of financial development and financial literacy* (ADB Economics Working Paper Series No. 613, March). Asian Development Bank.

Pranata, N. (2019). The role of digital payments fintech in accelerating the development of MSMEs in Indonesia. In N. Nemoto & N. Yoshino (Eds.), *Fintech for Asian SMEs.* Asian Development Bank Institute.

PwC. (2019, September). *Indonesia's Fintech lending.*

RM. (2020a). *Peer-to-peer lending—Global market trajectory & analytics.* Research and Markets. https://www.businesswire.com/news/home/20201215005523/en/Global-Peer-to-Peer-P2P-Lending-Market-Trends-Growth-Opportunity-Report-2020-2025---ResearchAndMarkets.com

RM. (2020b). *The ASEAN Peer-to-Peer (P2P) lending market, 2020.* Research and Markets. https://www.researchandmarkets.com/reports/5174497/the-asean-peer-to-peer-p2p-lending-market-2020#relb0-5181490

Serrano-Cinca, C., Gutiérrez-Nieto, B., & López-Palacios, L. (2015, Oktober). Determinants of default in P2P lending. *PLoS ONE, 10.* https://www.ncbi.nlm.nih.gov/pubmed/26425854

Tambunan, T. T. H. (2018a). Micro, small and medium enterprises in ASEAN: Regional Focus. *International Journal of Small and Medium Enterprises and Business Sustainability, 3*(1), 99–132.

Tambunan, T. T. H. (2018b). The performance of Indonesia's public credit guarantee scheme for MSMEs: A regional comparative perspective: Research Note. *Journal of Southeast Asian Economic, 35*(2), 319–332.

Tambunan, T., Santoso, W., Busneti, I., & Batunanggar, S. (2021). The development of MSMEs and the growth of peer-to-peer (P2P) lending in Indonesia. *International Journal of Innovation, Creativity and Change, 15*(2), 585–611.

Thakora, A. V. (2019). Fintech and banking: What do we know? *Journal of Financial Intermediation, 41.* https://doi.org/10.1016/j.jfi.2019.100833

Toronto Centre. (2017, August). *FinTech, RegTech and SupTech: What they mean for financial supervision.* TC Notes. Toronto Leadership Centre. https://res.torontocentre.org/guidedocs/FinTech%20RegTech%20and%20S upTech%20%20What%20They%20Mean%20for%20Financial%20Supervision% 20FINAL.pdf

CHAPTER 7

Theoretical Contributions: General Conclusions

7.1 Theories on the Pattern of Change and Development of MSMEs

In discussing industrial systems and the role of MSMEs within the systems and their pattern of overall development, there are two different key theories, the so-called "classical" theories and the "modern" theories. The classical theories emphasized the relationship between income levels or economic development and the existence or development and growth of MSMEs. While the modern theories explicitly emphasize the importance of such as subcontracting networks, clustering, technologies, entrepreneurship, and innovation for the development of MSMEs.

The Classical Theories

The classical theories mainly focused on the manufacturing industry, and it started with the 1965's article of Staley and Morse (cited by Tambunan, 2009). In their substantial study, based on the experience of industrialized countries and developing countries, they identified three categories of conditions for the predominance of MSMEs: (i) location, (ii) manufacturing process, and (iii) market or type of product. With respect to the first category of condition, factories processing a dispersed raw material (mainly rural industries) and products for local markets and with

© The Author(s), under exclusive license to Springer Nature
Singapore Pte Ltd. 2022
T. T.H. Tambunan, *Fostering Resilience through Micro,*
Small and Medium Enterprises, Sustainable Development Goals Series,
https://doi.org/10.1007/978-981-16-9435-6_7

relatively high transport costs are two main important local conditions. Separable manufacturing operations, crafts, or precision handworks, and simple assembly, mixing, or finishing operations are the main important conditions for the predominance of MSMEs with respect to the second category of condition. The market condition is in the form of differentiated products with low-scale economies and industries serving small markets. The significance of these three types of conditions may be different for MSMEs in different sub-sectors. For instance, market condition is a particularly important determinant for the dominance of MSMEs in the industries serving small markets such as the wood and furniture industries, because total demand for these products is usually limited as compared to many other consumer goods such as food and beverages, footwear, and clothing. While the condition of factories which processed a dispersed raw material is considered as a significant explanation for the dominance of small-and medium-scale food industries in rural areas.

Among these conditions, Staley and Morse (1965), as cited by Tambunan (2009), argued that particularly separable or specific manufacturing operations (for example, MSMEs produce certain components for LEs) and differentiated products having low-scale economies are the most important explanatory factors for the presence of MSMEs in developing countries.

Another important article was from Hoselitz (1959) and Anderson (1982) (cited by Tambunan, 2009). They had developed a generalized typology of growth phases of MSMEs and LEs based on the experiences of industrialized countries to explain changes in size of the industry and industrial structure over time in developing countries. Accordingly, during economic development, the composition of manufacturing activities, if classified according to scale, appeared to pass through three phases. In phase one, at the "early" stage of industrial development, which was the main characteristic of agrarian economies, MSEs in manufacturing activities, often called in the literature as cottage and household industries, i.e., non-factory or craft-based enterprises, were dominant in terms of their total number of production units and share in total manufacturing employment.

This was a stage of industrialization in which a large number of MSEs (mainly in rural areas) coexist with a quite limited number of larger-scale industries (mainly foreign or state-owned firms located in urban areas or large cities). In this stage, MSEs were dominant in industries like garment, smithy, footwear, handicrafts, masons, industries making simple building materials, and various crop-processing industries. They are closely linked to agricultural production as providers of basic inputs and processing services for output from agriculture and to the non-food needs of rural populations. In developing countries, these industries are characterized by substantial ease of entry, especially for the clothing, food, and handicraft industries, the initial capital requirement is very low, and the producers involved do not need high expertise and a special workshop to carry out these activities. Perhaps, it is for this reason that activities are undertaken mostly by women and children as part time jobs. However, their income from running MSEs serves an important role as a source of secondary family income. Most of the companies in these activities are self-employed or one-person units in which the owners carry out all the activities.

In phase two, in more developed regions with higher incomes per capita, MEs started to emerge and increased at a comparatively rapid rate and acted to displace MSEs in several industries. There were some factors which might explain the expansion of MEs industries in this stage of development.

In phase three, at the "later" stage of development, LEs become predominant, displacing the remaining MSMEs in some industries. This phase was partly a product of phase two, since the recorded growth of output and employment in LEs could be divided into: (a) the growth of once SEs through the size structure and (b) the expansion of already LEs. However, the expansion of LEs in this stage may also be caused, to a certain extent, by new large-scale entrants, which was not thought by Anderson and his analysis.

In this final phase, factors such as greater use of economies of scale with respect to plant, management, marketing, and distribution (depending on types of products and production flexibility); superior technical and management efficiency; better productive coordination and access to supporting infrastructure services and external finance; and concessionary finance along with investment incentives, tariff structures, and government subsidies were powerful causes and incentives for firms to grow larger. In practice, these factors were more favorable for large or modern industries than for small and traditional ones and so they may explain the eventual better performance of larger enterprises than that of small ones in advanced stages of industrialization.

The output composition of MSMEs, especially in the manufacturing industry, also appeared to shift with development. As income per capita increased, the activities of MSMEs shifted from "light" manufacturing

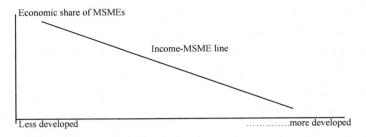

Fig. 7.1 "Classical" hypothesis on the link between the importance of MSMEs and economic development

with simple processing to intermediate and then to capital goods with more complicated processing ("heavy" manufacturing). In other words, the higher the income per capita, the lower the share of MSMEs (as a percentage of total employment in MSMEs) in light manufacturing and the higher their share in heavy manufacturing, especially in machine and transport equipment industries. Not only between manufacturing sub-sectors but also within a sub-sector a shift of MSMEs also took place with the process of development from producing "traditional" goods (i.e., kind of activities undertaken mainly by women and children) to making more sophisticated or "modern" goods. In other words, with the process of development, the share of MSMEs in industries producing "traditional" goods as a percentage of total employment or units in these industries declines.

To sum up, the "classical" theories on MSMEs predicted that in the course of economic development (reflected by the increase of per capita real income/gross domestic product [GDP]), the "economic" share of MSMEs (their shares in GDP, employment, sectoral output, and total enterprises), would decline steadily. Those of large and modern enterprises, on the other hand, would take off rapidly and finally they dominate the economy (Fig. 7.1).

The Modern Theories

It turns out that this classical theory estimate is not proven. Currently both in developed and developing countries, their economy is dominated by MSMEs not only in number but also in contribution to the formation

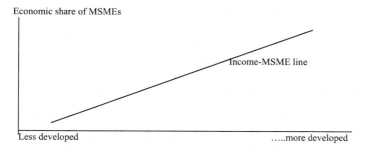

Fig. 7.2 "Modern" hypothesis on the link between the importance of MSMEs and economic development

or growth of GDP. Based on this fact, new ideas emerge regarding the factors that influence the dynamics of MSMEs. These new ideas, or often classified as modern theories of the growth of MSMEs, assume a positive relationship between the growth of MSMEs and the growth of GDP or the level of economic development (Fig. 7.2). The modern theories are in the fields of, among others, flexible specialization, entrepreneurship and innovation, internationalization, and company growth theories.

The concept of flexible specialization has been closely associated with Piore and Sabel's (1984) seminal work on the "second industrial divide" in which they discussed the re-emergence of craft-based regions in some countries in Europe, namely Italy, Austria, and Germany. In examining the development of craft-based regions in these countries, Piore and Sabel (1984) argued that MSMEs located in these regions have become the new dominant form of industrial organization. These industries are characterized by high and multi-skilled workers, "flexible" machinery which embodied the latest technologies and small batch production of a range of specialized products manufactured for the global market. There are four common organizational forms of flexible specialization identified in Piore and Sabel's (1984) study:

1. flexible and specialization: firms in the community could rapidly adapt their production techniques but remain specialized in the production of one type of good, for instance, garments;
2. limited entry: firms in the community form part of a bounded community from which outsiders are largely excluded;

3. high level of competitive innovation: there is continuous pressure on firms in the community to promote innovation in order to keep an edge on their competitor;
4. high level of cooperation: there exists limited competition among firms in the community over wages and working conditions, encouraging greater cooperation between them.

Since the publication of this Piore and Sabel's book in 1984, not only these new characteristics and modes of industrial organization have been widely discussed but several authors have attempted to assess the relevance of the flexible specialization paradigm in industrial districts dominated by MSMEs in developed countries. Many others have also attempted to assess the implications for industry, particularly MSMEs, in developing countries.

The main argument of the flexible specialization thesis is that MSMEs can grow fast or even faster than LEs with the process of development. In many developed countries such as Europe, Japan, South Korea, and the United States, MSMEs in some industries such as electronics and automotive have been found to be very significant as sources of invention, innovation, and efficiency. They have been found to be capable to stand the competition with LEs, and even to improve their current relative position in several instances.

The literature on the entrepreneurship and innovation theory emphasizes that MSMEs that carry out an innovation strategy are those that will be able to make competitive products, which means that they can survive and even develop rapidly. This new role of MSMEs can also be read from a paragraph in Audretsch's paper (2003) as follows:

> Such new SMEs deploying a strategy of innovation to attain competitiveness are apparently engaged in the selection process. Only those SMEs offering a viable product that can be produced efficiently will grow ... The remainder will stagnate, ... may ultimately be forced to exit the industry. Thus, in highly innovative industries, there is a continuing process of the entry of new SMEs into industries. (Audretsch, 2003)

Deshpandé et al. (2013) emphasize that by continuing to innovate, newly established companies are able to compete and survive in the market with established players or even with foreign companies. Other publications on the important role of innovation in the development of

MSMEs through their ability to compete in the market include Zahra et al. (2004, 2005) who state that family firms, which are mainly MSMEs, are widely recognized as a major source of technological innovation and economic progress. Yet, over time, some family firms become conservative and unwilling to take the risks associated with entrepreneurial activities.

Apart from innovation, the level of entrepreneurship or entrepreneurial orientation (EO) is also very important for the growth of a company. No doubt that EO has a positive effect on innovation activities in a company. In much of the literature EO is considered as one of the main resources that facilitate organizations or companies to find new ways to increase revenue streams, increase the chances of success in international markets and effectively utilize organizational resources (among others, Covin et al., 2006; Hussain et al., 2017). Hussain et al. (2017), for example, investigated empirically the effect of EO on the performance of MSMEs by conducting a field survey on 213 MSMEs in the manufacturing industry. The findings of their study revealed that organizational or company performance and EO are positively related to each other.

In internationalization theory, many experts such as Peng and Delios (2006), Abdullah and Zain (2011), and Scarborough (2012) emphasized that internationalization is a key determinant of the growth of a company. The strong reasons that justify this statement are as follows: the interests of the companies themselves to survive and thrive, the perception that they are threatened in the domestic environment, the awareness of the large business opportunities abroad, and the impact of various events and external forces. As stated by Zahra et al. (2005), the main reasons for doing or expanding a business abroad included market expansion, more financial gain, and learning new ideas.

In the case of MSMEs, as explained by Long (2003), there is no doubt that the contribution of MSMEs to exports, to some extent, is closely related to their ability to internationalize. This is also a very important factor that measures the level of global competitiveness of MSMEs. The low global competitiveness of MSMEs in developing countries in general can be a serious obstacle for them not only to penetrate the global market but also to be able to win the competition with imported goods in the domestic market, which means influencing their ability to survive in the domestic market or develop into a larger business scale. According to Matenge (2011), the internationalization of MSMEs can develop by itself (although not all MSMEs will give the same response) from the availability of new open markets through deregulations and competitions for these emerging markets.

Finally, the company growth theory identifies the determinants of company growth and the relationship between these factors and the company growth which is very complex. Recognizing this, several researchers in this area have developed various frameworks. Churchill and Lewis (1983; cited by Weldeslassie et al., 2015), for instance, developed a growth model by breaking a company's growth continuum into developmental stages. At every stage in the life of a company, various factors such as the goals of the company owner, managerial skills, access to capital/credit, application of technology, and other resources are generally understood as determinants of growth.

According to Mao (2009) and Degenhardt et al. (2002), the theory of company growth is based on three sub-theories, and the first is the scale limit theory that reflects transaction costs to explain the reasons for company generation and determine the scale of the business. The second is the life cycle theory which considers a company as the body of life. The third is the gene combination theory which involves a biological corporation concept in which a company is seen as an organism. From a life cycle perspective, the growth of MSMEs is divided into three stages: "initial" growth (startup), established regeneration and "expansion", and "diversification" stages of aging and "death".

Figure 7.3 illustrates the theory of company growth based on this life cycle theory. In the early stages of growth, a business is formed/started, products are developed, experiences are created, and the company experienced a relatively low rate of production or turnover or profit growth. After successfully passing the initial stage, the company started to enter the next stage, namely the expansion stage, marked by a rapid increase in production volume, income or profit, and the number of workers. Then after some time (the length of which could be a year or several years depending on many factors, especially market conditions or the level of competition in the market and changes in technology and tastes or behavior of the general public or consumers who have been buying the company's products), reached an established stage, or saturation, marked by the point at which the initial business ideas and concepts will no longer warrant further dynamic expansion. Therefore, the growth rate of the company either declines and dies or is forced to advance to a broader business concept from the diversification stage where products and services

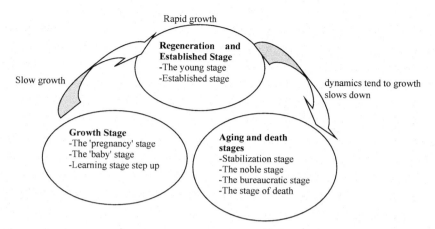

Fig. 7.3 Company growth theory based on life cycle theory (*Source* Degenhardt et al. [2002], Mao [2009], William [2017])

can go back through the growth process as before (Degenhardt et al., 2002).

In his dissertation, William (2017) discussed various theoretical models that have been developed that describe the growth of small businesses like MSMEs. One class of theoretical models focuses on the learning process, both active and passive, and the other models refer to stochastic and deterministic approaches. In the passive learning model, a company enters the market without knowing its own growth potential. Only after entering did the company begin to learn about the distribution of its own profitability based on information from realized profits. Continually updating such learning, the company decides to expand, contract, or exit the market. This learning model states that companies and company managers learn about their efficiency once they are established in the industry.

As described by Degenhardt et al. (2002), firms expanded their activities when managers observed that their estimation of managerial efficiency underestimated the level of actual efficiency. As firms grew older, the estimation of managerial efficiency becomes more accurate which reduced the likelihood that output will vary widely from one year to another. The implication of this theoretical model is that smaller and younger firms should have higher and more viable growth rates.

188   T. T.H. TAMBUNAN

Whereas in the active learning model, a company explores its economic environment actively and invests to increase its growth under competitive pressures from inside and outside the company. Potential and actual growth change over time in response to the investment returns of the companies themselves, and other actors in the same market. According to this model, business owners or managers can increase their efficiency through formal education and trainings which increased their knowledge or resources. Entrepreneurs or managers who are highly educated with a lot of work experiences and have attended many trainings are able, at least theoretically, to make their companies grow faster. In other words, a company grows if it has, or closes if it has not, successfully passed all kinds of obstacles in the earlier phase of its establishment (Degenhardt et al., 2002).

"Push" Versus "Pull" Factors

These theories, both classical and modern, did not pay much attention to the relationship between poverty and the growth of MSMEs, especially MSEs. MSEs in developing or poor countries are very different from MSEs in developed or high-income countries. In poor countries, most MSEs are low-income or seasonal activities with low productivity and produce very simple and low-quality goods at low prices which are mostly only sold in the local market. As explained in Chapter 1, the owners or entrepreneurs of MSEs as well as their hired workers mostly are low educated and come from poor families. Because they could not find better jobs elsewhere, they have no other choice than to do MSE activities (either as a primary or a secondary or a temporary/seasonal source of income) as a means for them to survive. Thus, they are "pushed", not "pulled" to do MSE activities (Fig. 7.4).

In other words, the above discussed theories are more relevant to socio-economic conditions in developed countries where poverty is not a serious problem. While in developing, especially low-income countries where most of the population is poor, the relationship between the growth in the number of MSMEs, especially MSEs and the growth in the number of poor people is positive (Fig. 7.5). When income per capita increases or poverty decreases, reflecting better employment opportunities elsewhere, less labor supply to MSEs or less people want to run own low-income generating economic activities.

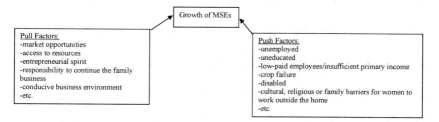

Fig. 7.4 "Pull" and "Push" determinant factors of the growth of MSEs in developing countries

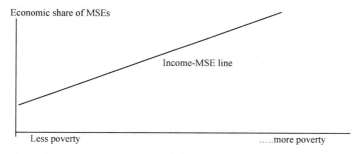

Fig. 7.5 Hypothesis on the link between the importance of MSEs and poverty

7.2 Theories on the Impact of Economic Crises on MSMEs

Chapter 5 has shown that different types of crises have different transmission channels through which the crisis affected MSMEs and pose different business risks, and therefore require different CMMs. So, an economic crisis may not affect all MSMEs in all sectors, it depends on the type of the crisis and therefore its transmission channels. For instance, the COVID-19 pandemic crisis could be considered as a combination of market demand and market supply (production) crises, as a result of the "anti-Covid-19 impact policy". From the market demand side, evidently, only MSMEs that made finished products (good and service) and were heavily dependent on offline marketing were hit hardly as people were staying at home. Whereas from the market supply side, generally, only LEs with large numbers of workers such as textile, apparel, electronics companies, and businesses which became a gathering place for many people such as cafes and restaurants, entertainment venues, cinemas, hotels, and malls that had to close during the pandemic period. Meanwhile, micro businesses that only employed less than 5 workers such as small car repair shops, small car washes, small shops, or business units without workers such as craftsmen, small traders, and food stalls remained open.

7.3 Policy Implications

Given the push and pull factors that affect the growth of MSEs in developing countries, it is then clear that the handling of MSEs in developing countries is different from that in developed countries. The handling of MSEs must also be different from the handling of MEs due to the factors of poverty, low education, and other limitations commonly suffered by the poor. Government intervention in MSEs is not enough to focus solely on funding, but also needs to pay attention to the improvement of skills of MSEs owners and workers as well as their innovation capabilities, and to help in the production process, procurement of raw materials, and marketing.

In the case of MSMEs during an economic crisis, based on the Indonesian experience with the 1997/98 Asia financial crisis and the COVID-19 pandemic crisis, this chapter has two policy implications. First, to increase the effectiveness of the fiscal stimulus package or other forms of government assistance, MSMEs most affected must be identified first. And for that, the type of the crisis and its main transmission channel as well as the types of related business risks need to be known in advance. Second, the form of stimulus must be in accordance with the CMM adopted by the target MSMEs. In other words, stimulus packages or other forms of government assistance must complement, not substitute, the adopted CMM. Different CMMs responding to different business risks require different policy approaches and therefore different forms of government assistance or fiscal stimulus packages.

REFERENCES

Abdullah, N. A. H. N., & Zain, S. N. M. (2011). The internationalization theory and Malaysian Small Medium Enterprises (SMEs). *International Journal of Trade, Economics and Finance, 2*(4), 318–322.

Audretsch, D. B. (2003). Entrepreneurship, innovation and globalization: Does Singapore need a new policy approach. In R. S. Rajan (Ed.), *Sustaining competitiveness in the new global economy*. Edward Elgar.

Covin, J. G., Green, K. M., & Slevin, D. P. (2006). Strategic process effects on the entrepreneurial orientation–sales growth rate relationship. *Entrepreneurship Theory and Practice, 30*(1), 57–81.

Degenhardt, S. S., Stamm, A., & Zehdnicker, M. (2002). *The growth gap: A small enterprise phenomenon*. Synthesis Document, The Donor Committee for Enterprise Development German, DCED Secretariat.

Deshpandé, R., Grinstein, A., Kim, S. H., & Ofek, E. (2013). Achievement motivation, strategic orientations and business performance in entrepreneurial firms: How different are Japanese and American founders? *International Marketing Review, 30*(3), 231–252.

Hussain, J., Abbas, Q., & Khan, M. A. (2017). Entrepreneurial orientation and performance: The moderating effect of market orientation. *Global Management Journal for Academic & Corporate Studies, 7*(1), 9–18.

Long, N. V. (2003). *Performance and obstacles of SMEs in Viet Nam Policy implications in near future* (Unpublished research paper). International IT Policy Program (ITPP), Seoul National University.

Mao, H. (2009). Review on enterprise growth theories. *International Journal of Business and Management, 4*(8), 20–22.

Matenge, T. (2011). Small firm internationalization—A developing country perspective. *International Journal of Business Administration, 2*(4), 103–111.

Peng, M. W., & Delios, A. (2006). What determines the scope of the firm over time and around the world? An Asia Pacific perspective. *Asia Pacific Journal of Management, 23*(4), 385–405.

Piore, M. J., & Sabel, C. F. (1984). *The second industrial divide*. Basic Books.

Scarborough, N. M. (2012). *Effective small business management: An entrepreneurial approach* (Vol. 10). Prentice Hall.

Tambunan, T. T. H. (2009). *SME in Asian developing countries*. Palgrave Macmillan.

Weldeslassie, H. A., Kibrom, G., Minwyelet, L., Tsegay, M., Tekola, N.H., & Gidey, Y. (2015, June). *Exploring the status, prospects and contributions of Micro, Small and Medium Enterprises (MSMEs) in Ethiopia*. Aksum University.

William, E. (2017). *Business constraints affecting the small and micro enterprises in Tanzania: A case of Bahi District in Dodoma region*. Ph.D. dissertation, St. John's University of Tanzania.

Zahra, S., Hayton, J., & Salvato, C. (2004). Entrepreneurship in family vs. non-family firms: A resource-based analysis of the effect of organizational culture. *Entrepreneurship Theory and Practice, 28*(4), 363–381.

Zahra, S. A., Korri, J. S., & Yu, J. (2005). Cognition and international entrepreneurship: Implications for research on international opportunity recognition and exploitation. *International Business Review, 14*(2), 129–146.

REFERENCES

Abdullah, M. A. (2002). An overview of the macroeconomic contribution of small and medium enterprises in Malaysia. In C. Harvie & B.-C. Lee (Eds.), *The role of SMEs in national economies in East Asia*. Edward Elgar.

Abdullah, N. A. H. N., & Zain, S. N. M. (2011). The internationalization theory and Malaysian small medium enterprises (SMEs). *International Journal of Trade, Economics and Finance, 2*(4), 318–322.

ADB. (1999). *Women in Sri Lanka*. Asian Development Bank.

ADB. (2001). *Women in Bangladesh*. Asian Development Bank.

ADB. (2009). *Key indicators for Asia and the Pacific 2009*. Asian Development Bank.

ADB. (2015). *Asia SME finance monitor 2014*. Asian Development Bank.

ADB. (2020, March 6). *The economic impact of the COVID-19 outbreak on developing Asia* (ADB Briefs, No.128). Asian Development Bank.

Adedayo, S. J., Salau, A. A., Abdulraheem, I., & Zekeri, A. (2020). An assessment of perceptions on entrepreneurship and self-reliance among cooperative societies in Kwara State, Nigeria. *Fuoye Journal of Agriculture and Human Ecology, 3*(1), 14–22.

Adekunle, O. A., Ola, T. O., Ogunrinade, R., & Odebunmi, A. T. (2021). The role of cooperative societies in advancing small and medium scale enterprises in Osun state, Nigeria. *Journal of International Business and Management, 4*(6), 1–13.

© The Editor(s) (if applicable) and The Author(s), under exclusive license to Springer Nature Singapore Pte Ltd. 2022
T. T.H. Tambunan, *Fostering Resilience through Micro, Small and Medium Enterprises*, Sustainable Development Goals Series, https://doi.org/10.1007/978-981-16-9435-6

194 REFERENCES

Afifiyah, S. (2020, April 11). *Jenis Usaha yang Justru Melejit Saat Wabah Covid-19* [The type of business that actually skyrocketed during the Covid-19 outbreak]. Tagar.id. https://www.tagar.id/jenis-usaha-yang-justru-melejit-saat-wabah-covid19

AKATIGA & the Asia Foundation. (1999, August). *The impact of economic crisis on Indonesian small and medium enterprises.* Study prepared for the United States Agency for International Development, Jakarta.

Alam, M. S. (2017). Participation of emerging markets in global value chains (GVCs) and factors hindering the operations of small and medium enterprises (SMEs). *International Journal of Small and Medium Enterprises and Business Sustainability, 2*(3), 1–21.

Amini, A. M., & Ramezani, M. (2008). Investigating the success factors of poultry growers' cooperatives in Iran's western provinces. *World Applied Sciences Journal, 5*(1), 81–87.

Amornkitvikai, Y., Harvie, C., & Charoenrat, T. (2012). *Factor affecting the export participation and performance of thai manufacturing small and medium sized enterprises (SMEs).* Research Online, Faculty of Commerce, University of Wollongong. http://ro.uow.edu.au/cgi/viewcontent.cgi?articicle=2090&context=commpapers

Anwar, K. (2020, April). *10.238 UMKM di Kota Serang Terdampak Wabah COVID-19* [10,238 MSMEs in Serang city affected by the COVID-19 outbreak]. https://banten.idntimes.com/business/economy/khaerul-anwar-2/10238-umkm-di-kota-serang-terdampak-wabah-covid

APEC. (2002). *Profile of SMEs and SME issues in APEC 1990–2000.* APEC Secretariat.

APEC. (2014). *Enhancing the competitiveness of SMEs through the innovative Cooperative Business Model (CBM).* Research Study, International Symposium and Workshop—Final Report, APEC Small and Medium Enterprises Working Group, March, APEC Secretariat, Singapore.

APEC. (2020, April). *Overview of the SME sector in the APEC region: Key issues on market access and internationalization.* APEC Policy Support Unit, Asia-Pacific Economic Cooperation Secretariat.

Arteaga-Ortiz, J., & Fernandez-Ortiz, R. (2010). Why don't we use the same export barrier measurement scale? *Journal of Small Business Management, 48*(3), 395–420.

ASEAN. (2015a). *ASEAN's external-relations.* ASEAN Secretariat.

ASEAN. (2015b, November). *ASEAN strategic action plan for SME development 2016–2025.* ASEAN Secretariat.

Audretsch, D. B. (2003). Entrepreneurship, innovation and globalization: Does Singapore need a new policy approach. In R. S. Rajan (Ed.), *Sustaining competitiveness in the new global economy.* Edward Elgar.

Bakare, A. A., & Akinbode, J. O. (2016). Development financial institutions and SMEs development in Osun state, Nigeria. *Fountain University Osogbo Journal of Management, 1*(2), 6–17.

Bakiewicz, A. (2004). Small and medium enterprises in Thailand: Following the leader. *Asia & Pacific Studies, 2*, 131–151.

Bari, F., Ali, C., & Haque, E. (2005). *SME development in Pakistan: Analyzing the constraint on growth* (Pakistan Resident Mission Working Paper Series, No. 3). Asian Development Bank.

Bavoso, V. (2019). The promise and perils of alternative market-based finance: The case of P2P lending in the UK. *Journal of Banking Regulation, 21*, 395–409. https://doi.org/10.1057/s41261-019-00118-9

Bayu, D. J. (2021). *Kemnaker Catat 96% Perusahaan Terkena Dampak Pandemi Corona* [Ministry of manpower records 96% of companies affected by the Corona pandemic]. Katadata.co.id. https://katadata.co.id/agungjatmiko/berita/5efc879e27b5b/kemnaker-catat-96-perusahaan-terkena-dampak-pandemi-corona

Bello, W. (1999). The Asian financial crisis: Causes, dynamics, prospects. *Journal of the Asia Pacific Economy, 4*(1), 33–55.

Belso-Martinez, J. A. (2006). Do industrial districts influence export performance and export intensity? Evidence for Spanish SMEs' internationalization process. *European Planning Studies, 14*(6), 791–810.

Berry, A., & Brian, L. (1999). Technical, financial and marketing support for Indonesia's small and medium industrial exporters. In B. Levy, A. Berry, & J. B. Nugent (Eds.), *Fulfilling the export potential of small and medium firms*. Kluwer Academic Publishers.

Berry, A., & Rodriguez, E. (2001). *Dynamics of small and medium enterprises in a slow-growth economy: The Philippines in the 1990s*. Research paper, June (Stock No. 37181), The International Bank for Reconstruction and Development/The World Bank, Washington, D.C.

Berry, A., Rodriguez, E., & Sandee, H. (2001). Small and medium enterprise dynamics in Indonesia. *Bulletin of Indonesian Economic Studies, 37*(3), 363–384.

Bhuyan, M., & Pathak, P. (2019). Entrepreneurship development and bridging gender gaps. *International Journal of Advance and Innovative Research, 6*(1), 56–65.

BIS & FSB. (2017). *FinTech credit: Market structure, business models and financial stability implications*. Bank for International Settlements. https://www.bis.org/publ/cgfs_fsb1.htm

BPS. (2017, November). *Analisa Ketenagakerjaan Usaha Mikro Kecil* [Micro and small business employment analysis], *Sensus Ekonomi 2016, Analisa Hasil Listing*. Badan Pusat Statistik Nasional.

REFERENCES

BPS. (2018, June). *Profil Industri Mikro dan Kecil 2017* [2017 Micro and small industry profile]. Badan Pusat Statistik.

BPS. (2020). *Profil Industri Mikro dan Kecil 2019* [2019 Micro and small industry profile]. Badan Pusat Statistik.

BRC. (2020). *Fintech global market opportunities and strategies*. The Business Research Company. https://www.thebusinessresearchcompany.com/report/fintech-global-market-report

Breckova, P. (2018). Export patterns of small and medium sized enterprises. *European Research Studies Journal, XXI*(1), 43–51.

Bruton, G. D., Khavul, S., Siegel, D. S., & Write, M. (2015). New financial alternatives in seeding entrepreneurship: Microfinance, crowdfunding, and peer to peer innovations. *Entrepreneurship Theory and Practice, 39*(1), 9–26.

Buckley, R. P., & Webster, S. (2016). *Fintech in developing countries: Charting new customer journeys* (UNSW Law Research Paper No. 2016–73). University of New South Wales. Retrieved February 11, 2018, from https://ssrn.com/abstract=2850091

Burhan, F. A. (2020, April). *Bisnis Anjlok akibat Pandemi Corona, UMKM Bisa Ubah Strategi Usaha* [Business drops due to Corona pandemic, MSMEs can change business strategy]. Katadata.co.id. https://katadata.co.id/berita/2020/04/15/bisnis-anjlok-akibat-pandemi-corona-umkm-bisa-ubah-strategi-usaha

Cardoza, G., Fornes, G., & Xu, N. (2012). *Institutional determinants of Chinese SMEs' internationalization: The case of Jiangsu province* (Working Paper No. 04–12). School of Sociology, Politics and International Studies, University of Bristol.

Chakraborty, P. (2012). *The great trade collapse and Indian firms* [Ph.D. dissertation, Graduate Institute of International and Development Studies].

Chandra, A., Paul, J., & Chavan, M. (2020). Internationalization barriers of SMEs from developing countries: A review and research agenda. *International Journal of Entrepreneurial Behavior & Research, 26*(6), 1281–1310.

Chantrasawang, N. (1999, September). *Current issues of SMEs in Thailand: Its linkages with FDI and the impact of the financial crisis* (pp. 28–3). Paper presentation, the International Conference on Small and Medium Enterprises at New Crossroads: Challenges and Prospects, Universiti Sains Malaysia.

Chesbrough, H. (2020). To recover faster from Covid-19, open up: Managerial implications from an open innovation perspective. *Industrial Marketing Management, 88*, 410–413. https://doi.org/10.1016/j.indmarman.2020.04.010

Chilipunde, R. (2010). *Constraints and challenges faced by small, medium and micro enterprise contractors in Malawi* [Thesis Master, Nelson Mandela Metropolitan University].

REFERENCES   197

Ciremaitoday. (2020, April 21). Kisah Perajin Batik Perempuan di Cirebon, Bangkit Ditengah Pandemi COVID-19 [The story of a female batik craftsman in Cirebon, Rising amid the COVID-19 pandemic]. *News.* https://kum paran.com/ciremaitoday/kisah-perajin-batik-perempuan-di-cirebon-bangkit-ditengahpandemi-covid-19-1tGcuTSTNoV/full

Claessens, S., Tong, H., & Shang-Jin, W. (2011). *From the financial crisis to the real economy: Using firm-level data to identify transmission channels* (NBER Working Paper No. 17360).

Cole, W. (1998a). Bali's garment export industry. In H. Hill & T. K. Wie (Eds.), *Indonesia's technological challenge.* Research School of Pacific and Asian Studies, Australian National University and Institute of Southeast Asian Studies.

Cole, W. (1998b). *Bali garment industry: An Indonesian Case of successful strategic alliance* (Research paper). The Asia Foundation.

Computer Business Review. (2016). *UK fintech VC investment booms to almost $1bn.* http://www.cbronline.com/news/verticals/finance/uk-fintech-vc-investmentbooms-to-almost-1b4820702

Covin, J. G., Green, K. M., & Slevin, D. P. (2006). Strategic process effects on the entrepreneurial orientation–sales growth rate relationship. *Entrepreneurship Theory and Practice, 30*(1), 57–81.

Cumming, D., & Schwienbacher, A. (2016). *Fintech venture capital* (SSRN Working Paper). http://ssrn.com/abstract=2784797

Dabić, M., Maley, J., Dana, L.-P., Novak, I., Pellegrini, M. M., & Caputo, A. (2019). Pathways of SME internationalization: A bibliometric and systematic review. *Small Business Economics, 55,* 705–725.

Das, D. J. (2000). Problems faced by women entrepreneurs. In K. Sasikumar (Ed.), *Women entrepreneurship.* Vikas Publishing House.

Dasaraju, H., Somalaraju, K., & Kota, S. M. (2020). MSMEs in developing economies and their role in achieving sustainable development goals in the context of Covid19: A theoretical exposition. *International Journal of Small and Medium Enterprises and Business Sustainability, 5*(2), 93–120.

DDLLC. (2018). *Closing the gap in fintech collaboration: Overcoming obstacles to a symbiotic relationship.* https://www2.deloitte.com/content/dam/Deloitte/global/Documents/Financial-Services/gx-fsi-dcfs-fintech-collaboration.pdf

De Dios, L. C. (2009, May 20–22). *The impact of information technology (IT) in trade facilitation on small and medium enterprises (SMES) in the Philippines.* Paper presented at the Regional Policy Forum on Trade Facilitation and SME s in Times of Crisis.

Degenhardt, S. S., Stamm, A., & Zehdnicker, M. (2002). *The growth gap: A small enterprise phenomenon.* Synthesis Document, The Donor Committee for Enterprise Development German, DCED Secretariat.

198 REFERENCES

Deshpandé, R., Grinstein, A., Kim, S. H., & Ofek, E. (2013). Achievement motivation, strategic orientations and business performance in entrepreneurial firms: How different are Japanese and American founders? *International Marketing Review, 30*(3), 231–252.

Devadas, S., & Young E. K. (2020, October). *Exploring the potential of gender parity to promote economic growth* (Research & Policy Briefs No. 39). The World Bank Malaysia Hub, The World Bank Group.

Dhameja, S. K., Bhatia, B. S., & Saini, J. S. (2002). Problems and constraints of women entrepreneurship. In D. D. Sharma & S. K. Dhameja (Eds.), *Women and rural entrepreneurship*. Abhishek Publications.

Dierman, van, P., Tambunan, T., Tambunan, M., & Wie, T. K. (1998, May). *The IMF 50-point program: Evaluating the likely impact on SMEs.* Draft report for the Asia Foundation.

Eugenia, O. A. (2018). Peer-to-peer lending: Business model analysis and the platform dilemma. *International Journal of Finance, Economics and Trade, 2*(3), 31–41.

EYGM Limited. (2017). *Unleashing the potential of FinTech in banking.* https://www.ey.com/en_gl/banking-capital-markets/five-challenges-for-banks-as-they-evolve-risk-management

Fakih, A., & Ghazalian, P. L. (2014). Which firms export? An empirical analysis for the manufacturing sector in the MENA region. *Journal of Economic Studies, 41*(5), 672–695.

Feng, Y., Fan, X., & Yoon, Y. (2015). Lenders and borrowers' strategies in online peer-to-peer lending market: An empirical analysis of ppdai.com. *Journal of Electronic Commerce Research, 16*(3), 242–260.

Frost, J. (2020). *The economic forces driving fintech adoption across countries* (BIS Working Papers No. 838). Monetary and Economic Department, Bank for International Settlements. https://www.bis.org/publ/work838.pdf

Ganesan, S. (2003). *Status of women entrepreneurs in India.* Kanishka Publications.

GEM. (2015). *Women's entrepreneurship.* Special Report, Global Entrepreneurship Monitor, The Center for Women's Leadership at Babson College.

Ghanem, E. (2018). *Banks and FinTech collaborate via different engagement approaches.* Capgemini Financial Services Analysis. https://www.capgemini.com/2018/08/banks-and-fintechs-collaboration-by-engagement/#_ftn

Goheer, N. A. (2003). *Women entrepreneurs in Pakistan—How to improve their bargaining power.* ILO /SEED.

Government Office for Science. (2015). *Fintech futures: The UK as a world leader in financial technologies.* UK Government Chief Scientific Adviser. https://assets.publishing.service.gov.uk/government/uploads/system/uploads/attachment_data/file/413095/gs-15-3-fintech-futures.pdf

REFERENCES 199

Griffith-Jones, S., & Ocampo, J. A. (2009, April). *The financial crisis and its impacts on developing countries* (Working Paper No. 53). International Policy Center for Inclusive Growth.

Gunawan, J. (2012). *Woman entrepreneurs in Indonesia: Challenging roles of an economic and social actor*. Riwani Globe.

Haddad, C., & Hornuf, L. (2016). *The emergence of the global fintech market: Economic and technological determinants*. https://www.researchgate.net/publication/307957382

Haddoud, M. Y., Beynon, M. J., Jones, P., & Newbery, R. (2018). SMEs' export propensity in North Africa: A fuzzy c-means cluster analysis. *Journal of Small Business Enterprise Development, 25*(5), 769–790.

Han, L., Xiao, J. J., & Zhi, S. (2018). Financing knowledge, risk attitude and P2P borrowing in China. *International Journal of Consumer Studies, 43*(2), 166–177.

Hani, F. F. (2015). Entrepreneurial motivation and challenges: A study on women entrepreneurs in Sylhet city. *Global Disclosure of Economics and Business, 4*(2), 111–122.

Harchegani, E. K., Solati, A., & Fataie, P. (2015). Identifying the factors affecting on SMEs' export performance (Case study: Sports equiments exporters). *Applied Mathematics in Enginnering, Management and Technology, 3*(3), 390–400.

Hartono, D. (2011). *Assessing policy effectiveness during the crisis: The case of Indonesia*. International Labour Organization (International Institute for Labour Studies).

Hatami, A. (2018). *Bank & FinTech collaboration models*. https://medium.com/@a_hatami/bank-fintech-collaborations-how-big-banks-plan-to-stand-up-to-the-big-tech-challenge-24eea57db095

Hendriyani, C., & Sam'un J. R. (2019). Business agility strategy: Peer-to-peer lending of Fintech startup in the era of digital finance in Indonesia. *Review of Integrative Business and Economics Research, 8*(4), 239–246.

Hermansah. (2020, April). *Simak strategi bertahan bagi UKM hadapi krisis akibat Covid-19 Pastikan bisnis Anda tetap berjalan dan mampu bertahan pada saat kondisi pandemi saat ini* [Check out the survival strategy for SMEs to face the crisis due to Covid-19 Make sure your business continues to run and is able to survive during the current pandemic conditions]. Alinea.id. https://www.alinea.id/bisnis/strategi-bertahan-bagi-ukm-hadapi-krisis-akibat-covid-19-b1ZLs9tpp

Hessels, J., & Terjesen, S. (2007, October). *SME choice of direct and indirect export modes: Resource dependency and institutional theory perspectives*. Scientific Analysis of Entrepreneurship and SMEs.

Hilbrecht, M. (2016). Self-employment and experiences of support in a work–family context. *Journal of Small Business & Entrepreneurship, 28*(1), 75–96.

200 REFERENCES

Hill, H. (1999). *Indonesia in crisis.* Unpublished draft postscript for the second edition of The Indonesian Economy since 1966, Cambridge University Press.

Hill, H. (2001). Small and medium enterprises in Indonesia: Old policy challenges for a new administration. *Asian Survey, 41*(2), 248–270.

Hine, D., & Kelly, S. (1997, April 6–7). *Tickets to Asia: Foreign market entry and sustained competitiveness by SMEs.* Paper presented at the 10th International Conference on SMEs.

Hoekman, B., & Shepherd, B. (2013, September). *Who profits from trade facilitation initiatives* (ARTNeT Working Paper Series, No. 129). Asia-Pacific Research and Training Network on Trade.

Hughes, K. (2006). Exploring motivation and success among Canadian women entrepreneurs. *Journal of Small Business and Entrepreneurship, 19*(2), 83–94.

Humphrey, J. (2009, March). *Are exporters in Africa facing reduced availability of trade finance.* Research paper, Institute of Development Studies Brighton.

Hurst, R., Buttle, M., & Sandars, J. (2010). The impact of the global economic slowdown on value chain labor markets in Asia. In A. Bauer & M. Thant (Eds.), *Poverty and sustainable development in Asia: Impacts and responses to the global economic crisis.* Asian Development Bank (ADB) and ADB Institute.

Hussain, J., Abbas, Q., & Khan, M. A. (2017). Entrepreneurial orientation and performance: The moderating effect of market orientation. *Global Management Journal for Academic & Corporate Studies, 7*(1), 9–18.

ILO. (2020a). *COVID-19 and the world of work: Impact and policy responses, ILO Monitor* (1st ed.). International Labour Organization.

ILO. (2020b). *COVID-19 and the world of work: Updated estimates and analysis, ILO Monitor* (2nd ed.). International Labour Organization.

ILO. (2020c). *COVID-19: Protecting workers in the workplace.* International Labour Organization. https://www.ilo.org/global/about-the-ilo/new sroom/news/WCMS_738742/lang-en/index.htm

ILO. (2020d). *MSME day 2020: The COVID-19 pandemic and its impact on small business.* International Labor Office file:///D:/FILE%20FEB%202018/FILE%2001%20FEB% 202018/DIKTI /BKD/ BKD%20FEB%202O21/SEDANG%20BERJALAN/JURNAL/SME %20CORONA%20journal%20global/coba%20UGM/MSME %20Day%202020_%20the%20COVID%20–19%20pandemic%20and%20its%20 impact%20on%20small%20business.html

Iman, N. (2020). The rise and rise of financial technology: The good, the bad, and the verdict. *Cogent Business & Management, 7*(1). https://doi.org/10. 1080/23311975.2020.1725309

IMF. (2019). *Financial inclusion of small and medium-sized enterprises in the Middle East and Central Asia.* International Monetary Fund. https://www. imf.org/en/Publications/Departmental-Papers-Policy-Papers/Issues/2019/

02/11/Financial-Inclusion-of-Small-and-Medium-Sized-Enterprises-in-the-Middle-East-and-Central-Asia-46335

Islam, N., Fariha, R., Shreya, N. Z., Sabaa, F. T., Faiaz, M. D., & Yusuf, I. (2019, December 10). *Socioeconomic factors of women entrepreneurship development in Bangladesh.* Paper presentation, International Conference.

Iyer, R., Khwaja, A. I., Luttmer, E. F. P., & Shue, K. (2016). Screening peers softly: Inferring the quality of small borrowers. *Management Science, 62,* 1554–1577.

Jagtiani, J., & Lemieux, C. (2018). Do Fintech lenders penetrate areas that are underserved by traditional banks? *Journal of Economics and Business, 100,* 43–54.

Jellinek, L., & Rustanto, B. (1999, July). *Survival strategies of the Javanese during the economic crisis.* Consultancy Report to the World Bank.

Jones, M. V., & Coviello, N. E. (2005). Internationalisation: Conceptualising an entrepreneurial process of behaviour in time. *Journal of International Business Studies, 36*(3), 284–303.

Joomunbaccus, S., & Padachi, K. (2019). The Impediments to small and medium sized enterprises' development in Mauritius. *Journal of Small Business and Entrepreneurship Development, 7*(2), 86–98.

Jovanovikj, B., & Georgievska, L. (2015). Transmission channels of the global economic crisis: Micro evidence for Macedonia. *Journal of Contemporary Economic and Business Issues, 2*(1), 5–20.

Julien, P., & Ramangalahy, C. (2003). Competitive strategy and performance of exporting SMEs: An empirical investigation of the impact of their export information search and competencies. *Entrepreneurship: Theory & Practice, 27*(3): 227–245.

Kane, J. (2009). What the economic crisis means for child labour. *Global Social Policy, 9*(Suppl.), 175–196.

KB. (2020, April 14). *Daftar Usaha yang Bisa Jadi Pilihan di Tengah Pandemi Virus Corona* [List of businesses that can be an choice in the middle of the corona virus pandemic]. Kumparan BISNIS, Bisnis. https://kumparan.com/kumparanbisnis/daftar-usaha-yang-bisa-jadi-pilihan-di-tengah-pandemi-virus-corona-1tDiIgDLASf/full

Kharel, P., & Dahal, K. (2020). *Small and medium-sized enterprises in Nepal: Examining constraints on exporting* (ADBI Working Paper No. 1166). Asian Development Bank Institute. https://www.adb.org/publications/sme-nepal-examining-constraints-exporting

Khor, N., & Sebastian I. (2009, December). *Exports and the global crisis: Still alive, though not quite kicking yet: ADB Economics* (Working Paper Series No. 190). Asian Development Bank.

REFERENCES

Kim, J., Kim, J., Lee, S. K., & Tang, L. (2020). Effects of epidemic disease outbreaks on financial performance of restaurants: Event study method approach. *Journal of Hospitality and Tourism Management, 43*, 32–41.

Kirkwood, J. (2009a). Spousal roles on motivations for entrepreneurship: A qualitative study in New Zealand. *Journal of Family and Economic Issues, 30*(4), 372–385.

Kirkwood, J. (2009b). Motivational factors in a push-pull theory of entrepreneurship. *Gender in Management: An International Journal, 24*(5), 346–364.

Klafft, M. (2008). Peer to peer lending: Auctioning microcredits over the internet. In *Proceedings of the 2008 International Conference on Information Systems, Technology, and Management.* IMT Business School Dubai.

Kompas. (2020a, May 9). Peluang Memanfaatkan Lonjakan Pengunjung Laman E-dagang [Opportunity to take advantage of e-commerce site visitor surges]. *Kompas Newspaper*, p. 9.

Kompas. (2020b, April 9). Jumlah Korban PHK Terus Bertambah [The number of layoff victims continues to increase]. *Kompas Newspaper*, p. 9.

Kompas (2020c, April 17), Stabilitas Sosial Dijaga [Social stability is maintained]. *Kompas Newspaper*, p. 1.

Laghzaoui, S. (2007). *Internationalization of SME: A reading in terms of resources and competencies.* Paper presented at the 3rd Iberian International Business Conference.

Leonidou, L. C. (2004). An analysis of the barriers hindering small business export development. *Journal of Small Business Management, 42*(3), 279–302.

Leonidou, L. C., Katsikeas, C. S., Palihawadana, D., & Spyropoulou, S. (2007). An analytical review of the factors stimulating smaller firms to export: Implications for policy-makers. *International Marketing Review, 24*(6), 735–770.

Li, Y., & Wilson, J. S. (2009, June). *Trade facilitation and expanding the benefits of trade: Evidence from firm level data* (Asia-Pacific Research and Training Network on Trade Working Paper Series No. 71). UN-ESCAP.

Lin, M., & Viswanathan, S. (2015). Home bias in online investments: An empirical study of an online crowdfunding market. *Management Science, 62*, 1393–1414.

Long, N. V. (2003). *Performance and obstacles of SMEs in Viet Nam policy implications in near future.* Unpublished research paper, International IT Policy Program (ITPP), Seoul National University.

Loscocco, K., & Bird, S. R. (2012). Gendered paths: Why women lag behind men in small business success. *Work and Occupations, 39*(2), 183–219.

Lukonga, I. (2018). *Fintech, inclusive growth and cyber risks: A focus on the MENAP and CCA regions* (IMF Working Paper No. 18/201). International Monetary Fund. www.imf.org/en/Publications/WP/Issues/2018/09/11/Fintech-Inclusive-Growth-and-Cyber-Risks-Focus-on-the-MENAP-and-CCA-Regions-46190

REFERENCES 203

Mabula, J. B., Dongping, H., & Chivundu-Ngulube, C. D. (2020). SME manager's perceived cooperative support, commitment and trust on learning and entrepreneurship orientation for firm innovation. *Human Systems Management, 39*(2), 233–250

Macphersona, A., & Holt, R. (2007). Knowledge, learning and small firm growth: A systematic review of the evidence. *Research Policy, 36,* 172–192.

Madushanka, H., & Sachitra, V. (2021). Factors influencing on export engagement of small and medium-sized enterprises in Sri Lanka: Resource based view. *South Asian Journal of Social Studies and Economics, 9*(3), 38–49.

Mahazril 'Aini Y., Hafizah H. A. K., & Zuraini, Y. (2012). Factors affecting cooperatives' performance in relation to strategic planning and members' participation. *Procedia—Social and Behavioral Sciences, 65,* 100–105.

Mahmood, B., Khalid, S., Sohail, M. M., & Babak, I. (2012). Exploring the motivation and barriers in way of Pakistani female entrepreneurs. *British Journal of Education, Society & Behavioural Science, 2*(4), 353–368.

Malaeb, O. R. (2017). *An investigation into the obstacles facing small and medium enterprises in Lebanon: Toward a national SME policy* [Master dissertation, University of Liverpool].

Mao, H. (2009). Review on enterprise growth theories. *International Journal of Business and Management, 4*(8), 20–22.

Matenge, T. (2011). Small firm internationalization—A developing country perspective. *International Journal of Business Administration, 2*(4), 103–111.

Mathews, A. (2018). *Mutually beneficial bank-FinTech collaboration models.* https://gomedici.com/mutually-beneficial-bank-fintech-collaboration-mod els/

Maulana, E. (2015). *Analisis Perkembangan Unit Simpan Pinjam di Koperasi Pegawai Republik Indonesia (KPRI) Dhaya Harta Jombang* [Analysis of the development of the savings and loans unit at the Koperasi Pegawai Republik Indonesia (KPRI) Dhaya Harta Jombang]. Prodi Pendidikan Ekonomi, Jurusan Pendidikan Ekonomi, Fakultas Ekonomi Universitas Negeri Surabaya.

Milne, A., & Parboteeah, P. (2016). *The business models and economics of peer-to-peer lending.* The European Credit Research Institute (ECRI). https://www.ceps.eu/ceps-publications/business-models-and-economics-peer-peer-lending/

Moktan, S. (2007). Development of small and medium enterprises in Bhutan: Analysing constraints to growth. *South Asian Survey, 14*(2), 251–282.

Morgan, P. J., & Trinh, L. Q. (2019). *Fintech and financial literacy in the LAO PDR* (ADBI Working Paper Series No. 933). Asian Development Bank Institute.

Mpunga, H. S. (2016). Examining the factors affecting export performance for small and medium enterprises (SMEs) in Tanzania. *Journal of Economics and Sustainable Development, 7*(6), 41–51.

Mupemhi, S., Duve, R., & Mupemhi, R. (2013, October). *Factors affecting the internationalisation of manufacturing SMEs in Zimbabwe* (ICBE-RF Research Report No. 62/13). Investment Climate and Business Environment Research Fund. Midlands State University.

Musa, A. (1998). *A study on access to credit for small and medium enterprises (SMEs) in Indonesia before and during the economic crisis (1997–1998)*. Study prepared for the Asia Foundation and the United States Agency for International Development, Jakarta.

Mustafa, R., & Mansor, S. A. (1999, October 30–31). *Malaysia's financial crisis and contraction of human resource: Policies and lessons for SMIs*. Paper presentation, the APEC Human Resource Management Symposium on SMEs.

Nembhard, J. G. (2014, February). *The benefits and impacts of cooperatives* (White Paper). Grassroots Economic Organizing (GEO). https://geo.coop/story/benefits-and-impacts-cooperatives

Nemoto, N., Storey, D., & Huang, B. (2019). Optimal regulation of peer-to-peer lending for SMEs. In N. Nemoto & N. Yoshino (Eds.), *Fintech for Asian SMEs*. Asian Development Bank Institute (ADBi).

Nemoto, N., & Yoshino, N. (Eds.) (2019). *Fintech for Asian SMEs*. ADBi.

Nguanbanchong, A. (2009, September 15–16). *Feminized recession impact of global economic crisis on women in Southeast Asia*. Paper presented at the seminar on Gender and the Economic Crisis: Impact and Responses.

Nurzaman. (2020, April). *Dampak Wabah Covid-19 UMKM (Usaha Micro Kecil Menengah) Banyak Gulung Tikar* [The impact of the Covid-19 outbreak MSMEs (Micro, small and medium enterprises) Many have been out of business]. KICAUNews.com. https://kicaunews.com/2020/04/07/dampak-wabah-covid-19-umkm-usaha-micro-kecil-menengah-banyak-gulung-tikar/

Nyatwongi, L. N. (2015, November). *Factors affecting the performance of importing and exporting small and medium enterprises in Mombasa country, Kenya*. School of Business. University of Nairobi. http://erepository.uonbi.ac.ke/bitstream/handle/11295/93235/Nyatwongi/20Linet/20N

OECD. (2015). *New approaches to SME and entrepreneurship financing: Broadening the range of instruments*. Organisation for Economic Co-operation and Development. https://www.oecd.org/cfe/smes/New-Approaches-SME-fullreport.pdf

OECD. (2020a). *Coronavirus (COVID-19): SME policy responses*. Updated 15 July. Organisation for Economic Co-operation and Development.

OECD. (2020b, April). *Evaluating the initial impact of COVID-19 containment measures on economic activity. OECD Policy Responses to Coronavirus (Covid-19)*. Organisation for Economic Co-operation and Development. https://www.oecd.org/coronavirus/policyresponses/evaluating-the-initial-impact-of-covid-19-containment-measures-on-economic-activity/

Oluyombo, P. (2013). Impact of cooperative societies savings scheme in rural finance: Some evidence from Nigeria. *Economic Review-Journal of Economics and Business, 11*(1), 22–35.

OSMEP. (2015). *The White paper on small and medium enterprises of Thailand in 2015 and Trends 2016.* The Office of SME Promotion.

Ottaviano, G., & Martincus, C. V. (2011). SMEs in Argentina: Who are the exporters? *Small Business Economics, 37*(3), 341–361.

Pasadilla, G. O. (2010, January). *Financial crisis, trade finance, and SMEs: Case of Central Asia* (ADBI Working Paper Series, No. 187). ADB Institute.

Pearson, R., & Sweetman, C. (Eds.). (2011). *Gender and the economic crisis.* Practical Action Publishing in association with Oxfam GB.

Peng, M. W., & Delios, A. (2006). What determines the scope of the firm over Time and around the world? An Asia Pacific perspective. *Asia Pacific Journal of Management, 23*(4), 385–405.

Perry, M., & Tambunan, T. T. H. (2009). Re-visiting Indonesian cases for cluster realism. *Journal of Enterprising Community: People and Places in the Global Economy, 3*(3), 269–290.

Petrit, G., Hashi, I., & Pugh, G. (2012, March). *The small and medium enterprise sector and export performance: Empirical evidence from South-Eastern Europe* (Working Paper No. 002). Centre for Applied Business Research (CABR). Staffordshire University Business School.

Piore, M. J., & Sabel, C. F. (1984). *The second industrial divide.* Basic Books.

Pranata, N. (2019). The role of digital payments Fintech in accelerating the development of MSMEs in Indonesia. In N. Nemoto & N. Yoshino (Eds.), *Fintech for Asian SMEs.* Asian Development Bank Institute.

Priyambada, A., Suryhadi, A., & Sumarto, S. (2005). *What happened to child labor in Indonesia during the economic crisis? The trade-off between school and work.* SMERU Research Institute.

PwC. (2019, September). *Indonesia's Fintech lending.*

Rahman, M. A. (2010). *An assessment of the factors affecting performance of women entrepreneurs in SMEs of Bangladesh* [M. Phil thesis, Department of Management University of Dhaka].

Rahman, R. (2020, April 16). 37,000 SMEs hit by COVID-19 crisis as government prepares aid. *The Jakarta Post.* https://www.thejakartapost.com/news/2020/04/16/37000-smes-hit-by-covid-19-crisis-asgovernment_prepares-aid.html

Raju, G. (2000). Women entrepreneurship development through DWCRA. In K. Sasikumar (Ed.), *Women entrepreneurship.* Vikas Publishing House.

Régnier, P. (2005). The East Asian financial crisis in Thailand: Distress and resilience of local SMEs. In C. Harvie & B.-C. Lee (Eds.), *Sustaining growth and performance in East Asia.* Edward Elgar.

206 REFERENCES

Revindo, M. D., & Ganb, C. (2016). Export stimuli, export stages and internationalization pathways: The case of Indonesian SMEs. *Economics and Finance in Indonesia, 62*(3), 191–205.

Revindo, M. D., Gan, C., & Massiel, N. W. G. (2019). Factors affecting propensity to export: The case of Indonesian SMEs. *Gadjah Mada International Journal of Business, 21*(3), 263–288.

Ribau, C. P., Moreira, A. C., & Raposo, M. (2018). SME internationalization research: Mapping the state of the art. *Canadian Journal of Administrative Science, 35*(2), 280–303.

Rihayana, I. G., Salain, P. P. P., & Adhik, N. R. (2018). Determining factors for marketing success in *endek* and embroidered textile industry through the integration of entrepreneurship orientation and customer relationship marketing in marketing capabilities. *Review of Marketing and Entrepreneurship, 2*(1), 31–48.

RM. (2020a). *Peer-to-peer lending—Global market trajectory & analytics.* Research and Markets. https://www.businesswire.com/news/home/202012 15005523/en/Global-Peer-to-Peer-P2P-Lending-Market-Trends-Growth-Opportunity-Report-2020-2025-ResearchAndMarkets.com

RM. (2020b). *The ASEAN peer-to-peer (P2P) lending market, 2020.* Research and Markets. https://www.researchandmarkets.com/reports/5174497/the-asean-peer-to-peer-p2p-lending-market-2020#relb0-5181490

Roomi, M. A. (2006). *Women entrepreneurs in Pakistan: Profile, challenges and practical recommendations.* School of Management Royal Holloway, University of London.

Roomi, M. A., & Parrott, G. (2008). Barriers to development and progression of women entrepreneurs in Pakistan. *Journal of Entrepreneurship, 17*(1), 59–72.

Saeed, S., Malik, N., Sohail, M. M., Tabassum, A., & Haq Nawaz Anwar, H. N. (2014). Factors motivating female entrepreneurs: A study conducted in major urban area of Punjab. *Mediterranean Journal of Social Sciences, 5*(4), 669–675.

Sallah, C. A., & Caesar, L. D. (2020, January). Intangible resources and the growth of women businesses: Empirical evidence from an emerging market economy. *Journal of Entrepreneurship in Emerging Economies.* https://www.emerald.com/insight/content/doi/10.1108/JEEE-05-2019-0070/full/html

Sandee, H., & Ibrahim, B. (2002, April). *Evaluation of SME trade and export promotion in Indonesia* (Background Report). ADB SME Development Technical Assistance. State Ministry for Cooperatives & SME.

Sandee, H., Andadari, R. K., & Sulandjari, S. (2000). Small firm development during good times and bad: The Jepara furniture industry. In C. Manning & P. van Dierman (Eds.), *Indonesia in transition: Social aspects of reformasi and crisis.* Indonesia Assessment Series, Research School of Pacific and Asian Studies, Australian National University, and Institute of Southeast Asian Studies.

Santoso, Y. I. (2020). *Menghitung dampak Covid19 terhadap dunia usaha hingga UMKM* [Calculating the impact of Covid19 on the business world to MSMEs]. https://nasional.kontan.co.id/news/menghitungdampak-covid-19-terhadap-dunia-usaha-hinggaumkm?page=all

Sari & Susanti. (2010). *Faktor-faktor yang mempengaruhi perkembangan Koperasi* [Factors that influence the development of cooperatives]. https://isjd.pdii.lipi.go.id/admin/jurnal/39962840.pdf

Sato, Y. (2000). How did the crisis affect small and medium-sized enterprises? From a field study of the metal working industry in Java. *The Developing Economies, XXXVIII*(4), 572–595.

Scarborough, N. M. (2012). *Effective small business management: An entrepreneurial approach* (Vol. 10). Prentice Hall.

Serrano-Cinca, C., Gutiérrez-Nieto, B., & López-Palacios, L. (2015, Oktober). Determinants of default in P2P lending. *PLoS ONE, 10*. https://www.ncbi.nlm.nih.gov/pubmed/26425854

Setyowati, D. (2020, April). *Siasat Empat UMKM Bertahan di Tengah Pandemi Corona* [Four MSMEs' tactics to survive in the midst of the Corona pandemic]. https://katadata.co.id/berita/2020/04/20/siasat-empat-umkm-bertahan-di-tengah-pandemi-corona

Shafi, M., Liu, J., & Ren, W. (2020). Impact of COVID-19 pandemic on micro, small, and medium-sized enterprises operating in Pakistan. *Research in Globalization, 2*, 1–14. https://www.sciencedirect.com/science/article/pii/S25900 51X20300071?via%3Dihub

Shah, H. (2013). *Creating an enabling environment for women's entrepreneurship in India* (South and South- West Asia Office Development Papers 1304). South and South-West Asia Office, United Nations Economic and Social Commission for Asia and the Pacific (UN ESCAP).

Shah, H., & Saurabh, P. (2015). Women entrepreneurs in developing nations: Growth and replication strategies and their impact on poverty alleviation. *Technology Innovation Management Review, 5*(8), 34–43.

Shakil, M. H., Munim, Z. H., Tasnia, M., & Sarowar, S. (2020). COVID-19 and the environment: A critical review and research agenda. *Journal of Science of the Total Environment, 745*(9). https://openarchive.usn.no/usn-xmlui/bitstream/handle/11250/2675634/COVID-19%2band%2bthe%2benviron ment%2bA%2bcritical%2breview%2band%2bresearch%2bagenda.pdf?sequence=2&isAllowed=y

Sharma, D. D., & Dhameja, S. K. (2002). *Women and rural entrepreneurship.* Abhishek Publications.

Shin, K.-Y. (2015). The two crises and inequality in the labour market. *International Union Rights, 22*(1), 3–5.

Sidek, S., Mohamad, M. R., & Nasir, W. M. N. W. (2019). Entrepreneurial orientation and SME performance: The serial mediating effects of access to finance and competitive advantage. *International Journal of Academic Research in Business and Social Sciences, 9*(9), 81–100.

Sinha, A. (2003). *Experience of SMEs in South and South-East Asia.* SEDF and World Bank.

Sinhal, S. (2005). *Developing women entrepreneurs in South Asia: Issues, initiatives and experiences* (ST/ESCAP/2401). Trade and Investment Division. UNESCAP.

Siregar, A. P. (2019). Dampak Otonomi Daerah dan Pemekaran Wilayah terhadap Perkembangan Koperasi di Indonesia [The impact of regional autonomy and regional expansion on the development of cooperatives in Indonesia]. *Agridevina, 8*(1), 58–71.

Siregar, A. P., & Jamhari (2013). Analisis Kinerja Koperasi Unit Desa di Daerah Istimewa Yogyakarta [Analysis of the performance of village unit cooperatives in the special region of Yogyakarta]. *Agro Ekonomi, 24*(2), 113–124.

SME Corp Malaysia. (2015, September). *Small and medium enterprise (SME) Annual Report 2014/2015.* SME Corporation Malaysia.

SMERU. (2009, November). *Monitoring the socioeconomic impact of the 2008/2009 global financial crisis in Indonesia* (Media Monitoring No. 04/FS/2009). SMERU Research Institute.

Suharyo, W. I. (2005, April–June). *Gender and poverty* (Gender and Poverty No. 14). SMERU Research Institute.

Sundari, L. S. (2020, April). *Dampak Pandemi Covid-19, Omzet UMKM di Kota Cimahi Turun 80 Persen* [The impact of the Covid-19 pandemic, MSME turnover in Cimahi City dropped 80 percent]. Galamedianews.com. https://www.galamedianews.com/?arsip=254042&judul=dampak-pandemi-covid-19-omzet-umkm-di-kota-cimahi-turun-80-persen

Suroso, A., Anggraeni, A. I., & Andriyansah (2017). Optimizing SMEs' Business Performance Through Human Capital Management. *European Research Studies Journal, XX*(4B), 588–599.

Suryahadi, A., Al Izzati, R., & Suryadarma, D. (2020). *The impact of COVID-19 outbreak on poverty: An estimation for Indonesia* (SMERU Working Paper). SMERU Research Institute.

Susanti, M. I. (2010). Peran Koperasi SerUsaha (KSU) "'Mitra Maju" dalam Meningkatkan Kesejahteraan Anggota di Kampung Sumber Sari Kabupaten [The role of "'Mitra Maju" multipurpose cooperative (KSU) in improving members' welfare in Sumber Sari district Village]. *Ejournal Ilmu Pemerintahan, 3*(2), 558–570.

Sushila Devi, R., Nurizah, N., Mohd. Shahron, A. S., Rafedah, J., & Farahaini, M. H. (2009). Factors influencing the performance of cooperatives in

Malaysia: A tentative framework. *Malaysian Journal of Co-operative Management, 5*, 43–62.

Sushila Devi, R., Nurizah, N., Mohd. Shahron, A. S., Rafedah, J., & Farahaini, M. H. (2010). Success factors of cooperatives in Malaysia: An exploratory investigation. *Malaysian Journal of Co-operative Studies, 6*, 1–24.

Suwandi. (2012, November 5). *Model Jaringan Ekspor.* Paper presentation, SEADI Seminar.

Tambunan, T. T. H. (1998, March 20–21). *Impact of East Asia currency crisis and economic development on Indonesia's SMEs and priorities for adjustment.* Paper prepared for the SME Resourcing Conference, ASEAN Chamber of Commerce and Industry.

Tambunan, T. T. H. (2006). *Development of small & medium enterprises in Indonesia from the Asia-Pacific perspective.* LPFE-Usakti.

Tambunan, T. T. H. (2009a). *SME in Asian developing countries.* Palgrave Macmillan.

Tambunan, T. T. H. (2009b). *Development of small and medium enterprises in ASEAN countries.* Readworthy Publications.

Tambunan, T. T. H. (2009c). Export-oriented small and medium industry clusters in Indonesia. *Journal of Enterprising Communities: People and Places in the Global Economy, 3*(1), 25–58.

Tambunan, T. T. H. (2009d). Women entrepreneurs in Indonesia: Their main constraints and reasons. *Journal of Asia Entrepreneurship and Sustainability, V*(3), 37–51.

Tambunan, T. T. H. (2010a). The Indonesian experience with two big economic crises. *Modern Economy, 1*, 156–167.

Tambunan, T. T. H. (2010b). *Global economic crisis and ASEAN economy.* Lambert Academic Publishing.

Tambunan, T. T. H. (2010c). *Trade liberalization and SMEs in ASEAN.* Nova Science Publishers. Inc.

Tambunan, T. T. H. (2011a). *Economic crisis and vulnerability: The story from Southeast Asia.* Nova Science Publishers Inc.

Tambunan, T. T. H. (2011b). The impact of the 2008–2009 global economic crisis on a developing country's economy: Studiesfrom Indonesia. *Journal of Business and Economics, 2*(3), 175–197.

Tambunan, T. T. H. (2013, December). *Constraints on Indonesia's export-oriented micro, small, and medium enterprises secondary data analysis and literature survey* (SEADI Working Paper Series No. 2). USAID.

Tambunan, T. T. H. (2015a, May). *Utilisation of existing ASEAN-FTAs by local micro-, small- and medium-sized enterprises* (ARTNeT Policy Brief, No. 45). ESCAP (UN).

Tambunan, T. T. H. (2015b). *ASEAN micro, small and medium enterprises toward AEC 2015.* Lambert Academic Publishing (LAP).

Tambunan, T. T. H. (2015c). Development of women entrepreneurs in Indonesia: Are they being 'pushed' or 'pulled'? *Journal of Social Economics*, 2(3), 131–149.

Tambunan, T. T. H. (2016, September). *The importance of credit guarantee scheme as a financing alternative for MSMEs in ASEAN in the era of ASEAN economic community*. The Study of Credit Guarantee Schemes in ASEAN Member States. Unpublished report, US-ACTI Grants Program. USAID.

Tambunan, T. T. H. (2017a). Women entrepreneurs in MSEs in Indonesia: Their motivations and constraints. *International Journal of Gender and Women's Studies*, 5(1), 88–100.

Tambunan, T. T. H. (2017b). Women entrepreneurs in MSEs in Indonesia: Their motivations and main constraints. *Journal of Women's Entrepreneurship and Education*, 1–2, 56–86.

Tambunan, T. T. H. (2018a). Micro, small and medium enterprises in ASEAN. Regional Focus. *International Journal of Small and Medium Enterprises and Business Sustainability*, 3(1), 99–132.

Tambunan, T. T. H. (2018b). The performance of Indonesia's public credit guarantee scheme for MSMEs: A regional comparative perspective, Research Note. *Journal of Southeast Asian Economic*, 35(2), 319–332.

Tambunan, T. T. H. (2019). The impact of the economic crisis on micro, small, and medium enterprises and their crisis mitigation measures in Southeast Asia with reference to Indonesia. *Asia Pacific Policy Study*, 6(1), 1–21.

Tambunan, T. (2020, Mei 20). *Dampak dari Covid-19 Terhadap UMKM*. Focus Group Discussion.

Tambunan, T., & Busneti, I. (2016). The Indonesian experience with two big financial crisis and their impacts on micro, small and medium enterprises. *Asian Research Journal of Business Management*, 3(4), 83–100.

Tecson, G. (1999). Present status and prospects of supporting industries in the Philippines. In *Present status and prospects of supporting industries in ASEAN (I): Philippines-Indonesia*. Institute of Developing Economies, Japan External Trade Organization.

Thakora, A. V. (2019). Fintech and banking: What do we know? *Journal of Financial Intermediation*, 41. https://doi.org/10.1016/j.jfi.2019.100833

Toronto Centre. (2017, August). *FinTech, RegTech and SupTech: What they mean for financial supervision*. TC Notes. Toronto Leadership Centre. https://res.torontocentre.org/guidedocs/FinTech%20RegTech%20and%20S upTech%20What%20They%20Mean%20for%20Financial%20Supervision% 20FINAL.pdf

Ubaidillah, A. (2021, February). *Ekspor Pisang 64 Ton/Bulan, Koperasi di Lampung Dipuji Menkop UKM* (Banana exports 64 tons/month, cooperatives in Lampung praised by coordinating minister for SME s). detik Finance. https://finance.detik.com/berita-ekonomi-bisnis/d-547 5517/ekspor-pisang-64-tonbulan-koperasi-di-lampung-dipuji-menkop-ukm

UNCTAD. (2020a). *The Covid-19 shock to developing countries: Towards a "whatever it takes" programme for the two-thirds of the world's population being left behind*. United Nations Conference on Trade and Development.

UNCTAD. (2020b). *Investment trends monitor: Impact of the coronavirus outbreak on global FDI*. https://unctad.org/en/PublicationsLibrary/diaein f2020d2_en.pdf?user=1653

UNDP. (2020a). *Assessment report on impact of COVID-19 pandemic on Chinese enterprises*. United Nations Development Programme.

UNDP. (2020b). *COVID-19: Looming crisis in developing countries threatens to devastate economies and ramp up inequality*. United Nations Development Programme. https://www.undp.org/content/undp/en/home/newscentre/news/2020/COVID19_Crisis_in_developing_countries_threatens_devastate_economies.html

UNDP. (2020c, April). *The social and economic impact of Covis-19 in the Asia-Pacific region*. United Nations Development Programme. file:///C:/Users/USER/Downloads/UNDP-RBAP-Position-Note-Social-Economic-Impact-of-COVID-19-in-Asia-Pacific-2020.pdf

UN-ESCAP. (2010). *The development impact of information technology in trade facilitation*. A Study by the Asia-Pacific Research and Training Network on Trade. Studies in Trade and Investment 69. United Nations Publication.

UNICEF. (2009). *Impact of the economic crisis on children: What the crisis means for child labour*. United Nations International Children's Emergency Fund.

Urata, S. (2000). *Policy recommendations for SME promotion in Indonesia*. Report to the Coordination Ministry of Economy, Finance and Industry.

Valodia, I., & Velia, M. (2004, October 13–15). *Macro-micro linkages in trade: How are firms adjusting to trade liberalisation, and does trade liberalisation lead to improved productivity in South African manufacturing firms?* Paper presented to the African Development and Poverty Reduction: The Macro-Micro Linkage Conference, Development Policy Research Unit (DPRU) and Trade and Industrial Policy Secretariat (TIPS).

Wattanapruttipaisan, T. (2005, May 19–20). *SME development and internationalization in the knowledge-based and innovation-driven global economy: Mapping the agenda ahead*. Paper presentation, the International Expert Seminar on "Mapping Policy Experience for SMEs".

WEF. (2007). *The global gender gap report 2007*. World Economic Forum.

WEF. (2015). *The global gender gap report 2015*. World Economic Forum.

WEF. (2020). *The global gender gap report 2020*. World Economic Forum.

Weldeslassie, H. A., Kibrom G., Lubak M., Mahlet Tsegay, N. H. T., & Gidey, Y. (2015, June). *Exploring the status, prospects and contributions of micro, small and medium enterprises (MSMEs) in Ethiopi*. Aksum University.

212 REFERENCES

Wengel, ter J., & Rodriguez, E. (2006). SME export performance in Indonesia after the crisis. *Small Business Economics, 26,* 25–37.

Wie, T. K. (2000). The impact of the economic crisis on Indonesia's manufacturing sector. *The Developing Economies, XXXVIII*(4), 420–453.

Wignaraja, G. (2012). *Engaging small and medium enterprises in production networks: Firm level analysis of Five ASEAN economies* (ADBI Working Paper 361). Asian Development Bank Institute. http://www.adbi.org/workingpa per/2012/06/01/5076.engaging.small.medium.enterprises/

William, E. (2017). *Business constraints affecting the small and micro enterprises in Tanzania: A case of Bahi district in Dodoma region* [PhD dissertation, St John's University of Tanzania].

Wiradi, G. (1998). *Rural Java in a time of crisis: With special reference to Curug village, Cirebon, West Java.* Paper presentation, the Economic Crisis and Social Security in Indonesia, Berg-en-Dal.

World Bank. (2009). *The global economic crisis: Assessing vulnerability with a poverty lens.*

Yasri. (1996). *Unit Usaha Simpan Pinjam Di Koperasi: Beberapa Faktor Yang Mempengaruhi Perkembangannya* [Savings and loans business units in cooperatives: Several factors that affect their development]. http://isjd.pdii.lipi.go. id/admin/jurnal/221971327.pdf

Yean, T. S., & Tambunan, T. (2018). *Accidental and international exporters: Comparing Indonesian and Malaysian MSMEs* (Trends in Southeast Asia, No. 5) ISEAS Yusof Ishak Institute.

Yoganandan, G., & Gopalselvam, G. (2018). A study on challenges of women entrepreneurs in India. *International Journal of Innovative Research & Studies, 8*(III), 491–500.

Yoshino, N., & Wignaraja, G. (2015, February 18). *SMEs internationalization and finance in Asia.* Paper presented at the IMF-JICA Conference on Frontier and Developing Asia: Supporting Rapid and Inclusive Growth.

Zahra, S., Hayton, J., & Salvato, C. (2004). Entrepreneurship in family vs. non-family firms: A resource-based analysis of the effect of organizational culture. *Entrepreneurship Theory and Practice, 28*(4), 363–381.

Zahra, S. A., Korri, J. S., & Yu, J. (2005). Cognition and international entrepreneurship: Implications for research on international opportunity recognition and exploitation. *International Business Review, 14*(2), 129–146.

Zulhartati, S. (2010). Peranan Koperasi dalam Perekonomian Indonesia [The role of cooperative in the Indonesian economy]. *Guru Membangun, 25*(3), 1–7.

Index

A
Amartha Mikro Fintek, 168
APEC, 5, 6, 14–17, 20, 38–40, 42, 63, 90
ASEAN, 38, 41, 68, 85, 86, 88, 118, 149, 150
Asian, 79, 83, 85, 88, 91, 118
Asian financial crisis, 13, 53, 75–77, 102–105, 109, 110, 115, 121, 126, 128, 135
Asia-Pacific (AP), 14–21, 39–42, 90

B
Bank credit, 91, 114, 148

C
Canada, 1, 5, 15, 39, 41, 63, 76
Channel, 102–107, 109, 112, 118, 119, 129–131, 135, 155, 170, 172–174, 189, 190
Chile, 39, 63
China, 16, 17, 41, 57, 67, 103, 130, 131
Classical theories, 179, 182
Cluster, 52
Commercial loans, 166
Commuter, 125, 126
Constraints, 25, 28, 29, 37, 39, 41–43, 77, 78, 89–91, 94, 96, 97, 108, 152, 157, 172
Cooperative, 48, 54, 56–60, 62–68, 154, 158, 173
Cooperative business model (CBM), 63
Covid-19, 102, 104, 105, 107–109, 121, 122, 125–127, 129–133, 137, 139, 162, 189, 190
Crisis mitigating measures (CMMs), 108, 109, 135–139, 189, 190
Customs, 41, 87, 90

D
Developing countries, 1–4, 7, 23, 24, 26, 28, 30–32, 37, 43, 62,

© The Editor(s) (if applicable) and The Author(s), under exclusive license to Springer Nature Singapore Pte Ltd. 2022
T. T.H. Tambunan, *Fostering Resilience through Micro, Small and Medium Enterprises*, Sustainable Development Goals Series, https://doi.org/10.1007/978-981-16-9435-6

214 INDEX

75–80, 83–88, 95, 106, 118, 149, 151, 153, 179–182, 184, 185, 189, 190

Development, 1–4, 11, 23–25, 28–32, 37, 38, 47, 50, 54, 59, 60, 62, 67, 68, 75–79, 83, 86, 87, 89, 93, 103, 111, 123, 129, 149, 150, 152, 153, 155, 156, 159, 163, 179–184

E

Economic crises, 101–105, 189, 190

Ecosystem, 147, 150, 151, 154, 155, 157, 165, 170, 173

Employers, 17, 78, 80

Employment, 1, 2, 4, 7, 18, 20, 29, 31, 32, 38, 79, 80, 84, 95, 96, 102, 104, 123, 128, 180–182, 188

Enterprise, 13, 93

Entrepreneur, 6, 7, 10–12, 17, 22, 24, 25, 67, 68, 75–81, 86–97, 157, 188

Entrepreneurship, 24, 25, 75–79, 85–89, 91, 93, 95, 179, 183–185

Export, 2, 37–44, 47–57, 62–68, 104, 105, 107, 112, 115, 118–121

F

Female, 11, 24, 77–82, 88–90, 93, 94, 97, 125

Financial technology (FinTech), 147–156, 158, 159, 167, 171–173

Foreign direct investment (FDI), 4, 47

Foreign tourists, 52–54, 120, 122, 123

G

Gender, 11, 18, 25, 76, 79, 80, 82–84, 86, 87, 89, 90, 92–94, 123–125

Gender Development Index (GDI), 82–84

Gender Inequality Index (GII), 82, 84

Gini Ratio, 129

Global Entrepreneurship Monitor (GEM), 25, 78, 88

Global Entrepreneurship Program Indonesia (GEPI), 80

Global financial crisis, 82, 102–104, 106, 118, 120

Global gender gap index (GGGI), 83, 85

Great Giant Pineapple (GGP), 57, 67

Gross domestic product (GDP), 14, 21, 25, 31, 37–39, 102, 110, 116, 117, 122, 163, 182, 183

H

Human development index (HDI), 82, 83

I

Indonesia, 4–11, 13–19, 21, 22, 24, 26, 28, 31–33, 37–39, 41, 43, 52–54, 57–61, 63, 66, 67, 75–81, 85, 87–91, 94–97, 101–105, 109–117, 119–124, 126–132, 147, 149–153, 157–160, 162–167, 170, 171, 173, 174

Investment, 3–5, 7, 24, 27, 28, 31, 101, 104, 153, 156, 167, 181, 188

Involutionary, 32

J

Japan, 1, 5, 16, 17, 63, 67, 103, 184

INDEX 215

K
KAN, 66
Korea, 63
KSP, 58, 66

L
Labor, 1, 11, 13, 18, 24–26, 31, 76, 78, 82, 87, 188
Large enterprises (LEs), 2–5, 7, 9, 11, 12, 14, 16, 19, 21, 25–28, 30, 31, 38–43, 47–49, 53, 56, 105, 106, 108, 114, 115, 119, 129, 180, 181, 184, 189
Last resort, 32
Life cycle theory, 186, 187

M
Macroeconomic impacts, 109, 121
Malaysia, 16, 18, 38, 41, 42, 57, 63, 67, 106
Manufacturing, 11, 30, 33, 42, 47, 49, 54, 63, 82, 83, 94, 95, 106, 107, 119, 128, 130, 158, 164, 167, 179–182, 185
Medium and large enterprises (MLEs), 18, 34, 75, 77, 78, 94
Medium enterprise (ME), 5–12, 14, 17, 21, 25, 27, 30, 181, 190
Micro and small enterprises (MSEs), 1, 2, 14, 17, 18, 21, 24, 27, 30–32, 34, 37, 38, 41, 42, 47–49, 54–56, 63, 64, 75–78, 81–83, 94, 95, 109, 148–152, 156–158, 162–164, 167, 168, 170, 171, 173, 180, 181, 188–190
Microenterprise (MIE), 5–12, 14, 17–19, 21, 25, 27, 30, 32, 39, 49, 90
Micro, small and medium enterprises (MSMEs), 1–7, 9–33, 37–44, 47,

48, 52–54, 58, 62, 63, 66, 78, 90, 91, 152, 159, 163–167, 171, 179–190
Millennium Development Goals (MDGs), 76, 77
Modern theories, 179, 182, 183
Motivation, 7, 9, 10, 43, 77, 78, 86–89, 94–96
MSIs, 28, 29, 49–52, 54–57, 63–66, 82

N
New Zealand, 40

O
OJK, 156, 158, 159, 161, 162, 168, 172
OPEC, 102

P
Papua New Guinea, 5, 41, 42, 66
Partnership, 47–49, 52, 54–57, 67, 76, 154, 155, 162, 163
Pattern of Change, 179
Peer-to-peer (P2P), 148–153, 156–160, 162, 163, 165, 167–174
Pelanusa, 67, 68
People's Business Credit (KUR), 48, 164, 168, 169
Peru, 15, 16, 63
Philippines, 15, 19, 38, 84, 85, 106, 149, 150
Poverty, 2, 4, 31, 32, 62, 76, 88, 102, 104, 111, 126–129, 188–190
Productivity, 4, 25–27, 152, 153, 188
Province, 22, 43, 49, 54, 60–62, 66, 67, 81, 89, 120, 128, 129, 152
Push vs Pull, 188

R

Regulations, 22, 28, 41, 48, 50, 54, 59, 60, 62, 68, 132, 154, 158, 159, 172

S

Satellite, 31, 156, 172
Seedbed, 3
Small and medium enterprises (SMEs), 3, 4, 7, 13, 17, 38, 54, 59, 60, 62, 68, 184
Small enterprise (SE), 5–12, 14, 17–19, 21, 27, 30, 49, 116, 181
Southeast Asia (SEA), 4, 38, 84, 85, 105, 118
Supplier, 3, 67, 106, 109, 131, 132, 151, 156, 158, 162, 164, 167–169, 172, 173
Sustainable development goals (SDGs), 4, 76

T

Thailand, 18, 19, 38–42, 63, 103, 106, 109
THMC, 67
Tourism, 58, 106, 119–122, 128, 131, 132

Trade, 3, 24, 33, 41, 43, 48, 54, 59, 68, 75, 76, 79, 90, 91, 95, 101, 105–107, 112, 118, 121, 128, 162
Transmission, 102–107, 118, 119, 131, 135, 189, 190

U

Underemployment, 123, 124
Unemployment, 2, 32, 104, 111, 114, 121–123

V

Vietnam, 6, 15–17, 19, 38, 63, 67, 84–86, 88, 118, 149, 150

W

Women, 4, 7, 9, 11, 18, 24, 25, 38, 58, 67, 75–97, 101, 119, 123, 159, 162, 168, 170, 181, 182
Women's Entrepreneurship Index, 25
Workers, 5, 6, 11, 14, 15, 17–19, 25, 31, 38, 48, 49, 68, 76, 78–80, 96, 101, 104, 107, 108, 119–121, 123, 125, 126, 135, 169, 183, 186, 188, 190
Working-age, 125

Printed by Printforce, United Kingdom